I0878672

HOLOCAUST HERO

DEDICATION

To Yosef Wosk, who believed.

"Rudolf Vrba deserves all the honors of mankind."

– Claude Lanzmann

HOLOCAUST HERO

THE LIFE & TIMES *of* RUDOLF VRBA

ALAN TWIGG

FIREFLY BOOKS

A FIREFLY BOOK

Published by Firefly Books Ltd. 2025

First printing

Library of Congress Control Number: 2025936113

Library and Archives Canada Cataloguing in Publication
Title: Holocaust hero : the life and times of Rudolf Vrba / Alan Twigg.
Names: Twigg, Alan, 1952- author
Description: Includes bibliographical references and index.
Identifiers: Canadiana 20250188449 | ISBN 9780228105718 (softcover)
Subjects: LCSH: Vrba, Rudolf. | LCSH: Holocaust survivors–Biography. | LCSH: Nazi hunters–Biography. | LCSH: Holocaust, Jewish (1939-1945) | LCGFT: Biographies.
Classification: LCC DS135.S553 T85 2025 | DDC 940.53/18092–dc23

Published in the United States by
Firefly Books (U.S.) Inc.
P.O. Box 1338, Ellicott Station
Buffalo, New York 14205

Published in Canada by
Firefly Books Ltd.
50 Staples Avenue, Unit 1
Richmond Hill, Ontario L4B 0A7

Cover and interior design: Hartley Millson

Printed in China | E

We gratefully acknowledge the financial support of the Government of Canada for our publishing program.

We are also grateful for the contribution by Yosef Wosk, which helped make publication possible.

CONTENTS

MINISTERSTVO NÁRODNEJ OBRANY

Čj. 15550/34/Vr-50 Kleg. 5. oddel. 1946

Vlastnoručný podpis majiteľa

Číslo partizánskeho preukazu: 4513

Meno a priezvisko Vrba Rudolf

narodený dňa 11.9.1924 Topoľčany

pol. okres Topoľčany, nár. slov.

je podľa zák. č. 34/1946 Sb

ČESKOSLOVENSKÝM PARTIZÁNOM

Bol príslušníkom partizánskej jednotky "Stalin-Brunovský"

od 16.IX.1944 do 7.IV.1945

a konal službu ako partizán.

Je oprávnený nosiť partizánsky odznak čís.

Here is Rudolf Vrba's name change and identity card rendered to him as a partisan fighter within the "Stalin-Brunovsky" brigade in 1945. It was uncovered by *Holocaust Hero* researchers Michelle Madden and Nicole LeCody in the Vrba Archives at the FDR Presidential Library in April of 2025.

Introduction

THIS FIRST VOLUME of a two-volume biography asserts there was much more to Rudolf Vrba than his escape from Auschwitz and his subsequent report that saved 200,000 lives. An outstanding medical researcher, Vrba submitted testimony to the Eichmann trial, pursued war criminals, served globally as a riveting public speaker, combatted Holocaust denialists and served as a consultant for prominent historians.

Under his birth name Walter Rosenberg, he survived 24 near-death experiences over a three-year period as a teenager outlined below. At 20, he fought in ten, life-threatening battles as a Partisan in the mountains of Slovakia and became a decorated war hero. Rudolf Vrba was a Jew who fought back.

25 Near-Death Experiences

- At 17, Vrba was beaten nearly to death by Hungarian border guards when, while attempting to re-enter his native Slovakia, he was accused of being a spy.
- Taken to the border for "the usual treatment" (reduced to target practice as an alleged fugitive), Vrba avoided gunfire in No-Man's-Land by zig-zagging his way to safety in the darkness.
- Next, when apprehended by Slovak border guards, he was again severely beaten as a potential spy ("You dirty, bloody Yid") but he survived to be delivered to the Nováky transit camp.

- Ignoring the advice of older camp inmates, Vrba masterminded an escape from the Nováky labor camp with Josef Knapp, only to have his accomplice betray him, leading to a police chase.
- Recaptured a week later, Vrba was methodically beaten by Hlinka guards. Angry at him for making them look inept, they took turns with their fists, boots and rifle butts. In June of 1942, he was transferred by train to Majdanek, a concentration camp in Poland.
- On November 3, 1943, during a one-day killing fest code-named Operation Harvest, Nazis slaughtered all of Majdanek's prisoners but Vrba was not among them. He had volunteered, with 400 other men, to undertake "agricultural work" at an unknown place called Auschwitz.
- Farm work at Auschwitz entailed digging up 107,000 rotting corpses, including 20,000 Russian POWs. Of the 1,400 men in that labor force, only 300 would be alive when the job was finished – and they were promptly executed. His ability to speak German got him transferred when a supervisor named "*kapo* Franz" purchased him in exchange for a lemon.
- Vrba was transferred with 1,600 others to Block Eighteen where prisoners left their bunks at 3 a.m. for transport to the Buna construction site. Workers were forced to sprint carrying heavy bags of cement and many were beaten to death. He survived after a French contractor gave him and his Slovak friend Josef Erdelyi an easier job. "By the fifth week," Vrba recalled, "we were probably the sole survivors of the sixteen hundred."
- During a typhus outbreak in August of 1942, having not slept for 24 hours, Vrba and Erdelyi were forced by the malevolent *kapo* Jakob Fries to sprint on their wobbly legs to prove they did not have typhus. In the wee hours of the morning, they were placed in a line-up for execution until a sympathetic *kapo* switched them to a different lineup. "We turned just in time to see the typhus victims we had just left, slouching away to the crematorium."
- In August 1942, due to the influence of a fellow Slovakian prisoner named Laco Fischer, Vrba was reassigned to the *Aufräumungskommando* (the "clearing up" or "Kanada" commando), a duty that required Vrba to gather confiscated items from the mostly doomed

arrivals. First, to test his mettle, a deputy *kapo* named Isaac ordered Vrba to "run for that wire." Vrba knew he would be shot by the SS if he dared approach the electrified fence, but he had no choice but to obey. A German *kapo* recognized his predicament and called a halt to this suicidal test of obedience.

- The dangerous job of cleaning the filth and corpses from the railway cattle cars was overseen by trigger-happy SS guards. If prisoners spoke to arrivals, they could be severely beaten, shot or clubbed to death. Vrba survived on the *Aufräumungskommando* crews "for about ten months."
- After he became a laborer in the Kanada compound, Vrba survived 50 blows from a cane wielded by an SS torturer rather than betray a secret about a theft committed by someone else.
- As recorded by his friend Alfréd Wetzler, Vrba often did favors for others. On numerous occasions he brought his comrades something he'd surreptitiously taken from the ramp, or from Kanada. Twice it ended badly for him. The first time he got 25 blows with a stick, the second time he received 25 strokes with a whip. Some prisoners died from such beatings.
- While sifting through pilfered items in Kanada, Vrba glimpsed a page in a children's atlas that showed the location of Auschwitz in relation to the Sola River. He ripped out this page, took it with him to the latrine, memorized the geographical information and destroyed the page. If caught with the book, punishment could have been fatal, but he learned an escapee could reach the border of Slovakia by following the path of the Sola River.
- As a typhus epidemic killed approximately 15,000–20,000 prisoners, Vrba survived his severe bout of spotted typhus when he was hidden within the Kanada compound by female prisoners. This lifesaving respite enabled Vrba to receive a clandestine injection from Josef Farber, a hospital orderly who turned out to be a link to the Hungarian underground movement.
- Vrba's popularity was such that fellow prisoners sequestered him in Block 4 during his convalescence and gave him food that saved his life.
- Even after Vrba had witnessed *Unterscharführer* Hans Konig flog a prisoner to death for helping himself to an apple and some bread,

Vrba continued to take life-threatening risks by "organizing" [camp parlance for theft] gifts for others. Wetzler would describe a character named Val (Vrba) "taking risks again" by openly offering "the pleasure of a little sharp French tobacco."

- After finding a large amount of money stored inside a loaf of bread while cleaning the train cars, Vrba risked his life by tossing all the foreign currency into the latrines rather than turning it over to the Nazis.
- Vrba evaded death again during a pre-Christmas typhus inspection when he had to strip in the fierce cold, then repeatedly plunge into hot showers and dash out into the winter air again. "For two days we were left naked and without food which weeded out a few more." Many of those who survived the typhus test contracted pneumonia and died anyway.
- Vrba was scheduled to make an escape attempt with French army captain Charles Unglick on January 15, 1944 but when the Polish-born Block Senior in the Quarantine Camp failed to appear for a 7 p.m. rendezvous, Vrba prudently left their meeting place after 20 minutes. Unglick had bribed an SS accomplice to drive a lorry, with two Jews hidden inside, out of the camp. Instead, the SS man shot Unglick in the heart and pocketed a fortune in gold and diamonds. Unglick's body was left on display for two days.
- While Vrba and Wetzler were hiding in a narrow enclave within a woodpile during their escape, police dogs sensed their presence and started barking. The search party began dismantling the stack of lumber, only to be called away by a disruption that occurred in the vicinity.
- We now know that Vrba and Wetzler were supposed to allow two of the makers of the hideout inside after three days; Vrba and Wetzler refused to cooperate. Feeling double-crossed, the irate pair, unable to join them, took revenge by piling extra wood onto the hideout. Vrba and Wetzler barely had the strength to successfully extricate themselves.
- While completing their eleven-day trek to freedom, one night Vrba and Wetzler escaped a flurry of bullets. Vrba threw himself to the ground, pretending to be shot, before he was able to dash off into the woods.

- Having reached Bratislava and been accorded false identification papers, Vrba again risked his life in September of 1944. Wetzler and Ceslav Mordowicz went to Nitra to visit Wetzler's brother, only to be apprehended by local police who confiscated their identification papers. Mordowicz fired a shot with a handgun, enabling them to flee in opposite directions. Mordowicz made it back to Bratislava and pleaded with Vrba to go and rescue Wetzler. Vrba went to Nitra, found Wetzler in hiding and gave him a new set of false identity papers – and never took credit for doing so.
- Vrba could have remained undercover with his forged identity papers proving he was not a Jew. Instead, he volunteered to serve as a machine gunner for a Slovak Resistance unit led by Miloš Uher. As a Senior Sergeant at age 20, Vrba encountered severe antisemitism among his mainly Russian comrades but he survived ten battles to become a decorated war hero, receiving the Czechoslovak Medal for Bravery, the Order of Slovak National Insurrection and the Order of Meritorious Fighter.

Rudolf Vrba's "Partyzan" medal of honor.

AUTHOR'S NOTE

This volume is mostly concerned with the first 21 years of Rudi's life. It reveals new information about his escape; it explores why his friendship with Alfréd Wetzler eroded; it provides, for the first time, an investigation of his service and valor as a decorated Partisan soldier. Contemporary interview transcripts reveal private details of his character.

A second volume (covering 1946–2006) will examine his two marriages, as well as his role as a doting father to two daughters, a featured *Shoah* documentary interviewee, a Nazi hunter, a Holocaust educator, a *bon vivant,* a medical researcher (pharmacology and the brain) and a prosecution witness versus Holocaust denialists – plus more interviews.

Rudolf Vrba was a brave, remarkable and unforgettable person – a rare Holocaust hero. I have come to this conclusion after investigating Rudi's extensive archives at the Franklin Delano Roosevelt Presidential Library; reading 120 Holocaust-related books and hundreds of academic papers and newspaper articles; and visiting Holocaust education centers in North America and Europe.

I also knew him. Along the way I have conducted and recorded more than 40 essential interviews with others who knew him. Chiefly, I have interviewed his wife Robin Vrba, Rudi's research partner Gillian Bryant-Greenwood, Holocaust educator and psychiatrist Robert Krell and fifteen other people who were close to Rudolf Vrba when he lived in Vancouver. All would concede he was far from perfect; all would agree he was a great man – in short, he was a great deal more than a mere escape artist.

Anyone who survived almost two years in Auschwitz, anyone who became one of only six Jews ever to escape from Auschwitz, and anyone who also co-wrote a report that ended up saving 200,000 lives, is going to be different from the rest of us. In the shadow of his valor, I learned a great deal from Rudolf Vrba and I am hoping others will learn, too. On a sidewalk, Rudi once gave me the best advice I've ever received. "Alan, if you ever have a problem, just stop and ask yourself, 'Is this going to a problem for me a year from now?'" The task of writing this book has never been a problem. Taking five years to prepare a two-volume biography of Rudolf Vrba has been an engaging privilege and a dutiful pleasure.

– A.T.

A NOTE FOR HISTORIANS

There is now an alternate story as to how Vrba and Wetzler made their way out of Auschwitz. In a private interview conducted in 2023, Rudolf Vrba's wife (Robin Vrba) has verified previously undisclosed details about the escape that were uncovered by research for this book, undertaken among Vrba's private papers at the FDR Presidential Library archives. These details were not included in Vrba's 1963 memoir. He did, however, confide the truth about his escape to at least two other friends (Reverend Fred Metzger and Stanley Medicks) and shared the full details with his wife privately.

Rudolf Vrba was not really "the escape artist" as claimed by others.

The truth is:

1. Vrba and Wetzler did not build their hideout.
2. Vrba and Wetzler did not conceive of the escape plan.
3. Beyond the gates, Vrba and Wetzler followed the instructions of Soviet prisoner Dimitri Volkov as to how to remain uncaptured.
4. Polish builders of their hideout had needed two volunteers to risk their lives to test the safety of the hideout. Hence, Vrba and Wetzler agreed to act as guinea pigs for someone else's scheme. After they had managed to remain uncaptured for three days, the pair would then welcome two of the hideout's creators into the enclosure, whereupon the quartet would remain sequestered for another three days. All four men would then escape. But this plan was never enacted because Alfréd Wetzler was in no condition to remain in hiding for three more days.

Details are disclosed in Chapter Seven – How Vrba Really Escaped.

ABOUT ANTISEMITISM

The word antisemitism – deliberately spelled without the hyphen – appears nine times in the text. It has been employed sparingly as its over-use has long been problematic, dating back to Hitler. Historian Sir Martin Gilbert, a close friend of Rudolf Vrba, has provided a useful summation as to why this term should not be used indiscriminately in "First Steps to Iniquity," the opening chapter of his book *The Holocaust: A History of the Jews of Europe During the Second World War* (1985): "The word 'Aryan' was a linguistic term, originally referring to the Indo-European group of languages. Since before the end of the nineteenth century it had already been distorted as a concept by a number of writers, among them Houston Stewart Chamberlain, who gave it racial connotations, and used it to denote superiority over the 'Semitic' races. Yet *the term 'Semitic' itself was originally not a racial but a linguistic term, relating, not to Jews and non-Jews, but to a language group which includes Hebrew and Arabic.* None of these refinements troubled the new racialism. For Hitler, 'Aryan' was synonymous with 'pure,' while 'Semitic' was synonymous with 'Jew,' and hence 'impure.'"

This is how Auschwitz appeared to Rudolf Vrba when he arrived at 9 p.m. on June 30, 1942. Initially, he was encouraged by the motto, Arbeit Macht Frei – Work Brings Freedom. He hoped Auschwitz would be less barbaric than Majdanek, his previous concentration camp. "Everywhere I saw neatness and order."

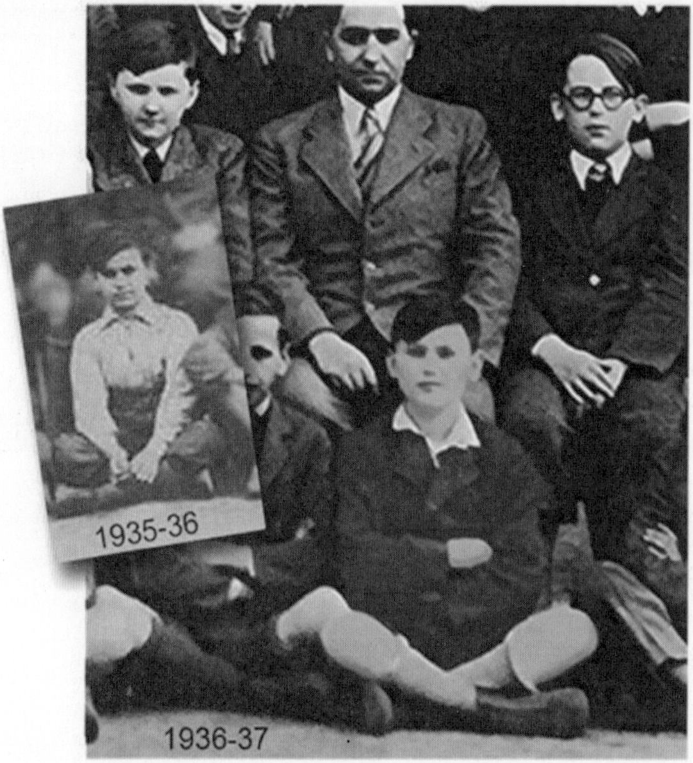

Class photos of Vrba as a schoolboy from 1935 (left) and 1937 (front row, arms folded).

CHAPTER I

The Early Years

On September 11, 1924, six years after Czechoslovakia was created as a new country in central Europe, Walter Rosenberg was born in the town of Topoľčany (*Nagytapolcsány* in Hungarian), in eastern Czechoslovakia. He would legally change his name to Rudolf Vrba 21 years later.

Walter Rosenberg was the sole progeny of his father Elias Rosenberg's second marriage. His mother, Helena Rosenberg, had been unable to conceive for the past ten years. He was raised with three much older siblings from his father's previous marriage – two half-brothers and one half-sister.

Precociously clever, Walter could do no wrong in his mother's eyes. His half-brother Sammy and his half-sister Fanči doted upon him. He was a gifted and determined child who excelled in science, literature and languages.

Vrba's mother, Helena Rosenberg, had been born midway between Topoľčany and Trnava, in the village of Zbehy, in the Nitra district, on September 16, 1895, to Bernhard Grünfeld (b. 1860) and Therese Grünfeldová (b. 1868). Vrba's surname for his post-Auschwitz identity was seemingly derivative of a Trnava region village now named Vrba or Vrbové, near Piešťany, where his maternal grandmother (née Just) had been born. With its current population of 6,000, this town in Hungarian was called Verbó; in German, it was Vrbau (modernized as Werbau). The translation of Vrba from Slovakian to English is "willow." Rudolf Vrba would tell his wife he would bend but he wouldn't break.

The name of Vrba's birthplace, Topoľčany, is derived from the Slovak word *topol,* meaning poplar tree. Birkenau, the world's most infamous

Five miles northwest of Piešťany, the village of Vrbové or Vrba was a WWII Jewish ghetto.

murder locale, was named after a stand of birch trees. The translation of *birke* from German to English is "birch." Vrba would refer to the camp as "Birch Tree Alley."

Only 48 kilometers from Topoľčany was the neighboring town of Trvana, birthplace of both Gerta (Gerti) Sidonová who would become his first wife, and of Rudolf Vrba's co-escapee from Auschwitz, Alfréd "Fred" Wetzler, born six years prior to Vrba. These two western Slovakian towns were about 250 kilometers southwest of an inconspicuous village in Poland called Oświęcim. Little-known until the Nazis transformed some former army barracks there into a concentration camp called Auschwitz, the hamlet of Oświęcim was soon expanded to incorporate more efficient crematoria nearby. This adjoining camp among the birch trees became the murder capital of mankind commonly known globally as both Auschwitz II or Auschwitz-Birkenau.

The largest city to the west of these small Slovakian towns was Bratislava, formerly known as Pressburg or Pozsony, some 80 kilometers east of Vienna. King Andrew II of Hungary granted Jews citizenship in 1229 and King Andrew III (last ruling member of the Arpád dynasty) granted

Jews the right to reside within the city's walls in 1291. Jews in Bratislava had a synagogue in the 14th century, but it was soon destroyed. Civil rights for Jews were rescinded by various decrees until Jews were forced by Count Pálffy to live outside the town in 1599. Known as the *Judengasse*, this Jewish settlement was uprooted again in 1840. Bratislava grew to accommodate approximately 15,000 Jews by 1930, making Bratislava home to the largest and most influential Jewish community in Slovakia.

At the time of Vrba's birth, Topoľčany was home to several thousand Jews. When Vrba was a toddler, the family moved to the village of Jaklovce (*Jekelfalva* in Hungarian) in eastern Czechoslovakia with fatal results. "My father was a timber exporter who owned a sawmill, some adjacent forests and a private railway line," Vrba wrote in a sworn statement when he applied to come to Canada from England. "My father's death occurred in 1928 and thereafter my mother continued to run the business until 1930 when it had to be wound up as the result of the 1929 economic slump and possibly also because of her lack of business knowledge."

The cause of his father's death, according to Vrba, was a liver ailment. He had recollections of visiting his father on his death bed.

After the family left Jaklovce, Vrba's mother made her living as a traveling saleswoman, offering lingerie she had made. "My mother was a strong-minded, self-reliant woman," Vrba recalled, "who had built up a small dressmaking business from more or less nothing."

From 1930 to 1933, Vrba was left in the care of his maternal grandparents in Nitra where he was tutored by his grandfather, Bernhard Grünfeld, who wanted young Walter to become a rabbi, and where he attended elementary school. "Grandfather's only son Alec had immigrated to the United States of America ... Grandfather wanted to have me with him as a replacement for his son."

It was in Nitra, on the same street where Rabbi S.D. Ungar lived, that young Walter was introduced to Orthodox Judaism. "I vividly remember Rabbi Ungar," he recalled, "who once, when I was eight years old, took me, on a particular occasion – it was meant to be a great distinction for a child – into his conference room. I was allowed to sit with grownups and was served tea and cake. Since this cake treatment, my relation to this Jewish group had always been cordial."

On Fridays, he was taken to the nearby river to participate, with his grandfather and other Jewish men, in ritual bathing in preparation for the Sabbath on Saturday. The Yeshiva of Rabbi Ungar was taken over by his son-in-law, Rabbi W.B. Weissmandel, who would play a pivotal role in Vrba's life about ten years later.

Most of the Jews in Nitra would be "resettled" by the Nazis. Vrba's maternal grandfather was murdered in Majdanek, but Rabbi Weissmandel and some of his pupils were permitted to remain in Nitra until fascist unrest prompted Weissmandel to relocate his Yeshiva to Bratislava so that, ostensibly, "it could be better protected." From this point onward, Vrba would look askance at Weissmandel as an easily manipulated puppet.

"The visibility of Yeshiva life in the center of Bratislava," he wrote, "less than 150 miles south of Auschwitz, was in my eyes a typical piece of Goebbels-inspired activity and brazen Nazi humor. There, before the eyes of the world, the pupils of Rabbi Weissmandel could study the rules of Jewish ethics while their own sisters and mothers were being murdered and burned at Birkenau. This Yeshiva in the center of Bratislava struck me as merely a circus with Rabbi Weissmandel as its main, albeit tragicomic clown."

Vrba's nurturing relationship with his grandfather came asunder when his grandmother suffered a bad fall. Even though he was not an orphan, Vrba was sent to a special boarding school for orphans in Bratislava, run by Jewish Secular Authorities. "My studies consisted mainly of Judaism and religious literature," he recalled, "the remaining subjects being considered of minor importance and only four hours a day were devoted thereto."

Bratislava proved advantageous because teachers there soon recognized that he was intellectually precocious and had a proclivity for languages. The school urged his mother, who remained in contact with him, to enroll her son in one of the city's better schools where he might excel academically. At age 11, in 1935, Walter succeeded in the entrance examination for the Gymnasium (high school) even though it meant losing the support of the Jewish Secular Authorities. Helena hired a woman to act as her son's guardian and created a permanent residence for him in Bratislava. At this point, he was shorn of the side-curls that identified him as a young Jew.

Walter blossomed as a student and divested himself of the Jewish traditions imbued in him in Nitra. One afternoon, he experimented by going into a restaurant and spending his lunch money on an order of pork. When nothing terrible happened to him, he understood that his indoctrination into the Jewish faith was a process that could not be trusted.

Increasingly, Walter would put his faith in science. When required to specify his preferred path for religious instruction from four categories, he chose the category "None" instead of Catholic, Lutheran or Jewish. He increasingly self-identified as Czechoslovak rather than Jewish. Maintaining an interest in learning other languages, he improved his facility in Russian and German, aptitudes that would hugely benefit him in Auschwitz.

In 1933, the Nazi Party had been declared to be the only legal political party in Germany and Adolf Hitler had made his first demand for the "return" of the ethnic German population of Czechoslovakia. At that time, Czechoslovakia was developing a progressive public school system that respected religious diversity. It was a parliamentary republic and the only de facto functioning democracy in Central Europe.

By 1938, Hitler demanded that Czechoslovakia must surrender Sudetenland on the grounds that the majority of the population had German ancestry. At the same time, the fascist Hungarian government was making a claim on southern Slovakia where the majority of the population had Hungarian ancestry.

The British Prime Minister sent Lord Runciman to investigate, but he could not speak the Czech language, so he mainly gleaned his information from members of the Germanic upper class. Neville Chamberlain came to Munich and met with Hitler and French Prime Minister Édouard Daladier on September 29, 1938, without any Czechoslovakian politicians present. The First Czechoslovak Republic was subsequently replaced by the short-lived Second Czecho-Slovak Republic when Czechoslovakia was forced to cede Sudetenland to Germany on October 1, 1938, as part of the Munich Agreement for "Peace in Our Time." The Republic was also forced to divest southern parts of Slovakia and Carpathian Ruthenia to Hungary as well the Zaolzie region of Silesia to Poland.

"The Holocaust did not begin only with the loading of victims into deportation trains," according to Slovak historian Ivan Kamenec, who attended school in Vrba's birthplace, Topoľčany. "... Applied to Slovakia, the Holocaust began already in the autumn of 1938 when the local Jewish population was gradually labeled as an open enemy of the Slovak nation."

"By means of the propaganda of hate," the Hungarian writer Sándor Török states in *Szenes-Interviews*, "it is possible to excite the masses to an uninhibited use of force and organized violence."

By this time, Vrba and his mother had relocated to Trnava, about 50 miles east of Bratislava. Vrba later stated that his mother had "married Ignac Reichsfeld, a local clerk who was also Jewish and I had been working as a laborer on building sites and in agriculture."

In the autumn of 1939, when he was 15 (or 14, as recorded by Gerta Sidonová), "Walter Rosenberg" (Vrba) had his formal education terminated because he was classified as a Jew. Much later, Vrba succinctly recalled his predicament: "By September 1939, the war had started. Czechoslovakia had been partitioned and Bohemia occupied. Slovakia, where I lived, became a satellite Nazi state ruled by a quisling government. The well-known Nuremberg laws were introduced and, as I was Jewish, I became prohibited from continuing to study and was precluded from working other than as a laborer at reduced wages."

Gerta recalled how she and approximately 20 other students arrived at their secondary school to find a large sign on the gate saying Jews were excluded. There was no explanation. The students rang the bell at the gate, but nobody came. After an hour, they realized the world had turned against them. Feeling betrayed and confused, they opted to take revenge. As a gesture of defiance, they vandalized some of the bicycles belonging to the other students, loosening screws, damaging the valves of the tires, inserting sharp stones in the tires.

Father Josef Tiso, the Catholic priest who headed the new republic, soon scapegoated Jews for the loss of territories to Hungary and Germany, and he pledged to "solve the Jewish question." The approximately 89,000 Jews in Czechoslovakia were most easily harassed and corralled in the cities. Tiso did not object strenuously when the First Vienna Award allocated a section of Magyar-populated southern Slovakia to Hungary on November 2, 1938, as devised by the foreign ministers of Germany (Joachim von Ribbentrop) and Italy (Galeazzo Ciano) following the signing of the Munich Agreement between the United Kingdom, France, Germany and Fascist Italy on September 30.

Trnava's two synagogues, for its 3,000 Jews, were destroyed by fire in December of 1938.

The Slovak Republic officially became autonomous as a puppet state on March 14, 1939.

The following day, German troops marched into Bohemia and Moravia without encountering any resistance.

Hungarians had already annexed the border territories of southern Slovakia. Thereafter, civilian life was disrupted for the "wandering Jews" who were rendered stateless and lived in tent camps along the Slovak-Hungarian border, homeless, relegated to an open field.

Formal education was denied to all Jews in keeping with Slovakia's eventual adherence to the Nuremberg Race Laws first announced at a Nazi Party rally in Nuremberg, Germany, on September 15, 1935. No written record has ever been found in which Adolf Hitler specifically made a decree for the introduction of these "race laws," but they marked a major turning point in Hitler's strategy to implement the "Final Solution."

The Nuremberg Race Laws were not applied to Slovakian society until 1939. There were two main components with regards to the initial curtailment of civil liberties for Jews. The Law for the Protection of German Blood and German Honor banned marriage and sexual relations between Germans and Jews. The Reich Citizenship Law made it illegal for Vrba and other Jews to continue with their formal education. It was also illegal for a Jewish family to hire a tutor or to encourage Jewish children to pursue studies at home.

Hitler cordially greets Slovakian leader Father Josef Tiso in Salzburg in 1940.

“Do not be the servant of the Jew. Whoever consorts with the Jew will die.”

CHAPTER 2

Persecution in Stages

The Jews of Slovakia were forced to wear the yellow Star of David in public after the Slovak Assembly in Bratislava unanimously adopted Law 1/1939. Forced to work as a laborer in Trnava, Vrba wore the Star of David on his jacket, but he disobeyed the Slovak People's Party dictates and taught himself chemistry, as well as foreign languages, much to the consternation of his mother, Helena Rosenberg, who wanted her son to learn a trade.

Slovakia joined the Axis coalition in November of 1940 when Slovakian leaders signed the Tripartite Pact. According to a census taken in December of 1940, there were 88,951 Jews in Slovakia at the time. In September of 1941, the Slovak government passed a Jewish Codex to further restrict Jewish activities. Slovakia would officially declare war on Britain and the United States in December of 1941, having already declared war on the Soviet Union in June.

The governing Hlinka Slovak People's Party (HSL'S) generated home-grown antisemitism without any direct urgings from Hitler. As Kamenec has documented, Prime Minister Vojtech Tuka and his equally radical Minister of the Interior, Alexander Mach, proposed deportation as the "solution" to the Jewish problem as early as March 3, 1942. Only a few days later, Tuka would suggest, "The Jewish question should be solved gradually by resettling them into the territory of the Ukraine. They have already indicated to us where they should be located. The Jews, by leaving the territory of our state, will cease to be nationals of the Slovak Republic."

In Trnava, some of the young Jews who had been denied formal education began to meet regularly, but surreptitiously, at a meadow outside of town called "the pond," so-named because there had once been a pond there. A mild-mannered friend from school who was also expelled, Erwin Eisler, had managed to disobey the order for all Jewish students to return their textbooks. Consequently, Vrba and Erwin were able to educate themselves with a book on chemistry by Czech scientist Emil Votoček. Vrba converted a shed in the back of his mother's garden into a laboratory for chemistry experiments.

It was at the pond that Vrba came to know 13-year-old Gerta Sidonová who would become his wife. Born in 1926, Gerta was the only child of Max Sidon and Josephine Frank. Her mother had a workshop where she manufactured Venetian blinds while her father, and her grandfather's brother, operated a kosher butcher shop called Sidon & Sons. The family were not highly devout Jews, but they kept the high holidays.

Gerta's life had been relatively happy until Jewish children were prevented from attending school in 1939 and her best friend, a non-Jewish girl named Maruska, had suddenly refused to have anything to do with her. When Jewish shop owners were forced to accept Aryan managers and turn over financial control to a non-Jew, it was Maruska's father who obtained managerial control of Gerta's father's butcher shop as a result of "Aryanization," the Nazis' official term for legalized theft.

The Jewish students who met at the pond read Marx, Lenin and Trotsky when they were not hotly debating the merits of Zionism, a movement that engendered some self-esteem in young people who were forced to endure daily humiliations at the hands of their Slovak neighbors. Democracy, as a possible solution to the oppression of the Nuremberg Laws, ranked as a less likely option. Most of their non-Jewish former friends who were still at school had embraced Fascism and belonged to the Hlinka Youth, the Slovak equivalent of the Hitler Youth.

Only five of the approximately 20 youths who met regularly at the pond would survive the war.

Initially, the new laws curtailing Jewish civil rights were not deeply concerning to Vrba. "They were introduced discreetly," he recalled, "falling almost imperceptibly around us, like gentle snow." Soon, teenagers were not allowed to go to the theaters or the skating rink. Walter pursued self-education as an antidote to loss of freedom. His mother thought her son's desire to learn English was eccentric, but when he proceeded to teach himself some Russian, she found this behavior so bizarre that she took him for a medical check up. The doctor was himself a reader of Russian literature, so Vrba's autodidacticism prevailed. In Auschwitz, it would be his ability with languages, especially German, that would help make the difference between life and death.

Following the death of the conservative Catholic priest Andrej Hlinka, in 1938, the Slovak People's Party – officially called Hlinka's Slovak People's Party – sided with the Nazis under the leadership of Jozef Gašpar Tiso. Under Tiso, freedom continued to be lost in increments. Jews were paid lower wages; jobs were first allocated to non-Jews; travel by Jews was restricted.

In February of 1942, Vrba finally had enough when he was reclassified as a Jew, not as a Slovak. "I simply would not stomach the suggestion that I was no longer a member of the community and that therefore I would have to be cordoned off, like a North American Indian," he recalled. "The only difference between us, indeed, was that the Indian was left in his own country."

The following month, Slovakia gained the dubious distinction of becoming the first Axis partner to formally consent to the deportation of its Jews when Slovakian government officials signed an agreement with Germany to expedite deportations of able-bodied, young Jewish men to Poland.

A *National Geographic* article, published on January 14, 2020, has outlined where and when the Holocaust began in Czechoslovakia when a trainload of 999 Slovak girls and young women, including Wetzler's future wife, Eta, was sent to Auschwitz on March 25, 1942.

These Slovak girls were on the first train exclusively carrying Jews to Auschwitz.

"One morning we woke up," recalled Edith Grossman at age 95, "and we saw outside on the street glued on the sides of the houses an announcement that all the Jewish girls, unmarried girls, from 16 and up, have to come to the school [on] the 20th of March 1942 for work." At 17, she dreamed of becoming a doctor. Her 19-year-old sister, Lea, wanted to be a lawyer. But the government of the Slovak Republic had begun implementing the Nazi Party's draconian laws against the Jews, forbidding education for Jewish children beyond the age of 14. "We couldn't even have a cat," she recalled.

Officials in Edith's hometown of Humenné assured families that girls would work as "contract volunteers" in a factory that was making boots for troops. When Edith and Lea walked out the door to register to become part of this new female workforce, she thought they'd be back for lunch. The girls gathered at the school to register with an SS official of the *Schutzstaffel* (Protection Squadron). A doctor ordered all girls to strip for a health exam. Although this was absolutely unheard of, they all obeyed. It was Friday and their parents were waiting outside, prior to Shabbat. The girls were whisked out the back exit of the school and herded towards the train station. There was no chance for the girls to say goodbye to their parents.

On their train ride through the Tatra Mountains, the girls tried to lift their spirits by singing the Slovak anthem. These nearly 1,000 young women were gathered at Poprad, about 75 miles west of Humenné. Eventually, after five days in a barracks, they were forced to board dank and empty cattle cars. The guards beat them until they cooperated. "I was with my sister and the closest friends of ours – we wanted to be together," she says. "There was nothing inside. There wasn't a bucket. No water. Not anything. Just a little window."

This was the first, official transport of the Holocaust. "The fascist government wanted to eliminate fertile bearers of the next generation of Jews," wrote Heather Dune Macadam in her *National Geographic* article. According to Slovak historian Pavol Mešťan, "it was easier to get families to relinquish daughters than sons. In addition, it was thought that the girls would entice their families to follow them to the relocation camps where Jews were being 'resettled' or 'rehomed' – Nazi euphemisms for killed."

After 12 hours in the frigid cattle car, they were forced to disembark at Auschwitz where mainly non-Jewish prisoners in striped uniforms used sticks to hurry them along. Until their arrival, Auschwitz had mostly been reserved for male prisoners of war, resistance fighters and political opponents of the Nazis. Edith's arrival with her sister marked a new era of unremitting horror that would later be dubbed the Holocaust.

When the deportations of young people in Slovakia began in 1942, the Slovak government agreed to pay Germany 500 Reichsmarks (about $245 USD) per Jew. In return, of course, as older Jews were shipped out of the country for resettlement, the properties and possessions of the deportees could be seized by the Slovak government. For the rest of his life Vrba would steadfastly identify theft of Jewish property and possessions, under the guise of "Aryanization," as one of the chief motivations for the Holocaust.

Soon, there were five main transit camps in Slovakia – at Patrónka, Nováky, Poprad, Sereď and Žilina. The deportation of entire families began on April 11, 1942. Approximately two-thirds of the Jewish population of approximately 89,000 were deported between March 25, 1942, and October 20, 1942.

This mass removal of an estimated 57,628 Jews in seven months was largely unreported in the international press. Slovak historian Eduard Nižňanský notes that the German ambassador to Slovakia, Hanns Ludin, had sent a telegram to Berlin on April 6, 1942, reporting, "The Slovak Government agreed on the transportation of all Jews from Slovakia without any pressure from the German side ... The transportation of Jews continues steadily, with no complications."

Czech historian Daniel Putík has estimated that only 1.5 percent (around 280 people) of the Jews deported from his country to Auschwitz in 1942 survived.

According to the U.S. Holocaust Memorial Museum, the Germans and their collaborators ultimately killed approximately 263,000 Jews who had resided in the territory of the Czechoslovak Republic in 1938. The museum corroborates the Slovakian estimate that approximately 57,000 Slovakian Jews were deported between March and October of 1942.

Non-Jewish Slovaks did the dirty work for the Germans. Members of the Slovak ethnic German paramilitary *Freiwillige Schutzstaffel* (Volunteer SS) initially worked alongside the Slovak People's Party's paramilitary wing, the Hlinka Guard, to "concentrate" Slovakian Jews, primarily men, in camps at Sereď, Nováky and Vyhne. All but 300 of these Slovakian internees were killed at Auschwitz, Lublin/Majdanek and Sobibór.

This massively successful mass murder spree ignited the Holocaust. The eradication of the large majority of Slovakian Jews did not go entirely unnoticed. Ivan Kamenec, in 1992, noted that the Vatican representative in Bratislava, Giuseppe Burzio, had written to Rome as early as March 9, 1942, just before the genocide was to begin: "The deportation to Poland of 80,000 people, who would be left at the mercy of Germany, is a death sentence for a large portion of them."

The purging of most Jews from Slovakia was anathema to Rudolf Vrba. There were no complicated arguments to be made, no analysis was required. In retrospect, he was not someone who deserves to be judged as peculiar or "hot-headed." Vrba was a rationalist. He refused to cast himself as a victim. He refused to obey, on instinct, the dictates of others and any such subservience struck him as lunacy.

"When it was announced to me," Vrba told French interviewer Claude Lanzmann in 1978, "from the Jewish community leaders that I would have to come and let myself be shipped to an unknown place, naturally it did not come into my mind to obey such a stupid instruction.

"They said first that only men from 16 to 30 would have to be resettled and if they go voluntarily nothing will happen to their families. And only those who were not married were supposed to go. All the contact was channeled through a so-called Center for Jews. That was the Jewish Council. I was surprised that everybody did obey."

Jews not wanted here.

Vrba on Civil Liberties Lost

"It is perfectly human to discriminate. I would say that everyone is inclined to a certain amount of discrimination. We know, very well, that the Scots have a certain antipathy towards the English. And the English can have a certain antipathy towards the Danish. And the Danish can have an antipathy to the Irish. And the Irish can have an antipathy to everybody. And so on.

"This is not discrimination. Everybody is entitled to like or dislike. It means nothing. But if, on the basis of this like or dislike, someone is excluded from the school, not on the basis of his achievements at the school, this is discrimination if it is done for reasons of race, religion, class.

"The first discrimination came with the introduction of the Nuremberg Laws. The first act of discrimination was my exclusion from the so-called gymnasium. In English terms, [this was] the so-called high school which meant an automatic right to enter any university.

"It was defined [by others] whether someone is Jewish or not, and it did not depend on what he professes to be. By law, he was defined without his will, without his approval, as a Jew. I think that to say it was racial would be nonsense because I can't see a common racial feature of the Jewish people of Europe. A Jew who is a Sheik in Yemen is certainly different than Lord Rothschild from Cambridge not by appearance, [but only] by habits, by cultural background.

"Jews, as such, actually don't exist. By that I mean, I think they would be difficult to define anthropologically. But then [nevertheless], there was a definition published, and then there was a law passed, based upon that definition, that anybody who falls within that definition [of being Jewish] is forbidden to go to school beyond elementary level.

"At age 14 I was given a paper that said I can't attend the next year of school. This was discrimination. This happened in 1939. This was in Bratislava, the capital of Slovakia. At that time, Slovakia was a so-called independent state.

"First, [Neville] Chamberlain gave a certain part of Czechoslovakia, Sudetenland, to the Germans, after the Munich Agreement in 1938. Then Bohemia was occupied; Prague was occupied. Slovakia was made a sort of socialist state called Independent Slovakia. But it was understood that the

Slovak people must be grateful to the great German nation for their freedom. Therefore, they accepted the Nuremberg Laws.

"The difference between Slovaks and Czechs was as big as the difference between Scottish and English. Even bigger. Slovaks speak their own language. It is similar to the Czech language, but they are two different Slavonic languages. Like the difference between Ukrainian and Russian. I considered myself Slovak by nationality. Under the old Czechoslovakian law, before the Second World War, you had the right to be a citizen of Czechoslovakia, or of Czech nationality, or of Slovak nationality. You could also say you are of Jewish nationality. Or you could say you are of German nationality. Or you could say you are of Hungarian nationality. It was a state of many nationalities. My nationality was officially Czechoslovak."

Rudolf Vrba on the Jewish Councils

"Before there could be deportations, there were two things. First, there were interviews. And then there was the marking of the Jews on the streets. The population should be warned on the street in advance [if a Jew was coming toward them]. A Jew has to wear a Jewish star. It has to be yellow. It was perfectly well-defined how large it should be. It was about six inches in diameter and the David Star had to have a minimum number of stitches.

"This created a bridge [divide] between the Jews and the other part of the people who were not very enthusiastic about the whole thing. [That's because] if someone was talking to a person with such a star, he was suspected of anti-state activities, of plotting with the Jews.

"The star was very important because those from the population in general who [at first] took the whole Jewish discrimination as a joke, suddenly they were visited [by fascists] for speaking with a Jew on the street. They could be exposed as people who liked Jews, who mixed with them and as people who were not aware of their [own] national identity. So that a division between Jews and the non-Jewish population has been created. It was suddenly risky to speak to a Jew in the street. Somebody could be labeled as a plotter against the regime. The regime of the New Europe, free of Bolshevism and Jewish plutocratism.

"So, the [general] population started to keep out, and keep off, of the Jews [keep away from the Jews]. At the same time, the government introduced a small Jewish star which was only one inch in diameter for those Jews who were very important. This gave a sign to the fascist street gangs not to touch a Jewish doctor, or a Jewish economist, or a Jewish businessman.

"Then it was said that the Jews had no right to offend, by their presence, whatever is public administration, any office, hospitals, schools. They should do that through their own Jewish council. So Jewish Councils were created and they [the people in those councils] were very important. They could travel freely and wear very small stars and [they] were equipped with papers that practically protected them from any sort of discrimination. Any rich Jew would provide for their favor [curry their favor] either by inviting them to their parties or by acting to gain their good will.

"But how could the Germans know who was a Jew and who was not a Jew? Only Jews knew. So, the Jewish Council was given the job, for administrative purposes, to make a list of Jews. And it was said that whatever Jew does not register himself will have committed a crime. So, I had to register myself and take out so-called Jewish papers that were issued by the Jewish Council. This means the Jewish Council had the list of all Jews.

"And then came the order that the Jewish Council should make a list of all properties owned by the Jews.

"And then came the order that the Jewish Council should make a list of the Jews who were very important for economical reasons for the country.

"And then it was said that the nation is fighting against Judeo-British plutocracy and Judeo Bolshevism and the Jews are not being widely represented in the army and this is not justice [not right]. So perhaps it would be good if the Jews would do something useful just as well. Why should they take the advantage? In this mortal fight for saving the civilization of Europe against those two big enemies? The threat of Jewish Bolshevism from the east and the threat of Jewish plutocracy from the west.

"So, they [the Jews] should do something [contribute] as well. They can't be trusted with arms but perhaps they can work. So perhaps it would be good if those Jews, perhaps between the ages of 16 and 30, who could actually serve in defense of civilization against those uncivilized enemies in the east and the west, could be re-educated to work. And so they should be sent to places where they would be given the opportunity to prove themselves as worthy of enjoying civilization, and the blessings of the civilization, by contributing manual work and not with those Jewish tricks.

"The Jewish Council was given the order to make the list of those young Jews who are between the ages of 16 and 30, and who are not absolutely necessary to be kept in Slovakia for economic reasons, who will be sent, to suitable places, in Poland probably, where they can contribute by [to] the war in a creative manner.

"This list was drawn by the Jewish Council and handed over and thus these people were called up. This means that letters had been issued saying you should come on that-and-that day, at that-and-that hour, to that-and-that place. You can take with you 25 kilos but you are not supposed to take any gold, or something like, because gold has to be given to the state. Gold which has been acquired by Jewish tricks. It belongs to the Slovak nation. Gold should be distributed to the local fascist leaders. It should be given voluntarily.

"And as long as they do so voluntarily, naturally the Slovak state will protect them from some antisemitic excesses. This means that their mothers or grandmothers and people like that will be given protection [in return] for their work outside the border, in Poland.

"It was obviously clear to me that if they can take me away, they can deport me. This was connected with a law for the loss of citizenship. A law for loss of citizenship was also issued. It appeared very innocent. It was only an administrative measure. But loss of citizenship means somebody can be deported. Anytime. So, they are not citizens anymore, but they are incorporated into the society on the basis of Christian humanity."

CHAPTER 3

Resistance & Rebellion

Walter Rosenberg as a street-smart teen.

DISGUSTED BY SLOVAK subservience and appalled at the prospect of being "deported like a calf in a wagon," Vrba, at 17, ripped the yellow Star of David from his shoulder in early March and set off from his hometown of Trnava, traveling east in a taxi, at the suggestion of his mother, who had given him 200 crowns, the approximate equivalent of $62 today, and reminded him to change his socks. He recalled that her face did not betray any emotion as he left.

A non-Jewish taxi driver risked his own neck to take him as far as the town of Sereď, where it was snowing heavily. When Vrba was unable to pay the fare of 400 crowns, the taxi driver took pity on him and charged 100 crowns instead. In return, Vrba gave him a note, written to his mother, asking her to make up the difference. From there, so as not to be detected, Vrba walked all night.

He had hatched a naïve plan: either join the Czechoslovak army-in-exile in England or else join the Titoists in Yugoslavia. Either way, not for the last time, he felt it was escape or die. In his immigration deposition made in

England decades later, Vrba would deftly eradicate any possible affiliations with the Titoists. "I considered the only way out of Europe to be through Yugoslavia and on my way there attempted to cross the Slovak-Hungarian border, illegally."

At dawn, he reached the home of a friend in the Hungarian border town of Galanta. At the time, anyone caught sheltering a Slovak would be jailed immediately, allegedly for helping a spy. They were not delighted to see him. Vrba gratefully accepted a quick bath and breakfast as elaborate precautions were taken to buy him a second-class train ticket for Budapest.

Four hours after his arrival in Galanta, the would-be Slovak resistance fighter was given 30 *pengő* (Hungarian currency) to supplement his remaining 100 crowns along with a copy of a local, antisemitic newspaper. In this way, he could best conform and disguise himself as a Hungarian.

Vrba successfully boarded the train for Budapest buoyed by the knowledge that he had the name of a Socialist underground worker in Budapest. Unfortunately, this man was out of the city, so Vrba was shunted off to meet this man's brother who had become a member of a local Fascist organization to fit in. The brother sympathetically sheltered Vrba in his home for 10 days until Vrba's hopes were severely dashed by his visit to the headquarters of a local Zionist organization. There a Zionist official was upset by the fact that Vrba was hoping to gain work by acquiring false Hungarian documents. It was then that Vrba realized, with disgust, that this Zionist, a fellow Jew, was actually a threat and might turn him in.

"Had I torn up the Talmud and jumped on it," Vrba recalled, "I do not think I could have shocked him more."

Denied help from his fellow Jews, Vrba agreed with his host that he would be better off returning to Trnava. There he could await the procurement of false documents to identify him as an Aryan instead of a Jew. Budapest, he was told, would be too dangerous without the false documents.

Armed with a copy of another Fascist newspaper, Vrba backtracked towards Slovakia. Three hours later he found himself once more on the outskirts of Galanta, this time plodding his way through a muddy field. Here he experienced the first of many beatings. He had been meandering homeward in the darkness until he heard voice shout "Halt!" He wanted to run, but after he was shot at by Hungarian border guards, he surrendered.

First, he was captured and severely beaten in the moonlight. Then, when ten border guards had assembled, a corporal hit him in the face with the butt of his revolver. Accused of being a spy, the teenager was beaten semi-conscious for half an hour; then taken for interrogation by an officer. Vrba wrongly assumed the worst was over. Instead, his inquisitor beat him even more severely with a truncheon for another hour or so.

When the officer believed Vrba was relatively inconsequential and harmless, he was put back into the custody of the border guards. As he was being marched back into the woods expecting to be shot, Vrba remembered he had successfully hidden his money, sewn into the fly of his trousers. He offered it to his captors, hoping to save his life – but that was not why he survived. The two members of the Hungarian border militia were afraid they had taken Vrba too far over the border into Slovakia. A gunshot could endanger their own lives. With a bayonet at his throat, Vrba listened to them argue about what to do. It was only then that Vrba realized his two Hungarian captors were as frightened as he was.

The guards let him get up and he began walking away, expecting a bullet in the back at any second. He recalled, "I walked fifteen yards and then I ran, zigzagging, ducking, weaving, waiting for a bullet that never came."

He ran about 100 yards into the darkness before he tripped and fell. Exhausted, beaten semi-conscious, he could never be sure how long he lay in the dirt before he woke with a dog panting in his face and a Slovak voice said, "Jesus, he's still alive!"

"You should be dead!" said another Slovakian border guard. "We always find them dead!"

But this was not a reprieve. The guards were Christians who despised Jews. After he received some brandy and some cursory medical treatment at a local inn, Vrba was taken to a prison cell at a local police station for questioning. His troubles were just beginning and yet somehow Rudolf Vrba was always able to retain a science-minded equilibrium throughout his travails.

Reproduced herein is Vrba's account of how the erosion of his civil liberties had led to mass murder. Instead of responding emotionally to the past, as most Holocaust survivors tended to do, he was capable of turning his own nightmarish experiences into a civics lesson with seeming ease.

Rudolf Vrba on Caste Distinctions

"From my exclusion from school to the deportation was a period of about three years. There was a sequence of discriminatory laws. First, for instance, there came a law which defines the Jews as such and says they are different from other peoples. This was based on the Nuremburg Laws that were biological nonsense, based on some mystical beliefs. No modern biologist would accept them.

"Then there was the edict that Jews cannot be in schools. Then, slowly, a Jew can only travel near his town. You had to give a reason why you wanted to go from one town to another. Then came a ruling that Jews can only travel in certain parts of the train, so that the population at large is not to be contaminated or offended by their presence because it might offend the public. The next part of the discrimination was that Jews could not live on certain streets.

"As far as discrimination is concerned, I would like to tell you one thing. It is very important for understanding what happened next. The discrimination was not uniform. There were, already, from the very start, introduced for Jews, different degrees of discrimination for various Jews. This was a very important part of the whole process for introducing discrimination subsequently.

"For instance, there was a law that a Jew cannot travel from one place to another. They said, in principle, that Jews shouldn't travel because it offends the non-Jewish public. By mixing in a train. Therefore, they should travel only when it is absolutely necessary. They should ask for a permit and they can travel in a particular wagon [train car]. However, there were certain Jews who were very necessary. For whom travel is very necessary. As a part of their function in society. Therefore, it was immediately said that those who are lawyers, or doctors of medicine, or connected with production of agriculture, should get a permanent travel permit and don't need to apply. This means they were traveling quite freely.

"So, you have already, immediately, the introduction of the discrimination: two groups of Jews. Of those who were discriminated against, and those who were [only] discriminated [against] formally, because they had a paper that said they were exempt from discrimination. So, there was immediately a division. It was natural that the most influential part of the Jews, those who had influence according to their social status, were officially discriminated [against], but not practically. They were more amenable to approve of this discrimination. This was a very important process, this process of division between the Jews, because it was continuously amplified.

"This was the first thing.

"The second thing was that they said that Jews were not to be allowed to enter an office of the Catholic Slovak state. Don't forget that in Slovakia it was Catholic. The new president was a Catholic minister. Monsignor [Jozef Gašpar] Tiso. The population, on the whole, was Catholic and Christian. So, if they had any doubts about something, if something is right or wrong, because it was Catholic, they would not doubt if something is right as long as Monsignor Tiso said so. As long as it is known that the Pope, in public, does not condemn Monsignor Tiso. On the contrary, he receives his envoys.

"So, the population, which was Catholic says, well, if Tiso, who is a Catholic priest, is approved by the Pope, he can't be wrong.

"Now the division.

"The next thing is that the Jews are not allowed to live on the main streets. They have to vacate the flats on the better streets. It is still said they can live where they want, except on certain streets. This meant that many flats on better streets became available to people who were able to collaborate with the new regime.

"Then came an edict that a Jew cannot be trusted for running a business. Therefore, the business should have an Aryan advisor. In other words, each Jewish shop has got an advisor who had access to the till. And everybody knew that an advisor's job is to take a cut of the deal [business].

"Certain Jewish shops were just closed. But the better shops are considered too important to be closed. So, these have Aryan advisors. Here, again, the Jews were divided between those who were important and those who were unimportant. Some Jews didn't have to close if they could get an Aryan advisor.

"This way some people [Jews] in a good business continued to make very good money. It was wartime and some people did well. There can be a certain economical boom. You have to sell buttons to soldiers [uniforms]. You have to sell shoes to soldiers. There's a trade in leather. There's a trade in rags.

"The small fellows, they were closed. But the big fellows, well, this shop is very important for leather and so on. It is important for the system.

The Jew knows how to run the shop, but he cannot be trusted so they have an Aryan advisor who usually was a member of the Fascist party. And very rarely knew anything about the business. This enables the Jewish businessman to carry on his business by giving part of his profit, a modest part of his profit at the start, to the Aryan advisor, who, usually before that, did have nothing. Or was a member of the underworld. Suddenly he had enough money for going to coffee houses or throwing parties. He could buy drinks for his friends. He wore a uniform. He was very important for protecting the nation against the Jews.

"The caste distinctions were enormously important. Finally, as time went on, you had groups who were excluded from school, and you also had Jewish doctors who were excluded from any discrimination because they were needed. Slovakia did not have too many doctors."

Hlinka guardsmen force Slovak Jews onto a train in 1942.

Rudolf Vrba last glimpsed his older brother, Sammy, at Majdanek (above), a crude forerunner to the more efficient killing grounds at Auschwitz. In November 1943, all of its 18,000 Jewish prisoners, male and female, were murdered and buried in mass graves. The day-long killing spree, code-named Aktion Erntefest [Harvest Festival], was recorded in copious detail by Erich Muhsfeldt, chief of the crematoria staff, who was hanged in 1948. "Erntefest" occurred at two other locations, bringing the death toll to 43,000, the largest camp massacre in one day of the Holocaust.

CHAPTER 4

Nováky & Majdanek

THE MORNING AFTER his arrest, Rudolf Vrba was taken to a barbed wire compound in nearby Nováky where he found himself to be the youngest of several hundred men marooned inside the kind of "resettlement camp" he had been hoping to avoid. The men were only allowed to go outside to visit the latrine, always in the company of an armed guard. Most of the inmates were dejected, fearing deportation to Poland, except for those in a portion of the camp reserved for a local work detail. Bribery was required to get transferred into this much preferred "safe" area.

It didn't take Vrba long to use his wits and get a job running errands. This enabled him to leave the barracks and explore escape opportunities. When he saw the perimeter of the compound was poorly guarded, he soon hatched an escape plan. First, he stockpiled clothing, one item at a time, with a sympathetic plumber in the work camp area who had a private locker. He then persuaded the Hlinka guards that he required an assistant for his food run errands. He selected Josef Knapp, also from Topoľčany, because he had access to money.

After several weeks of careful planning, the pair went under the wire and were soon running joyously into the woods. It was a Sunday, so they impetuously decided to attend the soccer match at the nearby stadium. Freedom! There they drank beer, ate sausages and winked at the girls. Sleeping in the woods after midnight, they were woken by a train whistle. Josef wondered aloud what it was carrying. Cattle? Coal?

"Or Jews," Vrba said.

The next day, as planned, they split up. It was important not to be recognized. Knapp went to nearby Vel'ké Uherce, where he was unknown, while Vrba caught a train to Topol'čany, where he had not been since infancy. There, Vrba was able to contact Knapp's girlfriend, Zuzka. But Zuzka's parents had mixed feelings about providing a hideout for Vrba so he gratefully assented to being housed in a garden shed, eating meals among the spades and forks and rakes. The town of Vel'ké Uherce was only half an hour away, but after two days Zuzka still had not returned from her visit to see Josef as they had planned.

Vrba began to realize that Knapp had left him in the lurch; his co-escapee had the money, his girlfriend and his freedom. Before catching a train to Trnava, Vrba thanked Zuzka's parents for their reluctant hospitality and explored the town of his birth. This betrayal by Knapp, a young man from his birthplace, would teach him an extremely important lesson: trust almost no one.

A kindly Jewish man listened to his story and gave him an excellent pair of shoes that had belonged to his deported son; they fit Vrba perfectly and boosted his spirits. There was still some time left to see the house in which he had been born. This proved to be his undoing. Suddenly, he heard the squeal of bicycle brakes behind him.

"Good morning," said a gendarme, with much formality. "May I see your documents, please?"

There followed a desperate chase scene, between a cyclist and a pedestrian, resembling a scene from an ancient Keystone Cops movie. The burly and capable policeman, a former military man, was not to be denied his prey.

Ultimately, Vrba was again pinned by an expert. The policeman explained why he was suspicious: earlier, when he saw Vrba inside a cafe, he had noticed Vrba was wearing two pairs of socks. That made no sense in warm weather.

His captor asked, "Are you a Jew or a thief?"

But this time there was no beating, at least not right away. "I don't blame you for running," said the policeman. "I did the same when the Cossacks came at me with sabers on the Russian front!"

The policeman dutifully, but not without some gentlemanly reluctance, escorted his otherwise unremarkable captive to headquarters.

The next morning, two Hlinka guards took Vrba to the train station. After he was guarded on his return trip to Nováky, he was methodically beaten to a pulp by a gang of camp officers who wanted to teach him a lesson he'd never forget, using their fists, boots and rifle butts.

Then he had his first meeting with an SS officer. This sealed his fate. Having successfully escaped from Nováky, Vrba could have been put to death as an example to others. Instead, the SS officer identified Vrba as a troublemaker who must be sent immediately to Poland.

"I think he probably felt the Hlinka men might kill me; if that happened, the news might filter through to the deportees and upset them. The SS did not want their charges upset; they wanted them to go nicely and cheerfully to the gas chambers without causing any hitch."

Vrba was deported in an overcrowded box car, without water, with only one shared bucket for human waste, for his arrival at the Nazi *Konzentrationslager* (concentration camp) in south-central Poland called Majdanek, on June 14, 1942. Nobody on the train was told their destination.

Vrba described the dehumanizing process of being transported to Poland in a talk he gave to the BBC. First, he described his journey from the Nováky prison camp in Czechoslovakia, onto Žilina and Zwardoń near the Polish border, eventually arriving at notoriously cruel Majdanek.

The One-Bucket Journey to Majdanek

"A train was one day drawn up to this transit camp. The crucial point was boarding the train. This was usually a special procedure ... but by that time, the younger people [men] were all gone [deported], so I am now boarding a train with thousands of women and children and old people.

"Only two or three guards were necessary for such a train. The old people watched the children; the children watched their parents. The whole bunch kept together. It [the process] was a bit slow. Here and there, somebody got hit in front of the children, so everybody tried to discipline [obey] because it upsets the children [if there is resistance].

"The only thing they had to do was put two soldiers with tommy guns by me. I was standing with my two guys with tommy guns who said, 'Well, mate, you see if you move you are a dead duck, so we are going to travel with you, and you won't move from your seat, and we do hope we don't have to use our arms in case you will try and stir up the peaceful population who understands discipline.'

"They started boarding people into the wagon [train car]. And again, more people into the wagon. And, again, more people into the wagon ... Until the wagon was bound up with people. Packages, parcels, men, women, children. And then there is an undisciplined gangster like me who is taking up special space at the expense of others. I would say, on the whole, it was not exactly a first-class train. There was not much sanitary conditions.

"On the way the train picked up still more people. Old ladies were hoisted into the wagon. I remember a very dignified old lady. Full of old-fashioned ornamentation. An Elizabethan-type lady. They had to hoist her into the train. She was very embarrassed because there was only one bucket for everybody. You know, those physiological things don't stop to function at such occasions. I think the old lady was very embarrassed. But she took it with some dignity and the train rolled on. It reached the Slovak border between Slovakia and Poland. The Slovak guards went away. And then I saw the SS and they boarded the train.

"Masses of young people had already been deported. Many people had received letters, written at gunpoint, from the people who had been deported to the people who had not yet been deported, informing them that the government had kept their promise, and so on. The older people had been promised, in the name of Christianity, to be 'united with their families.'

"A touch of Nazi humor: At the gas chambers, once, when they had transported thousands of people from Bohemia, when they were gassed, in the pocket of each of them was a ticket in which the German authorities [had] promised them that on their arrival 'everything will be done [so] that you shall be able to join the members of your family' – who were gassed in the same gas chambers a year before. So that promise was kept.

"The train was a very important part of the whole procedure. For the first part of the journey there was a discussion going on. Where are we actually going? And what for? And how will it be: It was forbidden to smuggle out gold. Someone came to me and asked what do you think I should do with this smuggled gold? Another one asked me what she should do with twenty cigarettes because it was forbidden to smoke, to take cigarettes. And one said, 'Even though I don't know if it's forbidden, I have got these new French letters [condoms].' This is not a breach of law. It is not gold. It is not silver. This went on for about twelve hours or so.

"After 24 hours or so, I took notice that the train was going very slowly. There were long stops. And I couldn't make out the route. It was a windy route without any logic. Unfortunately, when the train stopped, it was very far from any source of water. So, after 24 hours, there was not one drop of water. The children started to be thirsty.

"People, shall we say, had to perform the normal physiological functions. The whole wagon became suddenly a mess. There was a fight for the one and only bucket. It was not allowed to be emptied.

"The parents were obsessed to just quiet down the children just through the journey. The children shouldn't suffer too much. The old people shouldn't suffer so much. And people suddenly stopped to be preoccupied, either with the future or with the past. Just with surviving the journey.

"The thirst becomes overriding because food was allowed to be taken. And there was no water. There was no water for the children. There was a terrific desperation for water. You can imagine the wagon with about 60 percent of people resting on top of their luggage after two days. Those people got obsessed with why they are there. And water. Nobody thought anything about the past and nobody thought anything about the future.

"Suddenly you had hell on wheels. And no Slovak guards. And if you put your hand out the window, it was shot off. It was pretty clear: the slightest resistance was deadly. I explained constantly to the people, 'You are not going to be shot, but you have to be disciplined. It's not our fault that the train keeps stopping outside of the station, where there is no water, so be patient, be good.'

"So, slowly you get a dehumanization. Inside the wagon there starts a fight, a fight for access to the bucket, the inevitable bucket. Then the attempts to empty the bucket through some windows which were anyway closed with bars. Which led to soiling of somebody's luggage. Which led to quarrels about their future. Mutual accusations. About being considerate to children. About being considerate to old people. There was a question of moral issue: Who has moral preference? An 80-year-old lady or a one-year-old child?

"Some people believed an 80-year-old woman had the first right. Somebody believed a one-year-old child had the first right. The whole thing started to lose any semblance of civilization. That was the pressure of suffering of very small children, old people, of lack of sanitation, of torture by thirst, and the people slowly changed into something considerably different from what they had been at home."

Soon after he arrived at Majdanek concentration camp, situated three miles south-east of Lublin in German-occupied Poland, Vrba saw his brother, Sammy, 10 years older. They were able to briefly raise their arms in mutual acknowledgment. This muted hello was their final goodbye.

At Majdanek, Vrba's head was shaved, he was forced to wear a prisoner's uniform and wear wooden shoes and a cap that had to be removed every time he came within three yards of an SS officer. Here, too, he would learn that Zyklon B [cyanide-based pesticide first made in Germany in the early 1920s] had been used to murder prisoners at Majdanek since the winter of 1941. Mass murder using poison gas would only commence on a grander scale at Majdanek in October of 1942. It has been estimated that up to 500,000 people passed through Majdanek; 200,000 perished, and approximately 125,000 of these were Jews. Nobody can be certain.

Bullets and gas were spared at Majdanek; starvation was cheaper. "Not only were the living counted, but the dead, too," Vrba recalled. "They were piled up neatly behind us, a pathetic heap of corpses, some scraggy with starvation, some bloodstained from beating, and some who had died simply because they no longer had the will to live."

The next few days were instructive. Vrba observed *kapos* for the first time; often these were criminals who were strangely dressed in an assortment of odd clothing, a special class of subservients who were privileged to do the dirty work for the SS in return for survival. Every morning at roll call there were new corpses. Vrba would later describe Majdanek as his "preparatory school for the academy of Auschwitz."

Even though it was to become the first major concentration camp to be liberated, Majdanek never became well-known in the West, partially because it was not liberated by British or American troops. It was captured,

Majdanek was liberated by Red Army troops in 1944.

These preserved Majdanek furnaces attract relatively few visitors.

nearly intact, by the rapidly advancing Soviet Red Army on July 22, 1944.

Today, some of the crematoria in Majdanek, now located within the city limits of Lublin, remain in place, seemingly functional. Majdanek had as many as seven gas chambers – more than Auschwitz – as well as two wooden gallows and 227 structures. The Majdanek State Museum also oversees the remains of the Sobibór and Bełżec camps. Even though Majdanek is the best-preserved concentration camp of the Holocaust, these three camps attract only about 200,000 visitors a year.

By contrast, after the Nazis fled from Auschwitz, much of that complex was disassembled by local residents who pilfered as much of the remaining structures as they could. As well, the Nazis attempted to eradicate proof of their mass murder facilities before they fled, destroying the gas chambers and ovens.

The Auschwitz-Birkenau State Museum, created by Tadeusz Wąsowicz and other former Auschwitz prisoners in 1946, has undertaken invaluable research and archival restoration on behalf of the human race. Reportedly, a record 2.1 million visitors came in 2019 to receive tours in 20 languages. Figures naturally dropped during the Covid pandemic but rose back to 1.67 million visitors in 2023 according to the museum.

At dismal Majdanek, Rudolf Vrba was assigned to be a builder's laborer, but he only spent 12 days there. He wanted to escape at any cost. At the first opportunity, he naively volunteered for "farm work" at some unknown place called Auschwitz. He would later comment that conditions at Auschwitz were better than at Majdanek.

For the train journey to Auschwitz, 80 men would be crowded into each train car. The SS did not want the citizens of Poland to be frightened by gaunt scarecrows in prison pajamas, so they outfitted the cargo with dead men's caps and civilian clothing.

"Their motives worried me not a bit," Vrba said. "The cap made me feel as if I was off to a wedding!"

In the stifling heat, there was no water after 24 hours. The trip would take two-and-a-half days.

Rudolf Vrba clearly recalled the day he boarded a train at Lublin Station for Auschwitz. An SS officer with a whip cautioned them, "You are to be counted here and will be counted several times on the journey. If at any stage any man is missing, 10 men in his wagon will be shot."

CHAPTER 5

Auschwitz

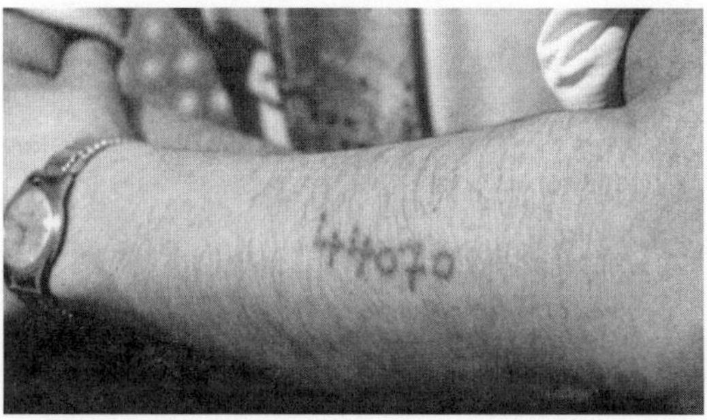

Rudolf Vrba was always willing to show his tattoo except once when he nervously re-entered Poland, by car, with a documentary film crew, on their way to Auschwitz.

WALTER ROSENBERG ARRIVED at Auschwitz at 9 p.m. on June 30, 1942, at age 17. The best way to learn about Vrba's time in Auschwitz is to read his book. It is not the intention of this biography to extensively reprise its riveting content. Here, for the record, is a much lesser-known summary of his journey to Auschwitz, transcribed from a BBC interview.

The Train to Auschwitz

"Imagine a train arriving in Auschwitz after an 11-day journey. I have been present emptying wagons where 30 percent of people were dead, and they had probably been dead for four or five days.

"There were great variations, but the basic principle was one and the same thing. To break the people during the journey in an anonymous way. So as to pretend that the people are exposed to the torture unintentionally. The SS is there only to keep order. It is not their fault that there is no water. It is not their fault if the train stops for 16 hours outside of a station.

It is not permitted for them to go and fetch the bucket. The doors are locked. So very soon there came a point where all those people inside were drawn near to insanity.

"It was not even announced that this was the last stop. Suddenly the doors are open.

"I have made the journey once. I couldn't make out anything about it. From my knowledge of geography, I could see that the train goes somewhere in the direction of Auschwitz, somewhere to the direction of the east. Then I suddenly saw through the window and we were going. In other words, the train was being shunted around. There was no free passage, so it looked, because military trains were passing by, and so on. The train was simply shunted out on some blind line. You never knew how long. But it was definitely kept out of reach of water. Or sometimes in reach of water but there was nobody to fetch the water. You could see water flowing in big streams, to a locomotive or something, or some transport that was passing by, but no water is available.

"The people fight with each other because they think, well, we are going to be resettled, and the organizers of this journey were obviously stupid, and they don't understand the problems of such a journey. That was the reaction. Because they wouldn't think that somebody would invent [this journey] to torture children with thirst.

"In other words, they considered it [the journey] as a special case of mismanagement. They didn't know this happened to thousands of trains. It happened to only one train, and that was the last he saw in his life.

"The train had stopped many times. This time something happened. Somebody opens the door. And there were machine guns in front of us. And somebody said, 'All men between 16 and 45, out. Quick. Anyone who won't come out will be shot on the spot.'

"Some women try to join their husbands. This was answered with shots. Or with clubs. Heads are broken. Hands are broken. Some children are killed. Things like that happen.

"But it was always said, 'This is not our principle [fault]. We are doing it only because you are making life difficult. We have ordered that the men should go [get] out. Can't you understand an order?'"

~

UPON HIS ARRIVAL at Auschwitz on June 30, at 9 p.m. Rudolf Vrba was at first impressed by the relative neatness and order of the camp. When he saw the famous letters in an arch across the main gate, *Arbeit Macht Frei* (Work Brings Freedom), still feeling young and strong, he was encouraged by the message. Later he'd write, "It was like some monstrous April Fool joke."

Soon, after everyone was paraded past the notoriously brutal and gigantic SS Oberscharführer Jakob Fries, Vrba received his tattoo number 44070, on the top of his left forearm, and his zebra stripes. It was nearly always dangerous to be noticed in Auschwitz, often deadly to be singled out, so prisoners became their numbered selves for much of the time.

Soon, he learned the true nature of the "agricultural work" he had volunteered to do. The work was to unearth and burn 107,000 corpses, mainly Jews, but also including 20,000 Russian prisoners of war. At this site, drunken and merciless SS overseers with whips, bolstered by one bottle of schnapps per day each, as a reward for their ghastly supervision, were welcome to punish or kill the workers with abandon. As the putrefied bodies were removed from the mass grave and stacked in piles for burning, the stench of decomposing flesh would be sickening.

Only 300 out of the 1,400 prisoners in the work crew lived to the end of the job, and then they were killed anyway for knowing too much. With some noteworthy exceptions, it was the same for almost all of the *Sonderkommando* units who dragged the victims from the showers to the furnaces. The vast majority were annihilated at six-month intervals to ensure the truth about mass executions could never be divulged.

In his memoir, Vrba states he never had to undertake this ultra-grim "agricultural work." He was spared from laboring "knee-deep in decomposing flesh" by one very brief conversation that occurred on his second evening in Auschwitz when he and his barrack inmates were introduced to a burly and menacing-looking *kapo* named Franz. This seemingly cruel overlord had a red triangle on his tunic indicating he was a political prisoner.

"Let's have a look at you bastards!" Franz bellowed. Vrba recognized this man's Viennese accent because Vrba himself had been raised not far from the Austrian capital. Like someone shopping, examining the merchandise, *kapo* Franz punched Vrba lightly in the stomach to see if he was strong. Vrba didn't flinch. "Strong boy, eh?" said the seemingly menacing tormentor. The *kapo* then felt his bicep. Vrba flexed it. The *kapo* approved. When he asked, "Where are you from?" Vrba gave a one-word answer. "Slovakia." The *kapo* asked if Vrba spoke German.

"Yes."

"Well?"

"Fluently."

Franz proceeded to tap his own leg with a club, and he peered into Vrba's face. "Okay, you'll do," he said. "Come with me." Vrba followed him, in his wooden shoes, out of the barracks. Only later did Vrba learn that Franz purchased him from the Block Senior of the barracks for one lemon.

For a brief period, Vrba had a relatively safe job carrying goods to supply the SS food warehouse, as overseen by the sympathetic *kapo,* nicknamed Franz Marmalade, until Franz was suspected of cleverly filching foodstuffs with the complicity of some of his workers. [Franz was so admired and beloved that even the Nazis went soft on him for his solitary confinement punishment. He survived the war and eventually came to visit Vrba in Vancouver.]

The onset of a typhus epidemic in the camp radically altered the size of the workforce as nearly half of the prison labor – those who were unduly weak and/or were suspected of having typhus – were eliminated. Vrba and Josef Erdelyi (a friend from the Majdanek transport, whose girlfriend had been in school with Vrba) were transferred to Block Eighteen and reassigned to "disgusting and dangerous" work (according to Vrba) as laborers in the Buna command, a deadly construction zone to serve German industrial interests [such as I.G. Farben, Krupp, Siemens] with unpaid labor. By his fifth week, Vrba and Josef were "probably the sole survivors" from a contingent of 1,600 men who had been herded each day like cattle, at 5 a.m., to reach a slave labor wasteland in which men were reduced to behaving like "a pack of starving wolves."

Vrba's life was again spared by the intervention of an overseer. This time his companion Josef arranged for them to work under the guidance of a French-speaking contractor who afforded protection from vicious guards. Bizarrely, after the war, Vrba would be offered a job as an industrial chemist at the site of the Buna industrial compound. Instead, Vrba would join a collective lawsuit against the industrial giant I.G. Farben in 1961, for back wages. A West

German court eventually awarded him 2,500 marks (approximately $5,000 in 2020 funds) but no compensation was paid to the relatives and dependants of those who had not survived; hence approximately 90 percent of the slave labor force at Buna was not recognized in the lawsuit for reparations.

British POW Denis Avey's memoir *The Man Who Broke into Auschwitz* (2011) provides some descriptions of what it was like for laborers to survive within the massive construction zone of the Buna/Monowitz compound. Avey, however, as an English-speaking and non-Jewish soldier, had a much superior diet and better lodging than the Jewish prisoners for whom he felt much pity.

Vrba's life was spared when he gained a transfer to the so-called Kanada compound of Birkenau, a warehouse complex so-named because its storehouse of stolen goods approximated the vision of faraway Canada as a paradise on Earth. "One week in Kanada," he later wrote, "taught me more about the real purpose of Auschwitz than I had learned in the three months that had passed since my initiation."

Vrba subsequently believed the plunder of Jewish belongings, along with the seizure of properties and businesses, was the mercantile motive for the Holocaust that was generally under-recognized.

Vrba's transfer to the Kanada compound was orchestrated by a former Slovak dentist, Laco Fischer, who had already survived five months in Auschwitz and therefore knew the ropes. Vrba's memoir spares the reader the grim details of initially working within the "Cleaning Commando" but he was more overt about the conditions when interviewed by the United States Holocaust Memorial Museum:

"I was part of the selection committee," he said, "greeting the incoming trains and we had to clean up the mess. After each transport arrived, I realized this process was pre-planned. Transports of three or four to 16 a day would arrive. This went on for about two years. People inside the trains were degraded totally. They defecated in front of each other, women menstruated, children and others were throwing up. This caused fighting with each other. They didn't understand what was really going on. They were under unbelievable stress, thinking that all this would stop once the train stops. But that was not the case. This was all planned out well by the Nazis – very civilized, clean, white-gloved people.

"We, the prisoners in striped clothing, would not have been believed if we were to tell them ahead of time that they are going to be gassed. So, as they got out of the wagons quickly, they were met with SS encircling them, and if a word was said, without warning they were shot. There was a cleaning commando, which I was part of for about 10 months. This was the cleaning up team. When a transport arrived, the SS unlocked the locks. The commando opened the doors. They were not to talk to the people in the wagons (train cars), not give any signs, punishable by instant death. Two SS men standing at the wagon ordered people to get out quickly. Anyone not moving fast was hit with a walking stick.

"Sometimes they used a different technique. They told the people to please step out, not take their luggage with them because these criminals standing around would take their trunks, but make sure their names are on the luggage, so it can reach them. Women with their children were sent off to the gas chambers together because women would have caused problems if their children would have been snatched away from them. The healthy men and women were selected out fast. The people selected for the gas chambers were hauled off in a truck to the nearest chambers, the truck was raised, the door opened, the people got out, got undressed to go to the showers. They were told they will get water and food after the shower, which of course never happened.

"We, the prisoners, couldn't protest because if we did, a few things could happen. Either one would be clubbed, beaten, or men would smile and write down our number and once whatever we were doing would be finished, we would be slowly clubbed to death. We couldn't warn people at their arrival even if we were not clubbed to death immediately. We were watched. When we were attending to the crippled and wounded, when we had to get them onto the trucks which could carry them to the gas chambers, we couldn't even put them on a blanket. We either had to drag them or, if they could run, make them run until they dropped, then drag them onto the truck. No resistance was possible. The possibility might have existed many months before they were to enter the train cars. Perhaps they could have saved themselves somehow."

STRIPED-TROUSERED PEONS HAD to efficiently and thoroughly empty and clean the railway cars filthy with corpses and excrement. Manhandling newly-dead carcasses, removing gold from teeth, pilfering and sorting all Jewish possessions – it was like some lost and found department in Hell. Belief in any benevolent God was also a casualty.

Vrba has stated he was present for the arrival of nearly every train for 10 months. As verified by those who knew him, he had what is often referred to as a photographic memory. He was able to commit to memory the arrival of each train and the approximate number of deportees in each new shipment of human cargo. This task gave him an additional reason for staying alive.

In June of 1943, Vrba was accorded the much-desired job of registrar within the Quarantine Camp at Birkenau. This enabled him to converse directly, and even privately, with the new arrivals who were spared the gas chambers. Vrba's access to the approximately 10 percent of arrivals who were not selected on the platform for immediate mass murder enhanced his ability to keep track of their countries of origin as well as the sequence of tattoo numbers accorded to each new shipment.

From his tiny office alongside the route for trucks that took doomed arrivals directly from the railway sidings to Crematorium IV, Vrba was uniquely positioned to continue his self-imposed regime of memorizing the extent of the genocide in tandem with his countryman, Alfréd "Fred" Wetzler, a registrar in the morgue for the deaths of those inmates not murdered in the crematoria. Wetzler would be accorded the false name of Jozef Lánik when he went into hiding after their escape. After the war, he continued to use the name Lánik to publish his non-fiction account *Tomb of Four Million People*. He later reverted to using his birth name.

Accorded better lodging, better food and relative freedom of movement as a registrar, Vrba was able to have a love affair with a woman in the so-called Czech camp, a special section of Auschwitz in which a contingent of Czech Jews were able to keep their clothes and hair and live in relative comfort. This Czech camp was kept separate from the reality of the killing grounds in case the Nazis were ever required to show the conditions of Auschwitz to the outside world and, in particular, the Red Cross.

In January of 1944, as a new rail line was being built only 30 yards from his lavatory, Vrba overheard the SS jokingly refer to pending shipments of "Hungarian salami." He realized Auschwitz was anticipating almost "a million units" of Jews from Hungary. As well, according to Ruth Linn in *Escaping from Auschwitz* (2004), Vrba was told by a German *kapo* on January 15, 1944 that the new rail line was being constructed so that arriving Jews could be transported more efficiently to the gas chambers.

The extent of this imminent influx would later be measurable by the increase in the number of *Sonderkommandos* required to dispose of the corpses. Prior to Vrba's escape, approximately 400 *Sonderkommandos* had worked to prevent their own demise by hauling away the carcasses of the dead, sometimes their own loved ones. After Vrba's escape in 1944, the ranks of the *Sonderkommandos* or *Hilflinge* (helpers) at Birkenau would swell to 900.

In his sworn deposition for the trial of SS-*Obersturmbannführer* Adolf Eichmann in 1961, and in his memoir originally titled *I Cannot Forgive* in 1963, Vrba revealed that he and Wetzler gained their vital information

Sorting the loot for the Kanada compound warehouses

about the layout of the gas chambers and crematoria from *Sonderkommando* prisoner Filip Müller who worked there from May of 1942. This information was confirmed when Müller, born in Sered', Czechoslovakia in 1922, eventually published his own book, *Eyewitness Auschwitz* (1979).

When Rudolf Vrba received his honorary doctorate in Haifa in 1998, he delivered a 14-page speech explaining how the Holocaust was "accomplished for very rational purposes" and robbery was "an integral part of the Holocaust." Here is a truncated summary of his viewpoint from a verbatim transcript of a BBC interview.

Rudolf Vrba describes Kanada

"You see, in the mind of a Central European, Canada was a land of plenty. There was a lot of immigration from Slovakia, from Poland, to Canada before the war.

"It was known that peasants who could not make a good living in Slovakia or Poland, because of the catastrophic economic condition in Europe, found land in Canada and a better opportunity for life. The rumor came that it was a land of milk and honey.

"Obviously, in the Kanada Commando in Auschwitz, there was everything. There was money. There was food. There was anything you could imagine. In the middle of the war. The money ... it is difficult to describe how much, but there was an enormous amount of money.

"That's why it was called Kanada, actually, Land of Plenty. It was sort of a camp jargon. Money. You see the people were mostly often robbed before they entered those transports. But those people knew that they were going to be transported somewhere. They tried to exchange or to sell, as long as it was possible, their property, for currency which would always have value. Especially hard currency. Dollars. English pounds. This was before the inflation of the dollar. German marks were no good at that time. A lot of gold coins. So-called Napoleons. Because they carried a picture of Napoleon. And then there were the Russian coins. There was a picture of the Czar. And they were called swines. Because of the swine on the coin! [Such coins were] there in abundance in the Kanada Command because as the clothes were sorted out, before they were sorted out, there was a special group of people looking through the clothes.

"The money was collected in the luggage, and the luggage was collected and carried away every evening after the working hours finished. There was everything possible there. There are weights of various denominations. Diamonds. Gold rings. Gold watches. Whatever was called valuable. And sometimes the SS was carrying it away because we could not close the luggage. He stamped it in with his foot in order to be able to close the luggage. Millions were involved.

"Not everything went into the luggage. I remember once we were sorting out a transport from Grodno [Belarus], and it was of poor quality. I remember once during the work I picked up a piece of bread, and it did not have the right consistency. I broke up the bread and there was perhaps $20,000 inside. In $100 notes. So, the risk was to take this package of notes and risk the trip to the lavatory. And once nobody stopped me on the way to the lavatory, it was done. All I had to do was to throw it down there [toss it into the latrine]. This was sort of the right place for the money, I suppose [so the Germans could not have it]. I didn't need money there. This was connected to a grave risk. There were some who tried it. But to go back to the barracks, or even during the work, you could be subject to inspection. And if any money could be found on any prisoner, death would be for sure.

"So, the risk was to get it to the lavatory and throw it in. The value of the money obviously ended that way. As an act of spite, perhaps. I couldn't see any good reason, if I found this money, why I should give it to the Germans, if it could be destroyed. The owners of this money had been destroyed. But, of course, only a fraction of the money [that was found] was destroyed. Most of it went to the luggage [to the Germans].

"There was sort of a rotation within that working group, you know. For those taken to the train, it was considered very hard work. It was pretty dangerous. There was a considerable amount of mortality because of the SS losing their patience and so on.

"There were several hundred people [doing this work]. There was a detachment of about 20 women who did nothing else but press out all the toothpaste which was brought in. They were sitting on benches and taking one toothpaste after another and pressing it out. It was a full-time job for

SS-Hauptscharführer Bernhart Walter, as head of the Auschwitz photographic laboratory for the Erkennungsdienst [Identification Service], and his assistant Ernst Hofmann, took at least 193 photos, including this image of female members of the Aufräumungskommando sorting through shoes confiscated from Hungarian Jews from Carpathian Ruthenia who were mostly gassed at Auschwitz-Birkenau in May, 1944. According to the United States Holocaust Memorial Museum, a selection of these images was first published in *The Tragedy of Slovak Jews* (Bratislava 1949). Two Czech researchers who were also Auschwitz survivors rediscovered the negatives in Prague in 1955 and provided two sets of negatives to Yad Vashem and the Auschwitz Museum.

about 20 women. And in one out of 10,000 tubes there was a big diamond. Or a roll of bank notes ... in a condom ... Once upon a time, more often than you would think, diamonds or hard currency were inserted into the toothpaste, or inside a condom ... in the hopes that they could carry the toothpaste through the various controls.

"The Jews were supposed to deliver their valuables a long time before they were deported. But this was the last station. It was the end of the process. And there was the suspicion, which was quite justified, that those Jews might have been clever enough to hide the money somehow. And, so, they brought the rest of their money to Auschwitz."

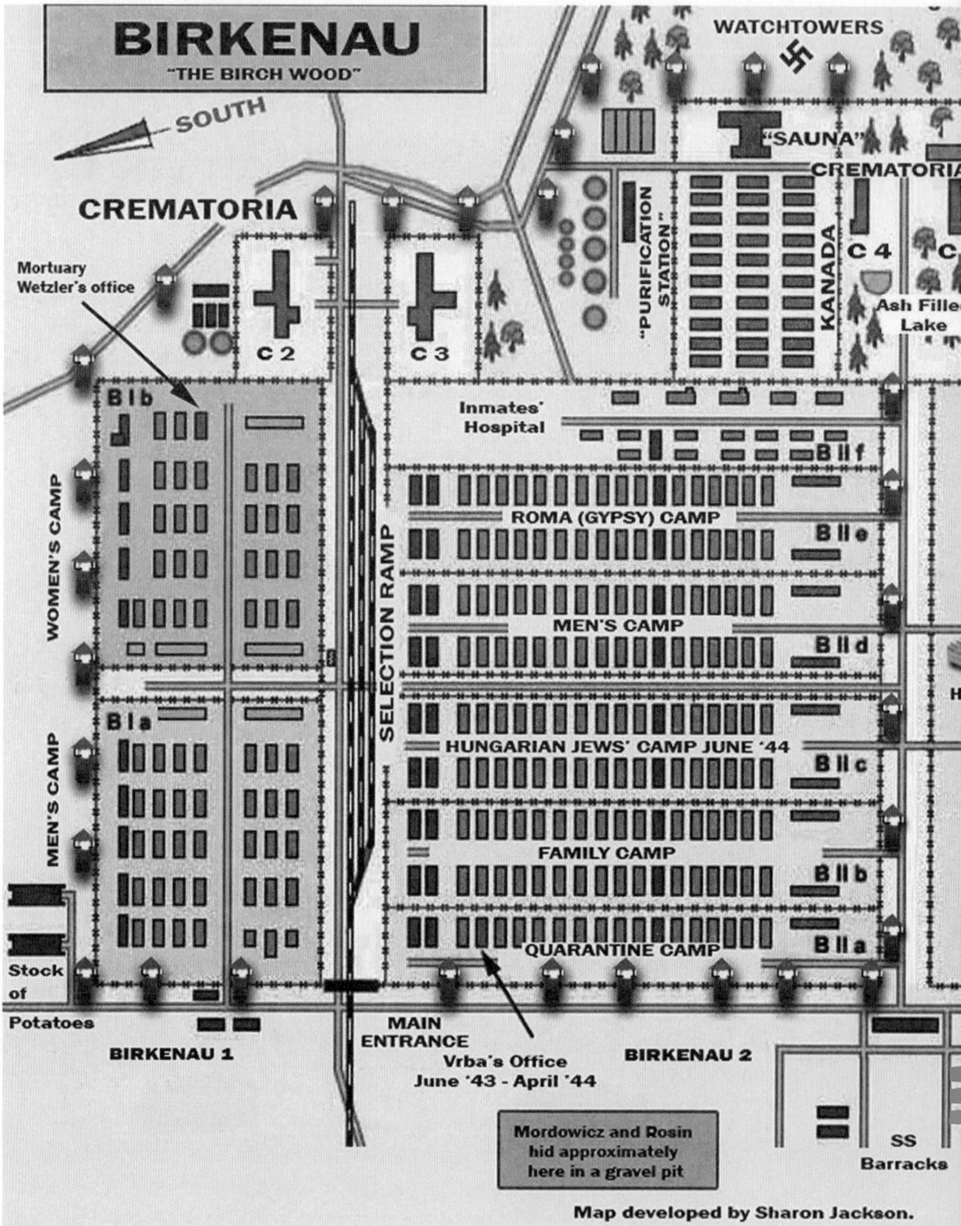

Map developed by Sharon Jackson.

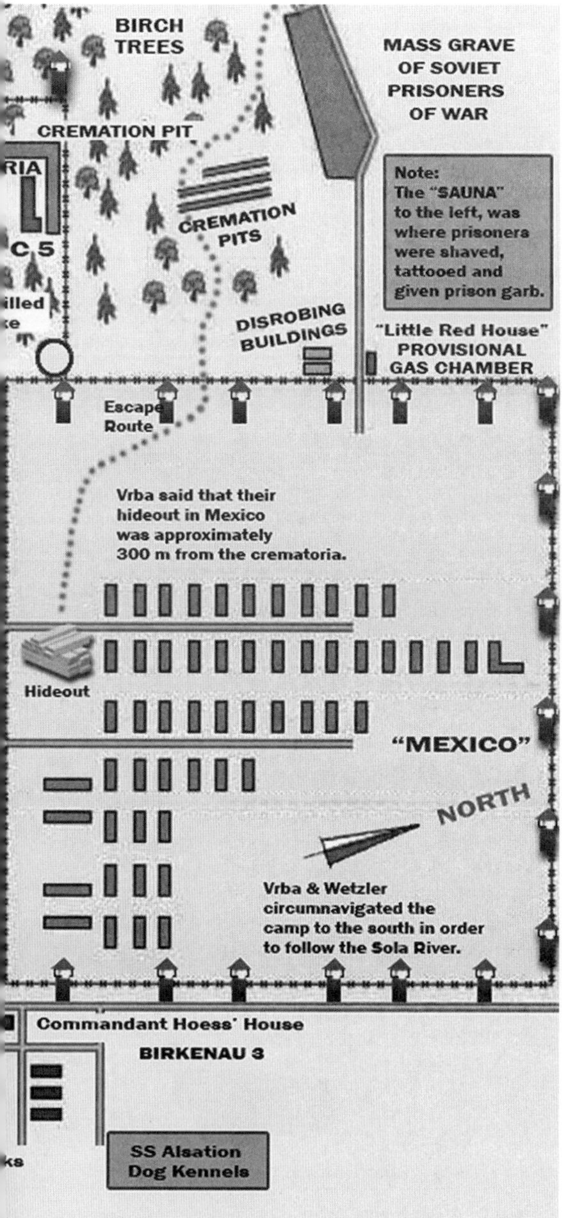

This diagram of Auschwitz II (Birkenau) shows the hiding place in "Mexico" (bottom right) where Rudolf Vrba and Alfréd Wetzler evaded capture for three days — within a lumber pile located "roughly 300 meters east of Crematorium V." It also locates the warehouse known as Kanada (top, center), the Selection Ramp (left, sideways text), Vrba's office, crematoria and other major features, as of 1944. There were three distinct sections of the overall prison complex known as Auschwitz. The first camp called Auschwitz I — (Stammlager) arose from a Polish army barracks at the town of Oswiecim. Auschwitz II (Birkenau), less than three kilometers away, was essentially a camp for mass murder built at the nearby village of Brzezinka. The third and largest complex, Auschwitz III (or Buna), was a slave labor compound at the village of Monowice (Monowitz). There, companies such as I.G. Farben worked prisoners to death. Rudolf Vrba was a rare prisoner who survived in all three. [Note: North appears on the right, South is shown on the left.]

Six Jews successfully escaped from Auschwitz I and Auschwitz II. Rarely mentioned is the lone Jewish female escapee, Cyla Cybulska, prisoner #29558, who was briefly in Birkenau before she escaped with Polish prisoner Jerzy Bielecki on July 21, 1944 from Auschwitz I. Married postwar, she lived in the United States as Cyla Zacharowicz. Little-known Jews who escaped from Buna/Monowitz (aka Auschwitz III) on July 22, 1944 are Josef "Pepi" Meisel (1911–1993) and Szymon Zajdow. As well, Max Drimmer and Mendel Scheingesicht [aka Herman Shine] were Jewish laborers who escaped from a Buna/Monowitz construction site with Polish civilian worker Józef Wróna on September 20, 1944.

See rudolfvrba.com for details.

Rudolf Vrba's first lover, Alice Munk, had been a teacher in the children's barrack at Terezín [aka Theresienstadt], 30 miles north of Prague, prior to their tragic tryst in Auschwitz. This graphic is from the cover of a rare, hardcover book published in Prague by the Council of Jewish Communities in the Czech Lands, in 1965. A copy was given to Vrba's partner in London, Gillian Bryant, by one of the contributors Erich Kulka, who Vrba knew from Auschwitz.

CHAPTER 6

Alice Munk & The Czech Family Camp

IT IS GENERALLY assumed that Rudolf Vrba's primary motivation for escaping from Auschwitz was to inform the world about the forthcoming mass murder of approximately 800,000 Hungarian Jews. A less noble explanation is that Vrba was heartsick over the murder of his first lover and therefore his escape from Auschwitz was a form of revenge against the Nazis.

Historians have tended to overlook the impact of Vrba's tragic love affair while he was still a teenager, but his affair with Alice Munk surely would have resulted in deep trauma. According to Vrba's memoir, she was gassed and cremated on the day after they had spent their first and last night together. We are told by Vrba that he stood for four hours outside the barracks, "tormented, until I saw the dark smoke mixed with a giant, yellow flame, rise up from the crematorium."

Alice Munk was introduced to Vrba by Fredy Hirsch who described the brown-eyed beauty as "one of my assistants." Although Vrba devotes 11 pages to the Czech Family Camp and Alice in his memoir, most critical writing about Vrba takes little notice of this personal tragedy. While Vrba's bravery was no doubt influenced by a desire to prevent the imminent mass murder of 800,000 Jews from Hungary, blowing the whistle on the Nazis was also the best way to avenge the murder of Alice Munk.

In Alfréd Wetzler's semi-fictionalized book, *Escape from Hell,* as the would-be escapees huddle in their Mexico hideout, even before the siren has sounded, Wetzler forestalls the getaway drama with a flashback to the mass-murder of nearly all the members of the so-called Czech Family Camp, including Vrba's lover Alice.

Further corroboration for Alice Munk's relationship with Rudolf Vrba has been provided by the Israeli academic Ruth Linn, by Vrba's first wife Gerta Vrbová and by the Terezín Memorial Museum. Also, supportive information can be found in the essential interviews conducted by documentary filmmaker Claude Lanzmann with Filip Müller and Rudolf Vrba.

Ruth Linn was contacted by the sister of Alice Munk after the war. This sister, Hanna Fabian, wanted to know if Linn could shed any further light on the disappearance of Alice in Auschwitz. Linn says she subsequently met Hanna Fabian at a home for elders in Haifa, somewhere around 2002 to 2005. Hanna confirmed that she had been in the Terezín (Theresienstadt) ghetto with her sister Alice, but it remains unclear as to why she, too, was not sent with her sister to the Czech Family Camp in Auschwitz-Birkenau.

At age 87 in 2014, Gerta Vrbová told British journalist Emily Ritter, "There had been a 'family camp' at Auschwitz, a place where families were kept together that the Nazis had set up only to fool the Red Cross in case they visited," she recalled. "There were 3,000 Jews there, and Rudi had fallen in love with one of them. Then one night, after six months with no sign of the Red Cross, the Nazis rounded them all up and gassed them. Children, women, everyone. That was it. He knew he had to escape. For himself, but also to tell the world what was happening. He'd heard rumors the Hungarian Jews would be next, and the Nazis were building new gas chambers."

Historian Radana Rutová at the Terezín Memorial Museum has provided access to a Czech document in the archive of the Jewish Museum in Prague that corroborates Alice Munk's role as a teacher within the children's barrack in Terezín. The document mentions some male teachers, including leader Moshe Stein. Then, in the top paragraph of the second page, according to a translation from Czech by Helen Karsai of Vancouver, it states: "We were strengthened by the arrival of Alice Munková, who became the head person of their barrack. She made sure that everything was in order in their barrack, and she looked after many ill people. There were hard times in their home, or barrack, which they called No. 9."

Nonetheless, Alice Munk remains largely a mystery. Evidently, she was born in Trutnov on November 30, 1920 and was raised in Hořice, presently a town of about 9,000 residents in the Hradec Králové Region of the Czech

Republic, approximately 170 kilometers west of Terezín. Vrba describes her as the daughter of wealthy industrialists "in a town north of Prague."

Her father, also named Rudolf, was born on November 2, 1876 in the Náchod district of the Hradec Králové Region and died or was murdered on November 1, 1940 at age 63. Her mother Emma (Emilie, born with the surname Spitzer on March 24, 1887) died alongside Alice in Auschwitz. Alice's twice-married, older sister Johanna Ottilie Munk (later married to Hans Fabian, later remarried to Otto Mautner) was born on November 14, 1911, and survived the Holocaust. She died at age 98 on October 7, 2010, in Israel where she met Linn.

According to the Terezín Ghetto Museum, Alice Munk was commandeered to be on Transport Ch, No. 173 (December 17, 1942, Hradec Králové Terezín). It is known she helped at the unsanctioned school in Terezín where Jewish children were educated. The fact that she was willing to serve in this capacity, at the risk of punishment, lends further credibility to Vrba's depictions of her in *I Escaped from Auschwitz*.

According to the Terezín Ghetto Museum, Alice Munk worked with children as a *Betreuerin* [responsible child minder] and took care of boys in Room IX (*heim L* 417). Children in Terezín lived separately from their parents in children's housing. "Alice worked there as a governess," according to Radana Rutová, "taking care of the children. Within these homes, the adults who cared for the children tried to provide them with some education and taught them in secret." [Czech-British historian Anna Hájková, as the author of the most recent book on Terezín, *The Last Ghetto: An Everyday History of Theresienstadt* (2020), was unable to provide any further information about Alice Munk when she visited Vancouver and delivered the biannual Rudolf Vrba Lecture.]

We can only speculate that Alice Munk might have been somehow related to the Prague physician Dr. Erich Munk who became chief medical officer at Terezín. A camp card states he was born on March 21, 1904 in Uherské Hradiště, 250 kilometers from Alice's birthplace. His parents were Berthold Munk and Ottilie Munk. His siblings were Max Munk, Olga Munk (Kapp) and Erna Munk (Jelinek). He married Emilie Freiberger and they were transported, on December 4, 1941, to the Thereseinstadt Ghetto [aka Terezín], 48 kilometers north of Prague, where Dr. Munk, a radiologist, was selected by the Jewish leadership to become chief of the Health Department and a Member of the Council of the Elders of the Jews. In 1943, Munk married Prague-born Emily Tausková (b. September 22, 1914) who later arrived on Ellis Island, New York, in 1951, and remarried to a Dr. Schliessner. She died near Los Angeles on April 7, 2012, at age 97. Dr. Erich Munk was eventually sent to his death at Auschwitz from Terezín on Transport Ev, No. 1786 on October 28, 1944. This occurred more than six months after the mass murder of the Czech Family Camp.

Alice was deported to Auschwitz on Transport Dl, No. 1472 (06. 09. 1943, Terezín Auschwitz) where she befriended the sisters Helena and Vera Rezek from Prague. With this pair, she served as an intermediary between the Auschwitz underground and the Czech family camp. There was a secret "tunnel of love" between the Family Camp and the main Birkenau men's camp but Vrba never used it. Still a virgin, he yearned for her from afar.

"For six months," Vrba recalled, "I had been in love with Alice – deeply in love. All that time, a few strands of wire had kept us apart. All that time, we had never so much as held hands." The situation would change soon after Vrba's main contact to the underground, Schmulewski, conveyed the news on March 4th that the *Sonderkommandos* had been told to prepare the furnaces for the incineration of four thousand prisoners on the night of March 7. Some 4,000 new Czech Jews had arrived from Terezín, so it was not difficult for the "old timers" in the camp to discern that the original batch of Czech inmates who had been forced into "regular" accommodations were soon to be murdered.

It was these changing and dire circumstances that would enable Vrba and Alice to become lovers. "Suddenly, the SS moved all new prisoners out of Camp A," Vrba recalled, "leaving only members of the permanent staff, like myself. As soon as it was cleared, the four thousand Czechs who had arrived in September were moved in among us."

They shared a first kiss in Vrba's room. "It was not much of a kiss because I had never had a great deal of practice in my life," he wrote, "but somehow my clumsiness did not seem to matter, and that night I fell asleep, thinking, soon, maybe, the war will be over." But the Nazis had a timetable that would take precedence.

In the morning, the resistance leader Schmulewski told Vrba that mass executions were likely to commence the next day. Vrba passed this dire news to Alice, Helena and Vera when they came to his room.

"I made no attempt to break the news gently, to soft-pedal," he recalled, "for now it was too late. Now we all had to think fast."

For an hour or so, the foursome discussed all aspects of the predicament, getting nowhere. Alice eventually stood and told the sisters Helena and Vera to leave, giving Vrba and Alice precious privacy. "We were alone," he recalled. "For me, it was the first time I had ever been alone with a girl in my bedroom ... She was curled up on the bed now, and I do not think I have ever seen anyone lovelier."

After making love for the first and only time, on the night of March 7, the young lovers' only hope was to help mount a resistance, to prepare for a fight. The veterans in the Auschwitz Resistance hastily decided that the charismatic German Jew, Alfred "Fredy" Hirsch (b. 1916), would be best suited to galvanize a revolt among the doomed members of the "old" Czech Family Camp. Vrba was designated by the Auschwitz underground to serve as their intermediary with Hirsch. The fact that Vrba was entrusted as the messenger between Fredy (the Family Camp) and the organized Resistance (or Underground) in Auschwitz is significant because it has been frequently suggested that Vrba was too much of a hothead, too unpredictable, to be fully integrated into the Resistance. After all, he was still a teenager. Therefore, the fact that he was selected to serve as the link in that situation would appear to negate such an accusation.

The unlikely duo conferred at about 11 a.m.

"Fredy, you're the only man who can do it," Vrba said. "The only man they'll follow."

Fraught with tense drama, this conversation brought forth an agony of indecision in Hirsch. He could not believe the Nazis would exterminate even the precious children who worshipped him as a teacher, as a friend, as a second father. Hirsch asked for an hour to think it over.

Alice was waiting outside. She and Rudolf talked about their future beyond Auschwitz, a future likely both knew was never to be. When Vrba returned to talk to Fredy Hirsch, he was lying on his bed, unconscious. "His heavy breath was growling in his throat," Vrba recalled. "His face was blue-gray. Flecks of froth hung from his lips, and I saw all the signs of luminal poisoning."

Unable to see his beloved children suffer, the athletic, Family Camp leader had taken his own life as the only antidote to suffering. Whether or not Vrba felt disdain for Hirsch's lack of bravery, or if he felt any regrets as the messenger who instigated Hirsch's suicide, remains a matter of conjecture.

To reduce panic, prior to the mass execution of the Family Camp Jews, the Nazis told the Czech internees that they were to be transferred to the new Heydebreck sub-camp that operated from April 1 to January 26, 1945. There were some minor attempts made by the doomed Family Camp members to resist, but mostly the mass executions went smoothly. On their way to their deaths on the night between March 8th and 9th, 1944, the victims sang the Czechoslovak anthem, the Jewish anthem *Hatikva* and the *Internationale*. Alice and nearly all of her Czech companions were murdered by the Nazis. There would be another mass execution of the incoming contingent of Czechoslovak Jews on July 10–12. These were the largest mass murders of Czechoslovak citizens during World War II.

Alice Munková was murdered at age 23.

~

BORN ON DECEMBER 15, 1920 – in Horná Mariková, Považská Bystrica District, Trenčín Region, Slovakia – Katya Singer was an assimilated Czech Jew who survived in the Women's Camp at Auschwitz as a secretary or *Rapportschreiberin* from September 1942 until her deportation to Stutthof in 1944. After the war, she moved to Prague, worked as an art dealer, married a physician and became known as Katherina Velenská. Before she died in 1995, she gave a recorded interview on July 21, 1991 at the Prague Intercontinental Hotel to camp survivor Susan Cernyak-Spatz in which she confirms that members of the Czech Family Camp knew in advance about the Nazis' planned mass execution.

It is possible that Alice Munk, as someone close to Fredy Hirsch, could have forewarned Rudolf Vrba about the planned annihilation of the Czech Family Group, rather than the other way around. Rather than assume that Vrba was intending to gallantly save her, one could also imagine that Alice Munk was desperate and pleaded with him to do something, anything, to somehow save her. This anti-romantic scenario must also be considered given that Rudolf Vrba later discussed Auschwitz with a lover he had from 1971–73, Betty Lambert, and she subsequently wrote an anti-romantic play depicting a female writer and a male-chauvinist character, named Gustav, who had been in Auschwitz.

So-called transactional sexual relationships were not uncommon in Auschwitz, the best known of which was between the beautiful Jewish prisoner Helena Citron and Austrian SS officer, Franz Wunsch, as chronicled in the documentary *Love it Was Not*. Heterosexual love affairs between Jewish prisoners were much rarer due to the separation of the male and female camps, but Helen "Zippi" Spitzer, a Slovakian Jew, did maintain an extended sexual relationship with David Wisnia, a Polish Jew, 10 years younger, whose operatic singing voice helped him survive. Spitzer's office mate and friend Katya Singer had an extended and forbidden affair with the sadistic SS officer, Gerhard Palitzsch.

"I often received information," Singer said, "that I could hand on. Once, I accidentally lifted the telephone receiver, and there was a conversation. I don't know who was talking, but the person said that an order had been issued [by the SS] to destroy the family camp. I, of course, immediately informed the camp inmates." Confirmation that the information was spread to Auschwitz-Birkenau was also made in a testimony by Polish inmate Anna Palarcyk. There is an extensive 1995 interview with her in the U.S. Holocaust Memorial Museum [wherein the first mention of Katya appears on page 73].

As Rudolf Vrba's most trusted academic confidante, Ruth Linn has recognized the importance of the so-called "Family Camp" or "Czech Family Camp" at Auschwitz with regards to Vrba's desire to escape. The underground movement in Auschwitz had deduced that when arrivals to the family camp were marked "SB6," this was a somewhat cryptic designation for Special Treatment of *Sonderbehandlung*. The abbreviation meant those who were privileged to receive the comforts of the Family Camp were meant to be murdered six months after their arrival.

During an interview for Israeli television, Linn provided a synopsis of Vrba's relations with the gay but universally admired Fredy Hirsch (translated here from the Hebrew):

Vrba's Relationship with Fredy Hirsch

"Auschwitz includes the story of one of the Germans' most successful organized deceptions – the so-called Family Camp that was built by the Nazis. About 4,000 Jews were brought from the Theresienstadt ghetto to Auschwitz on September 1943. All were exempted from the camp ordeal of tattooing, hair cutting, shaving and spraying. They were allowed to remain as families with their own clothing. They were also allowed to maintain some sort of social activities. Of course, no one could fully understand what motivated the Germans to preserve these families as families.

"Later, as we all know, this was just a misleading device of the Nazis – a conspiracy – so the Red Cross would not learn the true nature of Auschwitz. In March 1944, six months after their arrival, they were all gassed, and another transport of about 4,000 Czech inmates was brought to Auschwitz. This second family camp replaced the first one. In this second family camp, there was an admirable counselor named Fredy Hirsch. At the eve of the liquidation of this second family camp, it was Rudolf Vrba who came over to this camp, as a messenger of the underground in Auschwitz-Birkenau, and informed Fredy Hirsch that tomorrow the entire family camp was going to be gassed. Vrba assured him that the information came from the *zonder* [sic] commando and was based on their estimation of the amount of resources that would be needed for the liquidation.

"Vrba carried one message from the underground to Fredy: 'go and revolt.' Hirsch turned to Vrba and asked him, 'Whom should I revolt with? Children? Give me an hour to think about it.'

"Vrba returns after an hour and finds Hirsch dead. He could not make the decision. Maybe there are other interpretations. As has been noticed by Mark Bloch, the Jewish historian who also died in the Holocaust, war story is not just the story of shooting, cannons, and dead bodies. It is also a psychological story of individuals who are forced to make decisions within such hard conditions.

"And here comes the part that intrigued me: I could find Fredy Hirsch's story in many Hebrew history books, but Vrba's story was not. I also couldn't find his book in Hebrew. In Lanzmann's documentary, Vrba's short testimony was stunning but what was his personal story? We know that on the 7th of April, he escaped from Auschwitz-Birkenau with his friend, Alfréd Wetzler. But what else? The mystery fired up my curiosity ..."

Linn concludes with an assessment that rescuing the latest shipment of Czechoslovakian Jews was a primary motive for Vrba's escape. She is in good company. In a new biography about the Auschwitz escapee Mordowicz, *The Auschwitz Protocols*, Fred B. Bleakley provides a footnote in which he records that Martin Gilbert's wife, Lady Esther Gilbert, sent an email to him on July 26, 2017, in which she confided that her husband, Sir Martin Gilbert, privately believed that Rudolf Vrba's original and primary motive for escape was to possibly save the lives of the latest shipment of Czech Jews who constituted the new inmates of the Family Camp.

Hence, Ruth Linn and Sir Martin Gilbert were like-minded in this regard: Rudolf Vrba's love affair with Alice Munk was as much the major catalyst for this resolve to escape as the stated resolve to save 800,000 Hungarian Jews. At age 87, in an interview conducted by Emily Retter for an article that appeared in *The Mirror* on May 3, 2014, Vrba's first wife Gerta confirmed Gilbert's private opinion and Linn's public one.

Of the Jews sent to comprise the first, so-called Czech Family camp, it has been suggested that only 32 were not murdered. Claude Lanzmann's essential interviews with Filip Müller and Rudolf Vrba are the most powerful and persuasive evidence to support claims made by Gerta Vrbová and Sir Martin Gilbert that the fate of the Czech Family Camp was a primary motivation for Rudolf Vrba's desire to escape, but the majority of books and articles pertaining to the *Vrba-Wetzler Report* do not speculate on the impact of Rudolf Vrba's tragic love affair with Alice Munk.

The Nazis not only stole billions of dollars worth of properties, art, household furnishings, vehicles, gold, silver and art; they also plucked Vrba's first love from his arms, gassed her to death and incinerated her. If it is crass to include the fact that his first love literally went up in smoke, and that some of his teenage seed might well have been inside her when she was incinerated, well, one needs to be crass.

As much as the imminent deaths of possibly 800,000 Hungarians that he did not know could have been Rudolf Vrba's primary motive for escaping from Auschwitz – one might also speculate that escaping in order to blow the whistle on the Holocaust was the only way Rudolf Vrba could possibly avenge the death of Alice Munk.

To unveil the unparalleled audacity and breadth of the Nazis' streamlined mass murder methods was the first step towards exposing Alice's killers and making them criminally liable. "Vengeance is mine," saith the Lord. But Vrba was an atheist; so, he sought to generate vengeance with his own heroism. Blowing the whistle on the Holocaust was therefore also Rudolf Vrba's ultimate act of revenge.

In terms of maintaining Vrba's own sanity and self-esteem within a hideous landscape of cruelty and degradation, the family camp was a potent and constant reminder that "normal life" could still exist, that Auschwitz really was an aberration. Consequently, it is hard not to conclude that the suicide of the family camp's leading personality Fredy Hirsch, after Vrba had served as the chief intermediary between Hirsch and the camp underground, also would have had a significant impact on Vrba's psyche.

From all reports, Hirsch attended to the youths in the Family Camp with remarkable charm and wisdom; he managed to keep many of the Czech youngsters sane and even occasionally happy. Even the Nazis admired and liked him. Hirsch was something of a miracle worker. Mengele and Eichmann both visited his compound to witness the education of youngsters and they had voiced their approval. The death rate of children under his direction and care was near zero. Hirsch was such an inspirational figure that even the fact that he was openly gay did not provoke enmity.

Tasked with the mission of convincing Hirsch to serve as the leader of an uprising within the Family Camp, Vrba felt obliged to assert some pressure on Hirsch to comply as quickly as possible. After Hirsch demurred and instead chose to commit suicide, it is conceivable Vrba might have even imagined himself to be at least partially responsible for Hirsch's untimely demise. If he had succeeded in convincing Hirsch to lead a rebellion, could there have been – by some miracle – a different outcome for the Czech Family Camp?

Rudolf Vrba never wrote about such things. He did, however, describe and celebrate the positive aspects of both Munk and Hirsch. Vrba's love affair with Alice Munk, tenderly described with Alan Bestic's prose, affirmed for him – after more than a year of degrading and constant compromise to appease hostile captors within the boundaries of a collective nightmare – that his own feelings and thoughts could still triumph, that his heart could still serve as a compass. Alice Munk, in particular, served him as a beacon for a redemptive reality.

In his semi-fictionalized *Escape from Hell,* Wetzler interrupts the drama to recall how the families in Block-II B receiving "special treatment" were ultimately sent to the "Zyklon showers." Wetzler claims that one of the Czechs being sent on the 400-meter march to death had shouted out, "Avenge us!" Whether that outcry was really heard or not, it provides the narrator with the catalyst for this passage that immediately follows:

"There's nothing we want more than revenge. But how can such endless streams of people into the gas be avenged? Where would you find a just measure for revenge? Well, yes, there is the just measure of death for death. But death is only an instant, perhaps the most painless and most unexpected result. A full stop after suffering. But how do you avenge grief and unimaginable suffering? How indeed? When you have saved your life, too? Will you live in order to perform prolonged and frightful torture and then slow and frightful death? No, you could not live like that. But equally you could not live on this earth along with the murderers. So, what will you do to them? Of course, you will have your revenge. Somehow or other you will have your revenge."

Before he published his novel *What Dante Did Not See* in 1964, Wetzler first wrote *Auschwitz, The Tomb of Four Million People* in 1946.

CHAPTER 7

How Vrba Really Escaped

This rare 1944 SS photo of the "Mexico" section Auschwitz-Birkenau, known by the Nazis as Bauabschnitt III (Construction Sector III), shows the area where Vrba and Wetzler hid for three days inside a woodpile. This expansion of Auschwitz-Birkenau was undertaken to facilitate the anticipated mass murder of yet-to-be-transported, Hungarian Jews.

THE MOST IMPORTANT escape of World War II began on April 7, 1944, at 2 p.m. when Rudolf Vrba and Alfréd Wetzler huddled inside a pile of construction lumber, in a treeless zone of Auschwitz-Birkenau that was nicknamed Mexico ("Meksyk" in Polish). Such was the bleak humor of the most lethal death camp in history that overflow Auschwitz captives who were forced to sleep there – outside in the mud, often naked, with only a blanket – were nicknamed Mexicans. The *Sonderkommando* veteran Filip Müller confirms the origin of the name in *Eyewitness Auschwitz: Three Years in the Gas Chambers* (1979).

As registrars, Vrba and Wetzler reached their hideout in Mexico on April 7 by feigning errands. At section B-II-A, the quarantine hut, Vrba said he must deliver the identity cards for some transferred prisoners to section B-II-D. As a two-year veteran of Auschwitz, Wetzler reported at Section B-II-D that he must visit the hospital at Section B-II-F.

The pair's hideout-in-the-open was a stack of lumber situated, according to Wetzler, "near the *weberei* [weaving mill] where sealing for submarines was manufactured." In his essay entitled *The Preparations for the Holocaust in Hungary: An Eyewitness Account,* Vrba states, "we first remained hidden in Birkenau about 300 meters east from Crematorium V." Wearing Dutch suits, overcoats and boots obtained from the Kanada warehouse, Vrba and Wetzler would remain concealed outside the barbed wire perimeter of the Auschwitz prisoner barracks while they were simultaneously inside the external perimeter of guard towers that were usually only manned by Nazi guards during the day. While search parties with dogs were trying to locate the escapees for three days, those outer guard towers would be manned on a 24-hour basis; but after three days and nights of search parties, the regular routine would resume – at which time Vrba and Wetzler planned to run past the unguarded towers at night.

According to Vrba's memoir co-written with Bestic, three days later, when it finally came time for the weakened pair to remove their timber roof, Vrba and Wetzler ostensibly discovered they could barely manage to shift the weight of the wood overhead. We have been led to believe that without the inadvertent assistance of Nazi guards peeling away some of the timber during an aborted search, Vrba and Wetzler might have been trapped within their tomb. Given that both men would have been severely weakened by the adverse conditions, this version of events has not been questioned.

In fact, their escape story is more complicated.

~

ON APRIL 7, two accessories to the escape gambit helped Vrba and Wetzler swiftly remove layers of planks, affording them access to their hiding place; then timbers were replaced to make a continuous stack. These two helpers have been cited by historian Hendryk Świebocki as Polish Jews "who worked with Pawel Gulba in the digging crew."

Vrba's non-fictional account further states, "Nobody spoke, however. The Poles moved the planks and gave us an almost imperceptible nod . . . Our eyes soon got used to the gloom and we could see each other in the light that filtered through the cracks. We hardly dared to breathe, let alone talk." In his novelistic account of the escape, Wetzler would claim one of the Poles whispered, "Bon voyage."

The pair had sprinkled Russian tobacco, pre-soaked in petrol, outside their hideout, to deter the camp's 200 Alsatian search dogs and their handlers that would soon be searching for them.

Like two men in the same coffin, Alfréd Wetzler, age 25, and Rudolf Vrba, age 19, were able to lie side by side. Squeezed and immobilized, one next to the other, they had scarves tied around their mouths so as not to reveal where they were by accidental coughing. "The alarm would not be raised until 5:30." Vrba recalled, "and suddenly I realized I was longing to hear it. I felt like a boxer, sitting in his corner, waiting for the bell, or like a soldier in the trenches, waiting to go over the top."

Fluent in German and several other languages, both men from the eastern part of Czechoslovakia (Slovakia) were keenly aware there was more at stake than their lives. Having closely monitored the train arrivals for two years, they had correctly deduced that Auschwitz was expanding its operations to eliminate 800,000 Hungarian Jews – the last remaining major population of Jews in Europe.

"When a series of transports from the Netherlands arrived," Vrba wrote, "cheeses enriched the war-time rations. It was sardines when a series of transports of French Jews arrived; halva and olives when transports of Jews from Greece reached the camp, and now the SS were talking of Hungarian salami, a well-known Hungarian provision suitable for taking on a long journey."

Obviously, Hungarian Jews would be next. "Because it was close to Slovakia," he later wrote, "I thought it would be possible to give the warning."

The two fugitives calmed their nerves by wedging more tainted Russian tobacco, called *makhorka*, into the cracks of their refuge. Vrba later reported it took him "at least an hour to impregnate our temporary prison thoroughly with dog repellant."

Vrba then used a knife to scrape off a message, "Kiss our arses!", at the request of a preceding occupant Sandor Eisenbach, a fellow Slovakian who had left those words on one of the planks as a taunt to the Nazis, after which he was recaptured, tortured but not killed – a very rare case of a captured escapee being allowed to live.

Previous accounts of the Vrba-Wetzler escape have tended to neglect to mention that, at the time, the highest-ranking Nazi official for the three camps was the SS Senior Garrison Commander (*Standortältester*) Arthur Liebehenschel. When the order to replace Rudolf Höss was made by Himmler in November, Liebehenschel was put in charge of Auschwitz

I; the commander of Auschwitz II (Birkenau) would be Friedrich Hartjenstein and the commander of Auschwitz III (Buna) would be Heinrich Schwarz, but as the commandant of the *Stammlager*, the old main camp, Liebehenschel was therefore *Standortältester* (Head Garrison Officer).

The presence of Liebehenschel would be hugely significant for Vrba's escape because it was Liebehenschel's leniency that had enabled Eisenbach and three accomplices to survive after their failed escape attempt. Vrba would never have risked his life in the lumber pile if his fellow Slovakian had not assured him that nobody among his escape party had revealed, after they were captured, how the lumber pile had been converted into a hideout.

On April 7, a Friday, neither Vrba or Wetzler realized it was only a few hours before the onset of Passover, the annual festival for Jews to thank God for their liberty. Both escapees would remain atheists.

SS guards finally realized that two camp registrars were missing from their barracks during the 5 p.m. roll call but the shrieking siren of the alarm at Auschwitz was delayed, possibly because the news that two more Jews were attempting another escape would come as an embarrassment to the Auschwitz command.

Two French Jews had recently been caught trying to escape while carrying a loaf of bread containing diamonds pilfered from gassed victims. They were executed for theft. Even Liebehenschel could not be seen as someone condoning theft from the Third Reich. Then, on April 5, Siegfried Lederer [Vítězslav Lederer in Czech] had become the first Jew to escape from Auschwitz-Birkenau by donning the uniform of a high-ranking Nazi supplied to him by his Nazi accomplice Viktor Pestek, a German guard who had fallen in love with the beautiful Renée Neumann in the Czech Family Camp. Pestek had first asked Wetzler, and then Vrba, if either wished to join him as an escape partner; both had declined the offer (according to Vrba).

Renée Neumann had been unwilling to abandon her mother in the Czech Family Camp, so Pestek had made a complex plan that required a Czech-speaking accomplice. With Lederer's help, this likeable Nazi naively hoped to obtain false paperwork in order to extricate Neumann and her mother from Auschwitz. It was Lederer who eventually agreed to don the uniform of a high-ranking Nazi and accompany the German soldier on his lovestruck mission. After they somehow obtained false paperwork that would enable Pestek to return to Auschwitz and extricate the mother and daughter, purportedly to enable them to appear for a court case, Lederer could be a free man.

Pestek knew the guard duty protocol. Bizarrely, the pair were able to ride out of the main camp entrance on bicycles with Lederer as a higher-ranking officer who would not deign to address subordinates.

Unfortunately, when Pestek returned to Auschwitz with his false paperwork, Renée was still leery of her suitor's plan. The Nazis ultimately recaptured Pestek, who was promptly put on trial and executed. Lederer repeatedly tried to raise the alarm about Auschwitz; hardly anyone would believe him. He survived the war but carried the anguish of being disbelieved for the rest of his days.

~

ON APRIL 7, the shrieking siren of the alarm at Auschwitz was finally heard around 6 p.m. The warning that announced the pair's escape attempt lasted for 10 deafening minutes, but the Commandant of Auschwitz-Birkenau, Fritz Hartjenstein, would not be officially informed of this latest escape attempt, by teleprinter, until 8:33 p.m. He, in turn, waited until 11:30 to send a telegram to inform German police about the fugitives.

"No other siren has such a terrible wailing note," Wetzler would recall. "It was as if thousands of packs of wolves had come together in absolute silence to produce a howl that would make the air vibrate and freeze the blood in your veins ... One thousand two hundred SS men poured out of their barracks for the hunt."

Inside the hideout, the would-be escapists could hear the Nazis yelling orders to their vicious search dogs. Vrba kept glancing at his watch. "Then I disciplined myself to ignore it, grinning in the dark as I thought fatuously of my mother in her kitchen back home, shaking her finger at me and saying solemnly. 'A watched pot never boils.'"

Filip Müller, the most famous survivor of the *Sonderkommando* units, would describe the escape more than 30 years later: "In the area outside the barbed-wire fences ... another feverish hunt was in progress. SS men with Alsatian guard dogs were looking around in Mexico where the hiding place was, searching for the prisoners on the building sites, among building materials and in trenches. All through the night, furious barking and yapping of the dogs could be heard. Trained to attack, they could sniff out any unfamiliar smell and hear any sound."

The pair had bread, margarine and wine but could not bring themselves to eat. Their stomachs were knotted with stress. They took turns sleeping, pressing against each other for warmth, checking their wristwatches to keep track of the changing of camp guards in the watchtowers. Meanwhile, an international warrant for their arrest would soon be issued to all Gestapo stations, telegraphically, as well as to security police (*Sicherheitsdienst*), border guards (*Grenzpolizei*) and criminal police (*Kripo*).

Vrba would later staunchly maintain they did not carry any written evidence of Auschwitz's operations with them for fear of being searched. Wetzler, in his semi-fictionalized account of two fugitives with different names, first published as a novel, wrote that they did. Eastern European historians would tend to accept Wetzler's fictional account since he later became a communist, whereas Vrba's truthful account would be denigrated after he had defected to the West. Simultaneously, Yad Vashem in Israel was averse to publicizing Vrba's non-fiction account because Vrba was openly criticizing Jewish leadership for failing to adequately inform European Jewry of the contents of the *Vrba-Wetzler Report*.

On Sunday morning, their accomplice Adamek urinated against the pile and whistled to signal that all was well. That night, Allied bombs were dropped nearby; anti-aircraft guns fired into the sky. "The planks trembled with every salvo," Vrba recalled. Most prisoners in Auschwitz welcomed the idea of an Allied bombardment, even if their own lives would be endangered. At least they would have the relief of knowing the outside world had seemingly finally discovered where they were.

According to Vrba's account, once the hidden pair heard two German-speaking searchers climb onto their woodpile. They started heaving some of the planks aside. Vrba and Wetzler could hear every word that was said above them. One of the searchers was named Otto. As the pair remained huddled within their cocoon, Vrba would recognize the voice of *Unterscharführer* Buntrok shouting, "Look behind those planks!" Boots were atop the hideout, with barking dogs. Clutching their knives, the escapees were only inches away from being discovered.

Having already decided to never be taken prisoner, Vrba was determined to kill himself, with a knife or razor blade, if need be. But halfway through their task, the Nazi search party was distracted by some nearby disturbance and abandoned their task. "The stupid bastards," Wetzler supposedly whispered.

But there is much more to the story.

In early April, taking turns sleeping in furtive fits and starts, both men were increasingly weakened by fear. Conditions inside the woodpile were bone-chilling; the stress was draining their abilities to concentrate and remain still. As a result, the pair decided they had no alternative but to radically alter the escape plan. Vrba and Wetzler had, in fact, promised to allow two builders of the hideout to join them inside the cramped wooden cavern as soon as the Nazis had rescinded their search parties after three days.

When the pair of Poles arrived to be let inside the hideout, Vrba and Wetzler decided not to cooperate because they agreed they could not manage another three more days and nights inside the enclosure. They also knew that two prisoners standing alone in the expanse of the Mexico construction zone could only risk standing beside the woodpile for a minute or so.

In a fit of pique and revenge, the two Poles who were double-crossed hurriedly piled even more lumber atop the hideout. This way, if they couldn't use the hideout they had conceived and made, nobody else would be able to benefit from it either. This likely explains why Vrba and Wetzler had such extreme difficulty extracting themselves from the hideout.

Robin Vrba has verified this version of events in recorded interviews after hitherto unrevealed circumstances of the escape were uncovered within Vrba's private papers in the FDR Presidential Library archive.

There is a one-page document in the FDR Presidential Library archives that records a meeting between Vrba and Reverend Frederick W. Metzger at the University of British Columbia during which Vrba told Metzger that he and Wetzler had altered the original escape plan and opted to escape on their own, after enduring an excruciating three days and nights in the woodpile, thereby contravening the original plan to remain in hiding for six days.

Here is the relevant paragraph from Metzger's account:

> "Well," said Rudi, "there was more to the events than that. Actually, the Poles wanted to test the detection ability of the Nazi guards, so

that if the method worked, they would escape with us. So, we made a deal that we would be hidden for three days in a woodpile, and if we remained undetected by the Nazis, the Poles would get us out of the pile and we would all run away together. But after three days my companion could not stand it any longer, and he started to move some of the logs in order to break out. The Poles noticing this, got angry, and piled up so many more logs that it was impossible for us to move even an inch. Since we had broken our contract with them, they condemned us to death. On the same day something roused the suspicion of the Nazi guards, so that they came to our woodpile and started to scatter the logs. We were in danger of being discovered and to be shot on the spot. But just as the guards came to the last row of logs covering us, it happened that some disturbance and shouting occurred at the other end of the camp, so they stopped bothering with the woodpile and we were left free to escape into the night."

Stanley Medicks, founder of British and European Machal Association of volunteers who fought for Israel in 1948, also recorded that Vrba told him that once, at a swimming pool, "someone walked up to him, noticed the number tattooed on his arm and said, 'You are Rosenberg.'" The man at the swimming pool identified himself as one of the men who had masterminded

Stanley Medicks provided corroboration that Vrba and Wetzler did not engineer their escape.

the escape bunker. In 2008, Medicks wrote a letter to Martin Gilbert that reconfirmed, "One of Rudi's pleasures was meeting the man in Kanada who designed the bunker." Hence, Martin Gilbert would likely have been "in the know" about how Vrba and Wetzler had escaped for approximately eight years before he died in 2015.

ROBIN VRBA: "The only time I think Rudi ever compromised his ethics was when they were in the bunker and they were supposed to let the other two people in," she said. "Freddy [Wetzler] said, 'No' and Rudi didn't counteract that. It has nothing to do with [him] being younger or older. He knew that Wetzler was right – that they would never survive if they had to spend another three days in that bunker. Wetzler said to Rudi, 'If you let them in, I'm going out. I'm leaving.' And, so, Rudi let that go. He considered it an ethical compromise. Wetzler knew that Rudi would honor his word. But Wetzler couldn't do it any longer. They were up to here. That was almost a superhuman experience to go through that and survive three days in that bunker. I mean, he didn't say it, but they had to go to the bathroom; they had to live in this hell-hole. It was cold. It was pretty severe."

ALAN TWIGG: "You're saying Rudi would have kept his word to the other guys. But it was Wetzler who said, 'No, we gotta get out.' Is that correct?"

ROBIN VRBA: "Correct."

~

ANOTHER DETAIL THAT has been missing from preceding accounts of the escape is that Wetzler had a mental collapse as they were attempting to leave Auschwitz. This occurred after they had managed to extricate themselves from the hideout. According to Robin Vrba, her husband told her on several occasions that he had to rally Wetzler and persuade Wetzler to follow him beyond Auschwitz.

Ruth Linn has verified this detail. "I am well aware of the story," she wrote, on December 19, 2023, "since he told me. Yes, this is the truth. I cannot elaborate on why I did not include it in our version of the book."

One assumes Rudolf Vrba was reluctant to include this detail because it would cast his comrade in an unfavorable light. Regardless, the pair's bravery and endurance would ultimately result in one of the most important documents of the 20th century, the *Vrba-Wetzler Report.*

The search was officially called off on Monday night on April 10, 1944 at 6:30 p.m. when the pair of fugitives heard guards shouting, "*Postenkette abziehen!*" (Cordon down!). After three days of searching, the Nazis were assuming the prisoners had successfully fled the grounds. Once again, the watchtowers on the outer perimeter would be left unmanned for the night, as was the custom, after all prisoners within the barracks had been counted, and the area was surrounded by an inner perimeter of sentries.

The pair's luck held for 80 hours. They waited until around 9 p.m., then, with much difficulty, Vrba and Wetzler set about extricating themselves from the hideout. It was eerily silent. They could only stand erect in the moonlight with great difficulty. Gradually, their limbs became functional again.

"We scrambled out into the cold air and replaced the planks carefully in case someone else might be able to use the escape chamber later, and for a moment we sat on the pile of wood, motionless, invisible, gazing at the inner camp, which we were determined to never see again.

"For the first time, I was seeing Auschwitz from the outside, viewing it as its victims viewed it. The brilliant lights painted a soft yellow patch in the darkness, giving the whole place a mysterious aura that was almost beautiful. We, however, knew that it was a terrible beauty, that in those barracks, people were dying, people were starving, people were intriguing, and murder lurked around every corner.

"We turned our backs to it, slid to the ground, flung ourselves flat, and began to crawl slowly on our bellies, foot by careful foot, away from the toothless watchtowers and toward the small forest of birch trees that hid the old-fashioned pits of fire and gave Birkenau its name. We reached it, rose, and ran, stooping, through it until we came to open ground again and began to crawl once more."

In this way, they commenced their gruelling, 11-day trek to safety. The runaways made their way mainly by moonlight, walking parallel to the Sola River, heading for the Polish border with Slovakia 133 kilometers away as the crow flies.

During their escape, Vrba proved himself to be the opposite of a hothead. He made sure they adhered to the set of guidelines provided by Captain Dimitri Volkov, a bear of a man from Zaporizhia of the Don region (Ukraine) who had escaped from Sachsenhausen prison near Berlin and almost reached safety in Kyiv.

"As I wriggled forward, I remembered Dimitri Volkov's advice that the battle was just beginning. Although Volkov's advice was useful constantly," Vrba recalled, "he had never managed, however, to teach me how to see in the dark."

Volkov was one of a 100 Soviet soldiers who were captured on the eastern front and transferred to Auschwitz for additional punishment, and it was Volkov who supplied the vital tip about using petrol-soaked *machorka* to evade the dogs.

"He didn't want to know any details [of the escape]," Vrba later said, "because he was afraid I might name him as an accomplice if I was tortured."

Vrba had taught himself what he referred to as some "reasonable Russian" in his mid-teens so he had been able to gain Volkov's trust in Auschwitz during the pair's extended conversations about Russian literature. For his part, Volkov must have respected Vrba as a risk taker in his own right. At only 19, here was a youth who had already escaped imprisonment from Nováky and consummated a love affair within the confines of Auschwitz-Birkenau. [In 1987, the Soviet spy and author Ovid Gorchakov would contact Claude Lanzmann to let him know that the "Cossack" Dimitry Volkov had survived the war and was living in the Soviet Union. Gorchakov claimed to have written an article about the relationship between Vrba and Volkov for the Russian magazine *Rovesnik* and the Jewish monthly *Sovietishe Heimland*.]

The adverse conditions in the mountains were likely exaggerated in Wetzler's semi-fictionalized book that he published under his *nom-de-guerre* Jozef Lánik. The fictionalized protagonists Karol (wise) and Val (weak) continually encounter snowy conditions. It's now possible to retroactively check temperatures for particular dates in the area to prove the duo's privations were exaggerated.

Wetzler originally described his book, *What Dante Did Not See* (*Co Dante nevidel* Osveta, Bratislava, 1964), as a novel, hence he understood and admitted his account was a distortion of the truth. Unfortunately, this version of events has been misinterpreted as non-fiction and was used as the basis for a feature film.

To the same extent that their hideout had been completely constructed by others, beyond the barbed wire, it was Volkov's shrewdness that served as the pair's compass as much as their own. Adhering to his "Manual of What Every Escaper Should Know" – as Vrba put it – they would never carry meat. They would trust nobody. They would never carry money. "If you're starving," Volkov warned, "you'll be tempted to buy food." Volkov had also advised, "Never get drunk with freedom." They would live off the land. Steal. Keep away from people. "Don't be afraid of the Germans—there are many of them but each of them is small." Don't trust your legs because a bullet can always run faster. Take a knife for hunting or defending yourself. Never relax as long as you're in enemy territory. Take matches to cook what you can steal. Take salt because with salt and potatoes you can survive for months. Take a wristwatch to time your journeys to ensure you'll never get caught in the open. And take a razor blade for suicide."

"After their escape," Sir Martin Gilbert has summarized, "Vrba and Wetzler had worked their way southwards from Birkenau, without documents, without a compass, without a map, and without a weapon. Carefully avoiding the German 'new settlers' who live … in former Polish homes, who were often armed, and had the authority to shoot 'unidentifiable loiterers' at sight, they headed steadily towards the mountains, shunning all roads and paths, and marching only at night.

"One evening they were fired on by a German police patrol but managed to escape into the forest. Later they met a Polish partisan who guided them towards the frontier. On the morning of Friday, April 21, they crossed into Slovakia and found refuge with a farmer in the small village of Skalité."

Having crossed the Slovak-Polish border, exhausted and without food, after 10 days, the pair was discovered in the field of an unnamed pig farmer. Many years later he would be identified as Ondrej Čanecký. It was this Skalité farmer who listened to their story, then risked his own life to give them food and shelter. After he and his wife Agáta had allowed the pair to recover, Čanecký provided them with peasant clothing and led them to the local market in Čadca.

Ondrej Čanecký (above) saved the escapees [*Slovak Spectator*]. Village of Čadca (1940s).

In 2019, Čanecký became one of approximately 600 Slovakians granted the Righteous Among the Nations status by Israel and the Yad Vashem Holocaust Museum. Recipients are non-Jews who risked their own safety and lives during the Holocaust by hiding Jews or helping them escape, without expecting compensation or reward. Čanecký's name now appears on the Wall of Honor in the Yad Vashem Garden. More than 26,000 individuals from 51 countries have been recognized as Righteous Among the Nations. Wetzler's version of the escape narrative omits any mention of Čanecký, the pair's most significant helper enroute to freedom – adding credence to the claim that Wetzler's version must be considered as a work of fiction.

Čanecký escorted Vrba to the Čadca office of a Jewish doctor named Pollack who, in turn, could connect them to the Jewish Council in Žilina. On the doorstep, Čanecký offered money to Vrba; he declined. It turned out Vrba had met Dr. Pollack before – in Nováky where they had awaited deportation together. As the doctor put a bandage on Vrba's foot to counteract any suspicion for the visit, he learned the sickening news that his wife and children had not really been deported by train to anywhere safe, as the local Jewish Council had led them to believe. Dr. Pollack arranged for Vrba and Wetzler to sleep overnight in Čadca at the home of a relative of a Jewish Council member. Dr. Pollack escorted Vrba and Wetzer to meet leaders of the Jewish community of Žilina in the morning.

CHAPTER 8

The Unheralded Predecessors

Auschwitz Museum has preserved these Nazi images of Mordecai (Mordka) Cytryn, a planner for Vrba's escape with Wetzler.

THE MYTH THAT Vrba and Wetzler conceived their own escape continues to percolate. Having retold Rudolf Vrba's 1963 escape memoir with a bare minimum of recognition accorded to the protagonist's original text, British thriller writer Jonathan Freedland, author of *The Escape Artist,* told *Times Radio* that "Vrba spotted a loophole in the Nazi defenses" in order to escape. Freedland was well aware that Mordecai Cytryn (spelled by Freedland as Citrin) had conceived and built the cavern hideout, along with at least three other colleagues, because on page 156 of his first hardcover edition of *The Escape Artist,* he credits the Russian Jew "known only as Citrin" for discovering the crater in the ground, "perhaps a shell-hole."

Born in Warsaw on July 6, 1909, Cytryn (Prisoner #30980) was a Jew who had been brought to Auschwitz from the Pawiak prison in Warsaw on April 18, 1942. Cytryn's co-escapees were the Slovakian Jew Mendel (Sandor) Eisenbach (Prisoner #32704) and two Polish Jews, Getzel Abramowicz (Prisoner #27577) and Jacob (Kuba) Bałaban (Prisoner #86794).

It has been suggested that Cytryn and his accomplices drew lots to see who would serve as the guinea pig to test out their newly constructed hideout. Whether that is true or not, it was Cytryn who crawled inside, alone, on February 29, 1944, and allowed himself to be covered by planks.

If the SS failed to find him, Cytryn would then be joined inside the lumber pile by three others in due course. It was Cytryn who took the greatest risk, and it was seemingly Cytryn who chiefly conceived the escape plan.

It is not known whether or not these would-be escapees had obtained civilian clothes from the camp underground to conceal themselves if they managed to escape. It is now known that these men knew Alfréd Wetzler because they had the daily job of picking up the corpses of workers who had died and delivering them, on handcarts, to the morgue where Wetzler was the registrar. One advantage to this grisly work detail was that it afforded freedom of movement, relatively speaking, within the camp. As camp veterans who spoke fluent German, Vrba and Wetzler had been elevated in the camp hierarchy to become registrars. This meant they, too, could circulate more easily in Auschwitz-Birkenau than other prisoners. Their positions within the Auschwitz hierarchy of prisoners enabled them to stroll past the woodpile and reassure the sequestered quartet that "the coast was clear" once the escape attempt by the foursome was underway.

In his memoir, Vrba and his co-writer Alan Bestic failed to mention that Cytryn and his crew had carefully replaced the planks of the wood pile and fled from "Mexico" more than a month before they did – on March 5, 1944. After the war, escapee Kuba Balaban provided a roughly translated account made public by the Auschwitz Holocaust Museum. In this excerpt he describes how they were caught:

"At night we all set off to Brzeszcze. I was walking with Eisenbach at the front, while Cytryn and Ignac were about 100 meters behind us – for safety reasons. While walking along one of the Brzeszcze streets, a young girl bumped into me by accident and I, as a young man, accosted her and we started talking, ... walking around the town ... We were even discussing some political issues, and she confessed that she had a loved one in the camp in Auschwitz and when I saw her attitude, at some point I confessed that I had escaped from Auschwitz that night.

"When she asked how she could ... help, I answered that only with some good advice, how to reach the other side of the river. ... She decided to guide us herself by some winding paths to the river, to the place where the boat moors. In spite of the fact that it was winter and the ground was frozen, she seemed not to pay attention to any hardships and guided us to our destination. While saying goodbye I gave her a golden ring and a fountain pen as a souvenir of all four of us, the escapees from Auschwitz. Although she did not want to accept it claiming that we could always make use of it, I did not want to take her kindness for granted. I kissed her, she started crying and we parted. ... I wish I could meet this high-minded woman again and say thank you.

"All four of us got on the boat and safely reached the town of Kęty. We did not know exactly where to go, but we followed our instinct and headed in the direction of the mountains, where partisans were stationed. We marched all night long, and at dawn took a break in a forest. ... At dawn, when it cleared up a bit, we spotted a man who was passing on his bike on a forest path. Although we were not sure if he noticed us, we walked away about 300 meters from this place and fell asleep because we were very tired. After an hour the screams woke us up and then we found out that we were surrounded by gendarmes. They ordered us all to stand up, raise our hands and searched us to check if we did not have any weapons. They also told us to roll up our sleeves to see the numbers on our arms.

"They cuffed us and directed us to the police station in Porąbka via mountain paths. After three or four hours a car pulled up in front of the prison. ... Sitting inside we were sure that they were taking us back to Auschwitz, and at the time we decided that during the investigation, we could not in any event reveal the location of our bunker. I took on the responsibility for organizing the escape; the others agreed to say that it was me who had led them outside the camp."

It is not clear why Balaban would be willing to accept the responsibility for organizing the escape instead of Cytryn. Possibly, this could have been a fabrication to elevate his stature after the war. Regardless, in a nutshell, the foursome had made it past the guard towers, but they had been inadequately prepared to navigate and behave beyond the gates.

Even though Balaban had established contact with sympathetic Poles as they were heading for the town of Kety, they had soon discovered the local Polish population had been mostly evacuated and replaced by Germans who were loyal to the Nazis. Any contact was therefore exceedingly risky. Several days later, on the way to the Slovak border, in the vicinity of Porąbka [Porebka], they encountered a group of German foresters who were taken aback by their shaved heads and tattooed arms.

Before any gendarmes arrived, the Cytryn-Eisenbach-Balaban-Abramowicz quartet had wisely jettisoned all their valuables, correctly anticipating their capture. In advance of torture, they mutually decided they would say they had noticed a deserted guard post on the perimeter of Auschwitz and suddenly decided to flee. In this way they were able to succeed in maintaining the Mexico hideout as a secret.

In March of 1944, two other would-be escapees named Schwimmer and Zajoncz were awaiting their fate in the death block. They had been captured with valuables in their possession. Normally, all failed escapees were mutilated and publicly executed. But in this instance, when all six of the captured men were marched to gallows outside the Birkenau kitchen on March 17, only Schwimmer and Zajoncz were predictably lynched. For anyone familiar with the history of Auschwitz, it might seem preposterous that all four of Cytryn's crew were not hanged or shot – but that is, in fact, what happened.

An explanation for this bizarre circumstance can be found in Hermann Langbein's unparalleled book *People in Auschwitz*, originally published in German in 1995. In it, he records that on November 11, 1943, Camp Order 50/43 stated that Lieutenant Colonel Arthur William Liebehenschel would replace Höss as the senior garrison commander (*Standortältester*) of Auschwitz, thereby ranking him as superior to the commandants of Auschwitz II (Birkenau) and Auschwitz III (Buna) while he was simultaneously put in charge of Auschwitz I.

Langbein provides an explanation of why Himmler replaced Höss. According to a conversation overheard by the gardener in Höss's house, in the fall of 1943, Himmler was worried that the BBC was reporting too much about mass extermination of prisoners at Auschwitz. After the war, the loathsome Wilhelm Boger corroborated that rationale when he testified that Höss was forced to leave Auschwitz, by Himmler, due to "reasons of foreign policy." Ostensibly, Höss was given a promotion, but, in reality, he was reluctant to leave his wife and family who stayed behind (as depicted in the movie, *The Zone of Interest*).

Although the mass murders at the crematoria continued as "normal," Liebehenschel demolished the infamous Black Wall for executions, he

The relative leniency of Auschwitz overseer Arthur Liebehenschel was essential for enabling one of the Cytryn escapees to assure Rudolf Vrba that the hideout in Mexico was likely reuseable.

ordered the destruction of the stand-up cells (in which prisoners were forced to stand for 24 hours), he rescinded the order to shoot any prisoner trying to escape and, most radically, he ordered that prisoners who had been caught trying to escape would not be killed; instead, they could be transferred to another KZ. Aghast at the conditions he found, the commander wished to abolish capital punishment. He even declared that inmates should not be beaten during interrogations.

After the war, various testimonies from Auschwitz staff verified this was the case. A roll clerk named Erwin Olszowska testified at the Frankfurt trials, "When in the winter of 1943–44 the chief informer of the Political Department, Dorosiewicz, escaped and murdered an SS man, the new camp commandant ordered no reprisals." Another of Liebehenschel's underlings testified that the new commander did not insist that everyone must stand at attention in his presence, and when he visited a camp kitchen, he asked, "How does the soup taste?"

Liebehenschel stayed in charge only six months until Rudolf Höss reappeared and assumed the function of SS senior garrison commander on May 8, 1944. Three days later, Richard Baer replaced Liebehenschel as Auschwitz I commander. Most of Liebehenschel's reforms were rescinded but the fact remains that Vrba and Wetzler would not have escaped if Liebehenschel had not spared the lives of the Cytryn-Eisenbach-Balaban-Abramowicz foursome after they had been re-captured.

Höss returned to Auschwitz in May of 1944, whereupon Liebehenschel was appointed commandant of the nearly defunct Majdanek camp, soon evacuated. Liebehenschel was relocated to Trieste where he was head of a SS Manpower Office.

It was also during this "interlude of leniency" that Vrba and Wetzler were able to flee. Vrba and Wetzler would never have been able to reuse the Mexico hideout if Cytryn's quartet had been executed because they would never have gained assurance from Eisenbach that none of the foursome had revealed the location of the lumber pile. Therefore, approximately 200,000 Hungarian Jews would not have been saved from the crematoria due to the eventual distribution of the *Vrba-Wetzler Report*.

Despite his attempts to diminish cruelty, Arthur Liebehenschel was convicted of war crimes by the Polish government and executed in 1948. Cytryn and his crew have mostly fallen through the cracks of history. Wetzler and Vrba were hugely indebted to Cytryn's quartet for conceiving the escape plan, for testing the effectiveness of the petrol-tainted *machorka*, for preparing the hideout and for proving its viability, but Vrba saw fit to recognize only one of them by name – his fellow Slovak, Eisenbach. The preceding escape made by Cytryn is given very short shrift in *I Cannot Forgive*, subsequently reissued as *I Escaped from Auschwitz*:

"You know the planks the Poles have stacked for the new camp they're building?" Fred said. I nodded. It was to be Birkenau Three and it was being built parallel to Birkenau Two to accommodate the flood of Hungarians.

"Well, they've bribed some *kapos* [inmates, usually criminals, put in charge of the rest] to pile them so that there is a cavity left in the middle."

"I saw at once what they were trying to do. The planks were in the outer camp, which at night was undefended because all prisoners were securely behind the high-voltage wires and watchtowers of the inner camp. If they could remain hidden for three days, while all the guards stood to and the place was searched, they had a good chance; for at the end of three days it would be assumed that they had got beyond the confines of Auschwitz, and the job of finding them would be handed over to the authorities there. The guard that ringed the entire camp for those three days would be withdrawn and they would merely have to wait until night before sneaking away past the unmanned outer watchtowers."

It is possible to argue that Vrba failed to adequately credit those to whom he was indebted because Alan Bestic, who did nearly all of the writing based on Vrba's verbal accounts, had a somewhat cynical but practical attitude as a veteran Fleet Street journalist. In short, Bestic likely believed the general reader did not want a great deal of detail. Instead, they wanted drama. If Bestic had loaded Vrba's memoir with a barrage of strange or unpronounceable names [Olszowska, Dorosiewicz, Liebehenschel, Cytryn, Abramowicz, etc.], *I Cannot Forgive* might have sunk like a stone. Therefore, just as Vrba had been forced to be subservient to the editorial direction of Jewish elders when his famous Auschwitz report was drafted in 1944, almost 20 years later Vrba was obliged to once more yield to, and rely on, the craftsmanship of a senior authority for writing in English. *The Escape Artist* by Freedland tried to follow Bestic's lead in peddling the conceit that Vrba somehow orchestrated his own miraculous escape, as evidenced by a less than honest title.

The first edition of *The Escape Artist* cited Vrba and Wetzler as "the first Jews to break out of Auschwitz" and claimed they were "the first Jews to engineer their own escape from Auschwitz." Both statements are false.

Meanwhile, the Polish historian Josef Garliski has claimed Pawel Gulba and Sonderkommando David Szmulewski were involved in the planning, and it was Gulba who "concealed the two escapees in the Mexico area."

~

AFTER SANDOR EISENBACH survived torture within the notorious Block 11 compound (the Execution Block) under the command of SS *Rottenführer* Bruno Schlange, he was digging a ditch with his bare hands, as part of his penal labor punishment, when Vrba was ostensibly making his rounds as a registrar.

During a few precious seconds of forbidden conversation, Vrba was able to verify that the woodpile hideout was still unknown to the Nazis. According to Vrba, Eisenbach was also able to advise, "Steer clear of Porebka. It's stinking with soldiers."

Vrba's parents and Eisenbach's parents had lived in Vrba's hometown of Trnava. Vrba trusted Eisenbach completely. Eisenbach asked Vrba for a favor if they dared to reuse the hideout. Their dialogue is neatly truncated in Vrba's memoir. "We left a little memorial in the cavity," says Eisenbach. "A message scribbled on the planks. We signed it with our numbers, and if they find it, we're goners." Vrba promised to scrub it out and asked what the message said. Eisenbach replied, "Kiss our arses!"

In keeping with Liebehenschel's oddly liberal edict about not murdering escapees, Eisenbach's colleagues Bałaban and Abramowicz would eventually be transferred to Lieberose, one of the Sachsenhausen sub-camps, in Germany, in October of 1944. Both Balaban and Eisenbach survived the war.

Eisenbach is not to be confused with the much better-known Slovak prisoner named Ludwig Eisenberg. Vrba met the latter on the same day he received his zebra stripes. After being marched into the shower and told to strip among 400 others "in a room designed to hold no more than thirty," Vrba was met by a man who tattooed the number 44070 on the top of his left forearm. The numbers happened to contain the number 44 – the year of the momentous escape – and the remaining numbers are close to being 007. The tattooist was named Eisenberg.

Rudolf Vrba described the tattoo process in *I Cannot Forgive*. "Behind a table sat two more prisoners – one, a Frenchman known throughout the camp as Leo, the tattooist, the other a Slovak, called Eisenberg. They were cheerful fellows, who joked about the whole business, asking the cattle politely where they would like their numbers branded – on the left arm or the right, underneath or on top. There was something strangely comical in being given the choice in circumstances such as these; it was rather like asking a man which side he would like his hair parted, before his head was cut off."

Vrba had encountered a Slovakian locksmith named Ludwig ("Lale") Eisenberg who had been in Krompachy and had arrived in Auschwitz in April of 1942. His tattoo number was 32407. Eisenberg was selected for the coveted job of tattooist because he, like Vrba and Wetzler, could speak multiple languages – in his case, Slovak, German, Russian, French, Hungarian and some Polish.

In 1945, Eisenberg was reunited with Auschwitz survivor Gisela Fuhrmannova in Bratislava. They promptly married and he changed his name to the more Russian-sounding Lale Sokolov. It was this man, Rudolf Vrba's tattooist, who served as the protagonist for the commercially successful novel, *The Tattooist of Auschwitz*, written by Heather Morris. The Auschwitz Memorial Research Center has criticized the story as "an impression about Auschwitz inspired by authentic events, almost without any value as a document" because it contains "numerous errors and information inconsistent with the facts, as well as exaggerations, misinterpretations and understatements."

A follow-up novel presents the life of Cecília Kováčová, a character in *The Tattooist of Auschwitz* named Cilka who had a sustained sexual relationship with SS-*Obersturmführer* Johann Schwarzhuber after her arrival in Auschwitz at age 16 in 1942.

After his terse conversation with Sandor Eisenbach, Vrba ostensibly proceeded to invite Alfréd Wetzler to be his escape companion, intending to reuse the yet-to-be-disassembled woodpile. Due to their age difference, Vrba had barely known Wetzler when they were growing up in Trnava. "I always admired him," Vrba later recalled, "if only for his casual, bohemian manner and his easy way with girls." In an address he gave in Germany, Vrba refined that comment: "We had known each other since childhood and there was absolute trust between us. We were also 650 men from the town of Tyrnau (Slovakian: Trnava), where we had all lived, but only the two of us were still alive. Something like that connects even more, especially since he had already lost three brothers and his father and mother in Auschwitz."

Both men were fluent in multiple languages, as well as unusually literate, but their escape attempt had not been officially sanctioned by the underground leadership who felt Vrba might be too young and impulsive to succeed. They would be, however, supplied with razor blades for their wrists in case they were apprehended. It was much better to die quickly. That way, tongues could not wag.

Every attempted escape from Auschwitz was a form of rebellion and a rekindling of hope. Even though some "60,000 trapped men and women" inside Auschwitz (according to Wetzler's estimate) knew they would be forced to stand at attention outside their barracks for hours and denied their meager rations, most welcomed the piercing sound of the alarm, so loud that most inmates still reflexively put their hands over their ears. Even if the rebel pair could only outfox their captors for an hour or two – and then likely everyone would have to watch the sickening aftermath of the captives being ridiculed, tortured, whipped, mutilated, stretched or hanged as a public spectacle – the audacity to even attempt to escape was a victory for the human spirit.

We now know from Robin Vrba that Wetzler did escape with some money, contrary to the advice received from Volkov. Whereas Vrba was a member of the camp underground and had access to Volkov as an advisor, Wetzler was not a member of the underground and therefore did not have access to Volkov as an advisor. Robin Vrba has since revealed that the temptation to use money to gain supplies during the harrowing escape had got the best of Wetzler, and the pair were shot at when they were forced to flee as a direct result. She says Vrba chose not to include this detail in his memoir because he did not wish to show Wetzler in a negative light.

A copy of the bulletin that was sent by Auschwitz officials to notify all Nazi jurisdictions in central and eastern Europe about the escape of Walter Rosenberg (Vrba) and Wetzler can be seen at right.

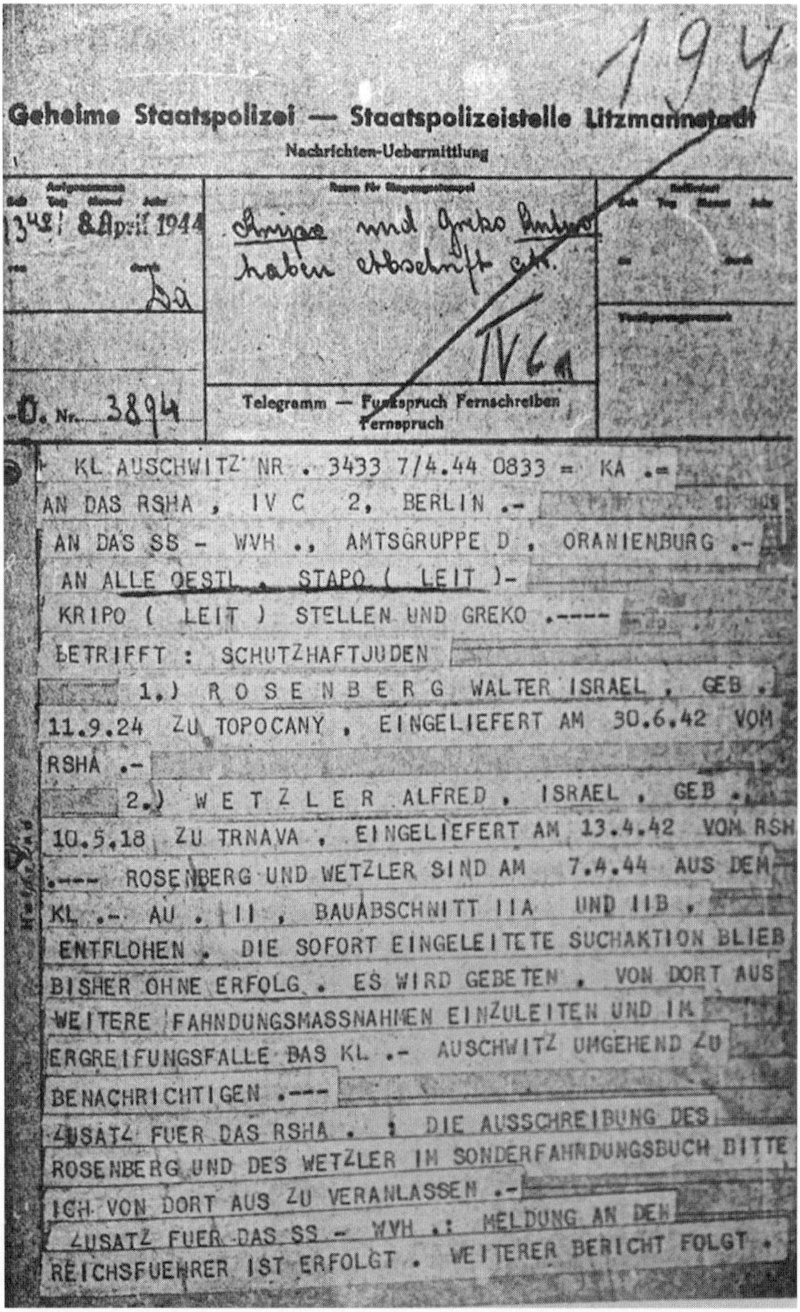

194

Geheime Staatspolizei — Staatspolizeistelle Litzmannstadt

Nachrichten-Uebermittlung

13[48] 8 April 1944

Kripo und Greko Lnlw. haben Abschrift erh.

Da

IV 6a

Nr. 3894

Telegramm — Funkspruch Fernschreiben Fernspruch

KL AUSCHWITZ NR . 3433 7/4.44 0833 = KA .=
AN DAS RSHA , IV C 2, BERLIN .-
AN DAS SS - WVH ., AMTSGRUPPE D , ORANIENBURG .-
AN ALLE OESTL . STAPO (LEIT)-
KRIPO (LEIT) STELLEN UND GREKO .----
BETRIFFT : SCHUTZHAFTJUDEN
1.) R O S E N B E R G WALTER ISRAEL , GEB .
11.9.24 ZU TOPOCANY , EINGELIEFERT AM 30.6.42 VOM
RSHA .-
2.) W E T Z L E R ALFRED , ISRAEL , GEB .
10.5.18 ZU TRNAVA , EINGELIEFERT AM 13.4.42 VOM RSH
.--- ROSENBERG UND WETZLER SIND AM 7.4.44 AUS DEM
KL .- AU . II , BAUABSCHNITT IIA UND IIB ,
ENTFLOHEN . DIE SOFORT EINGELEITETE SUCHAKTION BLIEB
BISHER OHNE ERFOLG . ES WIRD GEBETEN , VON DORT AUS
WEITERE FAHNDUNGSMASSNAHMEN EINZULEITEN UND IM
ERGREIFUNGSFALLE DAS KL .- AUSCHWITZ UMGEHEND ZU
BENACHRICHTIGEN .---
ZUSATZ FUER DAS RSHA . : DIE AUSSCHREIBUNG DES
ROSENBERG UND DES WETZLER IM SONDERFAHNDUNGSBUCH BITTE
ICH VON DORT AUS ZU VERANLASSEN .-
ZUSATZ FUER DAS SS - WVH .: MELDUNG AN DEN
REICHSFUEHRER IST ERFOLGT . WEITERER BERICHT FOLGT .

This bulletin was sent by Auschwitz officials to notify all Nazi jurisdictions in central and eastern Europe about the escape of Walter Rosenberg (Vrba) and Wetzler.

Obv. notársky úrad v TRENČÍN
Čís. evid. 185 /1944.
Pán Rudolf
narodený
dňa
zamestnaním bytom
TRENČÍN štátny občan,
je totožný s osobou vyobrazenou na nalepenej a pečiatkou opatrenej podobenke.
v TRENČÍN dňa
ved. notár
OBVODNÝ NOTÁRSKY ÚRAD
TRENČÍN
NMnV. 537

Rudolf Vrba's forged identity papers dated May 23, 1944

CHAPTER 9

The Famous Report

WHEN THE BEDRAGGLED duo of Vrba and Wetzler finally reached Slovakia on April 24, 1944, they were hidden in the basement of a former Jewish old folk's home in the town of Žilina. Their feet were bloodied and misshapen. A doctor was summoned. The malnourished pair recovered and soon cooperated with Jewish Council officials to produce an anonymous report that would be so detailed and emotionless that it could not *not* be believed. "No other single act in the Second World War," according to the World War II historian Sir Martin Gilbert, "saved so many Jews from the fate that Hitler and the SS had determined for them."

The pair's eyewitness reports were dictated over the course of three days. There were at least six drafts. Wetzler mainly composed the first section, Vrba mainly composed the third section and contributed drawings. The middle section was co-written.

"I had no doubts whatever as to my abilities to communicate the realities of Auschwitz to the outside world," Vrba recalled in 1997. "I believed that if I escaped the confines of Auschwitz and managed to get back into the world outside and spread the news about the fate awaiting potential candidates for 'resettlement,' I could make some significant difference by breaking the cornerstone of the streamlined mass murder at Auschwitz – its secrecy."

The reportorial process was overseen by two Jewish Council leaders from Bratislava, Oskar Krasňanský, a chemical engineer, and Oskar Neumann, a lawyer and writer. They had been contacted by Erwin Steiner, who also attended the summit along "with a man called Hexner," according to Vrba. While Neumann was ostensibly a Jewish official within the political infrastructure of the alleged "self-government" under President Jozef Tiso, sanctioned by the Third Reich, he doubled as the head of the secret resistance organization for Slovakian Jewry. Details of the reportorial process can be found in Neumann's autobiography, *In the Shadow of Death: A Factual Account of the Fateful Struggle of Slovak Jewry* (*Im Schatten des Todes*, Tel Aviv, 1956). According to Holocaust historian Raul Hilberg, Neumann's autobiography is possibly the only memoir written by one of the chiefs of the Slovak *Judenrat*, the *Ústredňa Židov* (ÚŽ).

The highly articulate escapees were interviewed in separate rooms, thereby enhancing their overall credibility. To verify their reportage, Krasňanský had brought with him identity cards for each individual deportee from Slovakia, as well as the date of their transport trains. Vrba and Wetzler were able to accurately provide information that matched his records for individual Slovakian Jews.

These interview sessions went on for hours. Vrba and Wetzler stayed indoors and slept in the basement at No. 9 Hollého Street to avoid detection. Ultimately, they were able to provide succinct estimates as to how many Jews were gassed and murdered in Birkenau from April of 1942 until they had escaped. Due chiefly to Vrba's memory techniques (later

This basement room at No 9 Hollého Street in Žilina is part of a Slovakian heritage site to honor the making of the *Vrba-Wetzler Report*. On the right is a vintage model of the typewriter used.

explained in detail to historian Martin Gilbert), the pair were able to calculate the "deaths by country of origin." For decades afterwards, Vrba repeatedly stated that their reportage, including maps he drew, were based on memory; the pair had NOT risked carrying any paper evidence hidden in cannisters.

Vrba and Wetzler reported that 300,000 Jews had been shipped from Poland by trucks, another 600,000 were delivered by trains. The other figures included Holland (100,000), Greece (45,000), France (150,000), Belgium (60,000), Germany (60,000), Norway & Italy & Yugoslavia (50,000), Lithuania (50,000), Austria & Bohemia & Moravia (30,000), Slovakia (30,000) and various others (300,000). Their eyewitness total was 1,765,000.

The duo's 32-page report in Slovakian was first typed by Ibolya Steiner (likely the wife of Steiner) on a typewriter manufactured by Seidel & Naumann of Dresden, Germany in the 1930s. Prior to its dissemination, Krasňanský, himself a good stenographer, translated the report into German with the assistance of Gisela Steiner [according to a 1946 report, *Oswiecim, hrobka styroch milionov l'udi*. Further details provided by Wetzler are in *Anatomy of the Auschwitz Death Camp*, Indiana University Press, 1994]. The first German version was completed by Thursday, April 27, 1944. Copies made in German are stored at the Vatican Archives (Report no. 2144. A.E.~S. 7679/44) and in the files of the World Jewish Congress, Geneva. There is also a copy at Yad Vashem, Jerusalem, in Hungarian, as well as an English version in the Roosevelt Library, Hyde Park, New York (War Refugee Board report, Box 61: General Correspondence of R. McClelland).

The testimonies of Vrba and Wetzler became the most significant part of the Auschwitz Protocols, now recognized as the first document that provided irrefutable proof about the extent and industrialized methods of mass murder at Auschwitz-Birkenau.

Vrba and Wetzler were far from being the first Auschwitz prisoners to attempt to generate an insiders' report about Auschwitz. According to the Auschwitz Museum: "Reports written by Polish escapees ... were another source of information on Auschwitz. In April 1942, Stefan Bielecki sent the Polish Home Army headquarters a report written by camp resistance leader Witold Pilecki. A month later, escapee Gustaw Jaster brought out another report. Kazimierz Hałoń, who escaped on November 2, 1942, reported on Auschwitz to the Krakow PPS leadership. Later, the socialist publication *Liberty* ran six articles probably based on his information:

"In April 1943, Witold Pilecki, Jan Redzej, and Edward Ciesielski escaped. Each of them compiled a report independently, and these were sent to AK headquarters. Stanisław Chybiński, who escaped a month later, wrote a report *Snapshots from Auschwitz* for AK headquarters. In mid-1944 escapees Konstanty Jagiełło and Tomasz Sobański sent the Krakow PPS organization secret messages and maps of the camps and SS deployments. None of these escapees' reports, with a few exceptions, was published during the war.

"Reports by other escapees were published and had an impact, however. The Pole Jerzy Tabeau escaped in November 1943. In a report to the leadership of the Polish underground, he discussed the events of the last year-and-a-half. His report was smuggled out of Poland. In Switzerland, it came to the attention of several diplomats and representatives of the World Congress of Jews. As the *Report by a Polish Major*, it reached the UK and the USA."

Eventually, it was the irrefutable information supplied by the two Slovakian Jews that resulted in a cessation of the trains carrying Jews to Auschwitz as of July 9, 1944. Whereas preceding eyewitness reports had been dismissed as implausible, the emotionless prose of the *Vrba-Wetzler Report* was so unerringly clear, including precise illustrations and exacting calculations as to the overall death toll, that the scale and methodology of the Holocaust was laid bare at last, but only after millions had already been murdered throughout Europe.

Vrba and Wetzler were initially credited (by Martin Gilbert) with saving at least 100,000 Jews when the veracity of their report finally reached the Allies. Other historians have since doubled that figure based on the input of multiple experts. Gilbert would eventually concur. Hence, the latest reissue of Vrba's memoir *I Escaped from Auschwitz* is now subtitled *The Shocking True Story of the World War II Hero Who Escaped the Nazis and Helped Save Over 200,000 Jews.*

The *Vrba-Wetzler Report*

Interviewed by *VGT Community News*, a news outlet near his home on the grounds of the University of British Columbia, Rudolf Vrba referred to the *Vrba-Wetzler Report* as "my first scientific document." It's an important remark. It shows that the complete lack of emotion in the document was purposeful.

While it is tempting to credit Vrba and Wetzler for retaining the presence of mind to refrain from any editorializing or personal remarks, having just completed one of the greatest escapes of the 20th century, the truth is somewhat more complicated. It was indeed an extraordinary show of restraint on their part not to editorialize or predict, but they were sternly advised to err on the side of facts by their hosts in Žilina.

Some of the establishment Israeli historians later tried to discredit Vrba by alleging that he ought to have included more explicit warnings about the imminent mass murder of Hungarian Jews. In fact, the teenaged Vrba and Wetzler were obeying the dictates of the Jewish elders who gave them refuge and it was only later that Vrba would be able to mention that he had overheard Nazis joking about the imminent arrival of "Hungarian salami."

The escapees were not only instructed to avoid predictions and options, they were also not permitted to include anecdotes that would unduly distress their readers. To this day, the original version of the report, in Slovakian, has not been found. Any warnings or explicit details that the pair might have tried to include could have easily been expunged in the translated versions that quickly followed. Regardless, Vrba and Wetzler jointly succeeded in sounding an alarm that gained meaningful responses from world leaders and ultimately helped save the lives of approximately 200,000 Hungarian Jews.

All other reports about the Holocaust prior to the *Vrba-Wetzler Report* had failed to force world leaders to take meaningful action to save the Jews of Europe. The pair's mathematical tallies (literally columns of numbers), along with their precise detailing of the camp's physical structures and their descriptions of the methodology of unprecedented genocide, provided an almost scientific perspective. It was this objective rather than subjective approach – offering bloodless and severely logical matching reportage devoid of moralism and outrage – that ultimately forced both

Winston Churchill and Franklin Delano Roosevelt to express their moral outrage to the Hungarian leader Admiral Horthy, demanding a cessation of trains bound for Auschwitz.

Here are some excerpts from the *Vrba-Wetzler Report* transcripts. Their eyewitness reportage was prefaced by a one-page foreword by Oskar Krasňanský who chiefly oversaw the process of recording the testimony of Walter Rosenberg and Alfréd Wetzler in April of 1944.

The *Vrba-Wetzler Report* – in Brief

Oskar Krasnynski's Foreword to *The Extermination Camps of Auschwitz and Birkenau in Upper Silesia*

> Two young Slovak Jews – whose names will not be discussed for the time in the interest of their own safety – have been fortunate enough to escape after spending two years in the concentration camps of BIRKENAU, AUSCHWITZ and LUBLIN-MAJDANEK, where they had been deposited in 1942 from SLOVAKIA.
>
> One of them was sent on April 13, 1942 from the assembly camp of SERED directly to AUSCHWITZ and then to BIRKENAU, while the other was sent from the camp of NOVÁKY to LUBLIN on June 14, 1942 and after a short stay there, transferred to AUSCHWITZ and, later, BIRKENAU.
>
> The following report does not contain everything these two men experienced during their captivity but only what the one or both together underwent, heard or experienced at first hand. No individual impressions or judgements are recorded, and nothing passed on from hearsay.
>
> The report starts with the story of the young Jew [Wetzler] who was removed from SERED. The account of his experiences in BIRKENAU begins at the time the second Jew arrived there and is therefore based on the statements of both. Then follows the individual narrative of the second Jew [Vrba] who was sent from NOVÁKY to LUBLIN and from there to AUSCHWITZ.

The declarations tally with all the trustworthy yet fragmentary reports hitherto received, and the dates given with regard to transports to various camps agree with the official records. These statements can therefore be considered as entirely credible.

Testimony Of the First Escapee [Alfred Wetzler]

"On the 13th April 1942 our group consisting of 1,000 men, was loaded into railroad cars at the assembly camp of SERED. The doors were shut so that nothing would reveal the direction of the journey and when they were open after a long while we realized that we had crossed the Slovak frontier and were in ZWARDON. The train had until then been guarded by Hlinka men but was now taken over by SS guards. After a few of the cars had been uncoupled from our convoy, we continued on our way arriving at night at AUSCHWITZ, where we stopped on the side-track. The reason the other cars were left behind was apparently the lack of room at AUSCHWITZ. They joined us, however, a few days later. Upon arrival we were placed in rows of five and counted. There were 643 of us. After a walk of about 20 minutes with our heavy packs (we had left Slovakia well equipped) we reached the concentration camp of AUSCHWITZ.

"We were at once led into a huge barrack where on the one side we had to deposit all our luggage and on the other side completely undress, leaving our clothes and valuables behind. Naked, we then proceeded to an adjoining barrack where our heads and bodies were shaved and disinfected with Lysol. At the exit, every man was given a number which began with 28,600 in consecutive order. With this number in hand, we were then herded to a third barrack where so-called registration took place. This consisted of tattooing the numbers we had received in the second barrack on the left side of our chest. The extreme brutality with which this was effected [sic] made many of us faint. The particulars of our identity were also recorded. Then we were led in groups of 100 into a cellar and later to a barrack where we were issued striped prisoner's clothes and wooden clogs. This lasted until 10 a.m. In the afternoon our prisoner's outfit was taken away from us again and replaced by the ragged and dirty remains of Russian uniforms. Thus equipped we were marched off to BIRKENAU.

"AUSCHWITZ is a concentration camp for political prisoners under so-called 'protective custody.' At the time of my arrival, that is in April of 1942, there were about 15,000 prisoners in the camp the majority of whom were Poles, Germans and civilian Russians under protective custody. A small number of prisoners came under the categories of criminals and 'work-shirkers.'

"AUSCHWITZ camp headquarters controls at the same time the work camp of BIRKENAU as well as the farm labor camp of HARMENSE. All the prisoners arrive first at AUSCHWITZ where they are provided with a prisoner's admittance number and then are either kept there, sent to BIRKENAU or, in very small numbers, to HARMENSE. The prisoners receive consecutive numbers upon arrival. Every number is only used once so that the last number always corresponds [PAGE TWO continued] to the number of prisoners actually in the camp. At the time of our escape, that is to say at the beginning of April 1944, the number had risen up to 180,000. At the outset the numbers were tattooed on the left breast, but later, due to their becoming blurred, on the left forearm."

Testimony of the Second Escapee [Rudolf Vrba]

<u>Majdanek.</u>

"On June 14, 1942, we left NOVÁKY, passed through ŽILINA and arrived at ZWARDON toward five o'clock in the evening. We were assembled, counted and SS men took over our convoy. One of these guards voiced his surprise at the fact we had made the journey without water by shouting, 'Those Slovak barbarians, give them no water!' The journey continued, and we reached LUBLIN two days later. Here the following order was issued: 'Those fit for work aged between 15 and 50 are to leave the cars. Children and old people remain.' We struggled out of the freight car and discovered that the station was surrounded by Lithuanians in SS uniforms all armed with automatic pistols. The cars containing the children and old people were immediately closed, and the train moved on. We do not know where they went and what happened to them.

"The SS troop leader in command informed us that we had a long way ahead of us but that whoever wanted to take his luggage with him could do so. Those who preferred to put it on a truck would certainly receive it later. So some of us dragged along our luggage whereas others loaded it on the truck.

"Behind the town stood a clothing factory called the 'Bekleidungswerke.' In the courtyard, waiting for their noon meal some 1,000 prisoners in dirty striped clothing, obviously Jews, were lined up and the sight of them was none too encouraging. Arriving on a small hill, we suddenly sighted the vast barrack camp of MAJDANEK surrounded by a three-meter high barbed-wire fence. No sooner had we gone through the entrance gate then I met Maco WINKLER from TRVAVA who warned me that all our personal belongings would be taken away. Around us stood Slovak Jews in a wretched condition, their heads shaven, in dirty prison clothes and wooden clogs or simply bare-footed, many of them having swollen feet. They begged us for food, and we gave them what we could spare, knowing very well that everything would be confiscated anyway. We were then conducted to the stockroom where we had to leave everything we possessed. At double time, we were herded into another barrack where we had to undress, were shaved and given a shower. After this, we were issued a convict outfit, wooden clogs and a cap.

"I was assigned to 'working section No. 2' as the whole camp was divided into three such sections separated by wire fences. Section No. 2 was occupied by a number of Slovak and Czech Jews. For two full days, we were taught how to remove and put on our caps when we met a German. Then, in the pouring rain, we practiced roll-calling for hours.

"The barrack accommodations were quite original to say the least. Three long tables (nearly as long as the barrack itself) had been placed one on top of the other. These comprised our "bunks" (four floors of them, that is ground floor plus the three tables). A small passage was kept open along the walls.

"Our food consisted of a fairly thick 'soup' early in the morning which had to be eaten with our hands. We got the same soup again at lunch. The evening meal consisted of a brew called 'tea,' 300 grams of bad bread and some 20 to 30 grams of marmalade or artificial fat of the worst quality.

"Great importance was attributed during the first few days to the learning of the 'camp song.' For hours we stood singing:

From the whole of Europe came
We Jews to Lublin
Much work has to be done
And this is the beginning.

To manage this duty
Forget all about the past
For in fulfillment of duty
There is community.

Therefore on to work with vigor
Let everyone play his part
Together we want to work
At the same pace and rhythm.

Not all will understand
Why we stand in rows
Those must we soon force
To understand its meaning.

Modern times must teach us
Teach us all along
That it is to work
And only to work we belong.

Therefore on to work with vigor
Let everyone play his part
Together we want to work
At the same pace and rhythm.

From the whole of Europe came
We Jews to Lublin
Much work has to be done
And this is the beginning.

To manage this duty
Forget all about the past
For in fulfillment of duty
There is community.

(A literal translation of the song).

Working section No. I	was occupied by Slovak Jews
Working section No. II	was occupied by Slovak and Czech Jews
Working section No. III	was occupied by Partisans
Working section No. IV & V	was being built by the Jews of Sectors I & II

"The Partisans in section III were locked up in their barracks without having to work, and their food was thrown at them as if they had been dogs. They died in great numbers in their overcrowded barracks and were shot at the slightest excuse by the guards who did not dare venture too near them.

"The 'Capos' were Reich Germans and Czechs; whereas the Germans were brutal, the Czechs helped wherever they could. The camp's eldest was a gypsy from HOLIC by the name of GALBAVY. His adjutant, a Jew from SERED called MITTLER, certainly owed his post to his brutal actions. He took full advantage of the power conferred upon him to torment the Jews who, as it was, already had their full share of hardships. The evening roll-call brought us more brutal treatment from the SS men and for hours we had to stand in the open after a hard day's work and sing 'the camp song.' A Jewish orchestra leader was forced to conduct from the roof of one of the barracks. This was the occasion of much hilarity among the SS men.

"During these 'concert parties' the SS guards were very generous with blows and physical punishment. A tragic end befell Rabbi ECKSTEIN from SERED who was suffering from dysentery and once came a few minutes too late for the roll-call. The group leader had him seized and dipped head first into one of the latrines, then poured cold water over him, drew his revolver and shot him.

"The crematorium was located between working sections I and II and all the bodies were burned there. With an effective strength of six to 8,000 men per working section, the mortality was about 30 a day. This figure later increased five and sixfold. In other instances, 10 to 20 inmates were removed from the sick room, brought to the crematorium and burned after having been put to death in a manner which I have not been able to find out. This crematorium was electrically heated, and the attendants were Russians.

"Illnesses increased as a result of the bad food and intolerable living conditions. Serious stomach troubles and seemingly incurable foot disease spread throughout the camp. The feet of the victims swelled up to the point where they could not walk. More and more of the sick were now being taken to the crematorium, and when on June 26, 1942 the number thus treated rose to 70, I decided to take an opportunity which was offered to me and applied for a transfer to AUSCHWITZ.

"On June 27, 1942, I discarded my prisoner's outfit and traveled to AUSCHWITZ in civilian clothes.

"After a journey of 48 hours during which we were cooped up in freight cars without food or water, we arrived at AUSCHWITZ half dead. At the entrance gate the huge poster 'Work brings freedom' greeted us. As the courtyard was clean and well kept and the brick buildings made a good impression after the dirty and primitive barracks of LUBLIN, we thought that the change was for the best. We were taken to a cellar and received tea and bread. Next day, however, our civilian clothes were taken away, our heads were shaved, and our number was tattooed on our forearm in the usual way. Finally, we were issued a set of prisoner's clothes similar to those we had worn in LUBLIN and were enrolled as 'political prisoners' in the concentration camp of AUSCHWITZ.

"We were billeted in 'Block 17' and slept on the floor. In an adjoining row of buildings, separated from ours by a high wall, the Jewish girls from Slovakia, who had been brought there in March and April of 1942 were quartered. We worked in the huge 'BUNA' plant to which we were herded every morning about 3 a.m. At midday, our food consisted of potato or turnip soup, and in the evening we received some bread. During work, we were terribly mistreated. As our working place was situated outside the large chain of sentry posts it was divided into small sectors of 10 x 10 meters, each guarded by an SS man. Whoever stepped outside these squares during working hours was immediately shot without warning for having 'attempted to escape.' Often it happened that out of pure spite an SS man would order a prisoner to fetch some given object outside his square. If he followed the order, he was shot for having left his assigned place. The work was extremely hard, and there were no rest periods. The way to and from work had to be covered at a brisk military trot; anyone falling out of line was shot. On my arrival about 3,000 people, of whom 2,000 were Slovak Jews, were working on this emplacement. Very few could bear the strain, and although escape seemed hopeless, attempts were made every day. The result was several hangings a week.

"After a number of weeks of painful work at the 'BUNA' plant, a terrible typhus epidemic broke out. The weaker prisoners died in hundreds. An immediate quarantine was ordered and work at the 'BUNA' stopped. Those still alive were sent at the end of July 1942 to the gravel pit, but there work was even still more strenuous. We were in such a state of weakness that, even in trying to do our best, we could not satisfy the overseers. Most of us got swollen feet. Due to our inability to perform the heavy work demanded of us our squad was accused of being lazy and disorderly. Soon after a medical commission inspected all of us they carried out their job very thoroughly. Anyone with swollen feet or particularly weak was separated from the rest. Although I was in great pain, I controlled myself and stood erect in front of the commission who passed me as physically fit. Out of 300 persons examined, 200 were found to be unfit and immediately sent to BIRKENAU and gassed. I was then detailed for work at the DAW (Deutsche Aufrustungswereke) where we had to paint skis. The prescribed minimum to be painted each day was 120. Anyone unable to paint this many was thoroughly flogged in the evening. It meant working very hard to avoid this punishment. Another group was employed at making cases for hand grenades. At one time 15,000 had been completed, but it was found that they were a few centimeters too small. As punishment several Jews (one of whom was a certain ERDELYI who is said to have relatives in BANOVCE) were shot for sabotage.

"Somewhere around the middle of August 1942, all the Jewish girls from Slovakia who lived next to our quarters, on the other side of the wall, were to be transferred to BIRKENAU. I had the opportunity to talk to them and was able to see how weak and half-starved all of them were. They were dressed in old Russian uniform rags and wore wooden clogs. Their heads were shaved clean. The same day we again had to undergo a strict examination, and those suspected of having typhus were removed to the Birch wood. The remainder was shaved fresh, bathed, issued with a new set of clothes and finally billeted in the barracks the girls had just left. By chance, I learned that there was an opening in the 'clearance squad' and I handed in my application. I was detailed to this task.

"This squad consisted of about a hundred Jewish prisoners. We were sent to a far corner of the camp, away from all our comrades. Here we found huge sheds full of knapsacks, suitcases and other luggage. We had to open each piece of baggage and sort the contents into large cases specially prepared for each category of goods; i.e., combs, mirrors, sugar, canned food, chocolate, medicines, etc. The cases were then stored away. Underwear, shirts and clothes of all kinds went to a special barracks, where they were sorted out and packed by Jewish girls. Old and worn clothes were addressed to the 'TEXTILE FACTORY' at MEMEL whereas the usable garments were dispatched to a collecting center in BERLIN. Gold, money, bank notes and precious stones had to be handed over to the political section. Many of these objects were however stolen by the SS guards or by prisoners. The head of this department was Albert DAVIDOVC from SPISSKA NOVA VES. He still holds this post and has become quite an expert in the matter. A brutal and vile individual who often struck the women is commander of this squad. He is SS 'Scharführer' WYKLEFF.

"Every day the girls who came to their work from BIRKENAU described to us the terrible conditions prevailing there. They were beaten and brutalized, and their mortality was much higher than among the men. Twice a week 'selections' took place, and every day, new girls replaced those who had disappeared.

"During a night shift, I was able to witness for the first time how incoming convoys were handled. The transport I saw contained Polish Jews. They had received no water for days, and when the doors of the freight cars were opened, we were ordered to chase them out with loud shouts. They were utterly exhausted, and about a hundred of them had died during the journey. The living were lined up in rows of five. Our job was to remove the dead, dying and the luggage from the cars. The dead, and this included anyone unable to stand on his feet, were piled in a heap. Luggage and parcels were collected and stacked up. Then the railroad cars had to be thoroughly cleaned so that no trace of their frightful load was left behind. A commission from the political department proceeded with the selection of approximately 10 percent of the men and 5 percent of the women and had them transferred to the camps. The remainder were loaded on trucks, sent to BIRKENAU and gassed while the dead and dying were taken directly to the furnaces. It often happened that small children were thrown alive into the trucks along with the dead. Parcels and luggage were taken to the warehouses and sorted out in the previously described manner.

"Between July and September 1942, a typhus epidemic had raged in AUSCHWITZ, especially in the women's camp of BIRKENAU. None of the sick received medical attention, and in the first stages of the epidemic a great many were killed by phenol injections, and later others were gassed wholesale. Some 15,000 to 20,000 mostly Jews died during these two months. The girl's camp suffered the most as it was not fitted with sanitary installations and the poor wretches were covered with lice. Every week, large 'selections' took place and the girls had to present themselves naked to the 'selection committee' regardless of weather conditions. They waited in deadly fear whether they would be chosen or given another week's grace. Suicides were frequent and were mostly committed by throwing oneself against the high-tension wires of the inner fence. This went on until they had dwindled to 5 percent of their original number. Now there are only 400 of these girls left and most of them have been able to secure some sort of clerical post in the women's camp. One of them, KATJA by Christian name (family name unknown) from POVAZSKA BYSTRICA, (where she has relatives by the name of LANGDELDER) has risen to the important post of chief recorder. About 100 girls hold jobs at the staff building in AUSCHWITZ where they do all the clerical work connected with the administration of the two camps. Thanks to their knowledge of languages, they are also used as interpreters. Others are employed in the main kitchen and laundry. Of late, these girls have been able to dress themselves quite well as they have had opportunities to complete their wardrobes which, in some cases, even include silk stockings. Generally speaking, they are reasonably well off and are even allowed to let their hair grow. Of course this can nor[t] be said of the other Jewish inmates of the women's camp. It just so happens that these Slovak Jewish girls have been in the camp the longest of all. But if today they enjoy certain privileges, they have previously undergone frightful sufferings.

"I was not to hold this comparatively good job with the 'clearance squad' for long. Shortly afterwards, I transferred to BIRKENAU on disciplinary grounds and remained there over a year and a half. On April 7, 1944, I managed to escape with my companion."

Careful estimate of the number of Jews gassed in BIRKENAU between April 1942 and April 1944 according to countries of origin.

Poland (transported by truck)	approximately	300,000
Poland (transported by train)	"	600,000
Holland	"	100,000
Greece	"	45,000
France	"	150,000
Belgium	"	50,000
Germany	"	60,000
Yugoslavia, Italy and Norway	"	50,000
Lithuania	"	50,000
Bohemia, Moravia and Austria	"	30,000
Slovakia	"	30,000
Various camps for foreign Jews in Poland	"	300,000
	approximately	1,765,000

Mordowicz, Rosin & Tabeau

A cumulative document containing the *Vrba-Wetzler Report,* now known as *The Auschwitz Protocols* or *Auschwitz Report,* was originally released as *The Extermination Camps of Auschwitz and Birkenau.* Not declassified by the U.S. State Department until 1964, it also includes the contents of a much shorter report [4 ½ pages] by the Auschwitz escapees Ceslav Mordowicz and Arnošt Rosin.

At a conference in Žilina in 2015, historian Eduard Nižňanský of Bratislava University provided a basic and yet oft-overlooked explanation as to why the audacious and heroic escape of Mordowicz (prisoner #84216) and Rosin (prisoner #29858) has long remained obscure: "Unlike the case of Alfréd Wetzler and Rudolf Vrba, the story of the escape of A. Rosin and

C. Mordowicz is virtually unknown. In my opinion, one of the reasons is that they, unlike the two previously mentioned, never wrote about it."

When it comes to making history by escaping from Auschwitz-Birkenau, bizarrely, not unlike a beauty contest, there was little to be gained by coming in second. When they buried themselves within a gravel pit, Ceslav Mordowicz and Arnošt Rosin had less oxygen than Vrba and Wetzler, as well as less provisions, and their freedom of movement in the camp had been severely limited in the aftermath of the Vrba and Wetzler escape, and yet the Mordowicz-Rosin escape remains a hundred times more obscure than the Vrba-Wetzler escape that was commenced 49 days earlier.

The Mordowicz-Rosin escape was equally dangerous and dramatic. By the time the pair had made their way into Slovakia on June 6, 1944, having escaped on May 27, it was D-Day, the day of the Normandy landing, and the pair was thrilled to believe that war might soon be over. Using some money they had smuggled out of Auschwitz, they went to a tavern to celebrate only to be arrested for contravening currency laws. It took eight days, with some involvement from Rudolf Vrba, before the local Jewish Council could pay their fines and bribe them out of jail.

Each escape would prove essential for enabling the Allies to understand the escalating murder rates at Auschwitz and Birkenau. Whereas Vrba and Wetzler had outlined the expansion of the camp infrastructure in anticipation of the influx of Hungarian Jews, it was the Mordowicz-Rosin reportage that confirmed the arrival of Hungarian transports in Auschwitz-Birkenau after the first deportation from Budapest had commenced on April 29, 1944. Upon their arrival in Slovakia, Mordowicz and Rosin were also interviewed by Oskar Krasňanský, this time in the home of Rabbi Boby Reich, a Jewish leader in Liptovský Mikuláš. On July 10, in Bratislava, Krasňanský then drafted a German-language report for the Allies, including their testimonial that deported Hungarian Jews had arrived in Auschwitz in early May. That first transport of Hungarians was assigned for labor detail. Thereafter, between May 15 and 27, between 14,000 and 15,000 Hungarian Jews were arriving daily; 90 percent were sent immediately to the gas chambers.

The *Auschwitz Protocols* also contained *The Polish Major's Report*, later attributed to Jerzy Tabeau, a medical student who had escaped in November of 1943 and soon afterwards compiled a testimonial that was circulated,

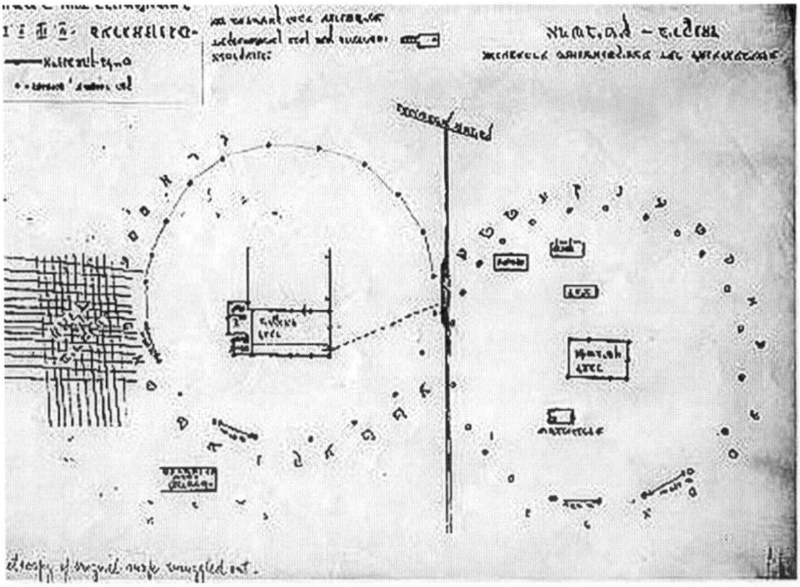

Robin Vrba has confirmed this map in the *Vrba-Wetzler Report* was provided by Rudolf Vrba because he was taught by a teacher to render maps with south at the top and north at the bottom. He also placed his own peculiar notation at the top of this map to identify it as his own [shaped like a key], knowing that he would not have his name attached.

early in 1944, with limited impact, even after Tabeau had made it all the way to London in March to provide in-person testimony about genocide at Auschwitz. His reportage was eventually copied in Geneva in August of 1944 and was incorporated in the *Auschwitz Protocols* as a 17-page document called "No. 2. Transport The Polish Major's Report." Tabeau (1918–2002) became a respected cardiologist in Krakow, but he was never properly celebrated for his heroism during his lifetime – a fate he shared with Vrba, Wetzler, Mordowicz and Rosin.

The map [above] within the *Auschwitz Protocols* was drawn in Žilina by Rudolf Vrba. Conventional placements of north and south have been reversed so they appear "upside down."

"This is the result of a peculiarity of the way my mind works," Vrba wrote in a letter to Martin Gilbert in 1980, "and until this day whenever I draw a location of a particular place, the north will be on the bottom of

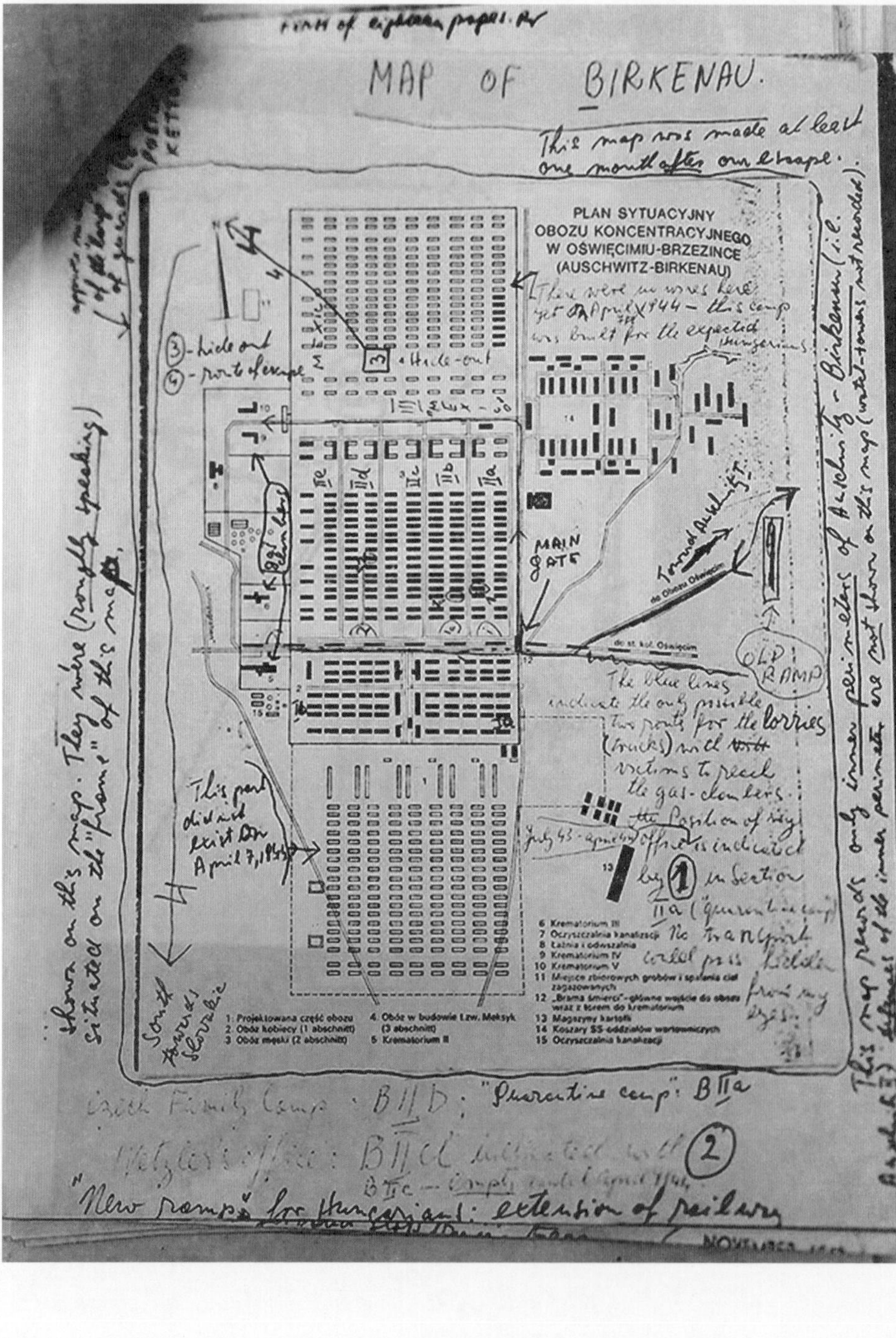
MAP OF BIRKENAU.
This map was made at least one month after our escape.
PLAN SYTUACYJNY OBOZU KONCENTRACYJNEGO W OŚWIĘCIMIU-BRZEZINCE (AUSCHWITZ-BIRKENAU)
MAIN GATE
OLD RAMP
1 Projektowana część obozu
2 Obóz kobiecy (1 abschnitt)
3 Obóz męski (2 abschnitt)
4 Obóz w budowie t.zw. Meksyk (3 abschnitt)
5 Krematorium II
6 Krematorium III
7 Oczyszczalnia kanalizacji
8 Łaźnia i odwszalnia
9 Krematorium IV
10 Krematorium V
11 Miejsce zbiorowych grobów i spalenia ciał zagazowanych
12 „Brama śmierci"-główne wejście do obozu wraz z torem do krematorium
13 Magazyny kartofli
14 Koszary SS-oddziałów wartowniczych
15 Oczyszczalnia kanalizacji

the map. This error is not inborn but originates from an error of a teacher of mine in my school who explained to me (at my age of 10) that our school is 200 yards south of [the] Danube. In fact, it was 200 yards north of [the] Danube and since then north in my maps appears on the bottom. I hardly ever doubted the wisdom of my teachers."

Vrba made a subsequent map [left] upon which he added personal notations. This second map was found in the Vrba archives at the FDR Library. His notation #3 [within a square box, below the word MAP] pinpoints the exact whereabouts of the woodpile hideout.

John J. McCloy, American "desk murderer" extraordinaire, TIME magazine (6/20/1949). Adolf Hitler appeared six times on the cover of TIME, Heinrich Himmler, thrice.

CHAPTER 10

Failures To Act

UPON READING THE uncredited report about Auschwitz by Vrba and Wetzler – generally combined with two other documents and referred to as the *Auschwitz Protocols* following the war – British Prime Minister Winston Churchill responded privately by writing, "There is no doubt this is the most horrible crime ever committed in the whole history of the world."

Meanwhile, on the other side of the Atlantic, guided by an unelected, behind-the-scenes fixer named John J. McCloy, President Roosevelt's hapless War Refugees Board had done its best not to save any Jews. The devils are in the details: The neophyte director of the War Refugees Board, John Pehle, had been obliged to consult with FDR's aging Secretary of War Henry Stimson, a Republican born in Manhattan in 1867. Disastrously out of touch with the plight of European Jews, Stimson had handed all his WRB responsibilities to McCloy, a civilian corporate lawyer who had watched the 1936 Olympics in Berlin from Hitler's private box and had represented clients who had business dealings with the German corporate giant I.G. Farben.

Few American citizens today – or then – have ever heard of the War Refugee Board, let alone its central fixer, John J. McCloy. As Anton Chaitkin's *George Bush: The Unauthorized Biography* makes clear, America's main comptroller for aid to war refugees (including Jews) had lived in Italy at the behest of his Wall Street law firm (Cravath, de Gersdoff, Swaine & Wood) and opened a Milan office to serve as an advisor to the fascist government of Benito Mussolini. Anyone who prefers to remain skeptical can visit the Desk Murderer section of rudolfvrba.com. Much of the extensive background information on McCloy and WRB has been gleaned from Kai Bird's invaluable McCloy biography, *The Chairman*.

By the summer of 1944, Allied bombers were well in range of Auschwitz, having repeatedly bombed industrial targets adjacent to the camps. The U.S. 15th Air Force had established full operations at its base in Foggia in Southern Italy in the spring of 1944, but military strategists were able to persuasively deflect any and all requests for any aerial interference to save or protect Jews by simply declaring that Auschwitz was out of the range of Allied bombers. This was false. The majority of Auschwitz inmates did not believe they were going to survive the war, and they were hoping some bombs could be redirected to destroy Auschwitz. Rudolf Vrba, however, said he was never in favor of bombing Auschwitz because he believed the Nazis would simply respond by slaughtering all their prisoners, as they had done in Majdanek and elsewhere.

The first formal request to bomb Auschwitz, in order to curtail its growth and save European lives, had been made to the RAF as early as January of 1941. A request had been written by non-Jewish Auschwitz prisoners in December of 1940 and delivered to the head of the RAF Bomber Command, Air Marshall Richard Peirse, by the Polish Prime Minister-in-exile, Wladyslaw Sikorski, who was also Commander-in-Chief of the Polish Army: "The prisoners implore the Polish Government to have the camp bombed. With the destruction of the electrified barbed wire, the ensuing panic and darkness prevailing, the chances of escape would be great. The local population will hide them and help them to leave the neighborhood. The prisoners are confidently awaiting the day when Polish planes from Great Britain will enable their escape. This is the prisoners' unanimous demand to the Polish Government in London."

The more disturbing question as to why the Allies never bothered to simply bomb the railway tracks leading to Auschwitz is far more complicated and beyond the purview of this biography. Readers can visit Desk Murderer at rudolfvrba.com for extensive background and correspondence on this issue.

Allied apologists or Vrba detractors have suggested that more Jews were not saved from Hungary because the unnamed authors of the *Auschwitz*

Protocols did not provide any clear and direct warning that Hungary's 800,000 Jews would be next. But we know from Vrba that the original versions of the *Vrba-Wetzler Report* did not contain specific warnings about the need to prevent the wholescale slaughter of Europe's largest remaining Jewish populace within a national boundary because, as relatively young men, Vrba and Wetzler, were prohibited by their elders in Žilina from making predictions as to what they believed could and would happen.

Having been well-placed within the camp structure to maintain an ongoing statistical tally of mass murder, Vrba and Wetzler were instead encouraged to accentuate their unique and astonishing mathematical tallies. It was a prudent strategy. The *Vrba-Wetzler Report* is so remarkably devoid of emotional responses to the horrors they had witnessed, and so limited in terms of any ghastly descriptions of the countless tortures and cruelties they observed, and almost devoid of predictions or opinions, that it is nearly impossible for any relatively sane person *not* to believe it must be true.

This objective approach – having two abnormally intelligent witnesses provide bloodless and severely logical and matching reportage, devoid of moralism and outrage – ultimately forced both Winston Churchill and Franklin Delano Roosevelt to express the moral outrage that was absent from the document.

For posterity, Churchill concluded "the most horrible crime ever committed" had been done with scientific machinery "by nominally civilized men in the name of a great State and one of the leading races of Europe. It is quite clear that all concerned in this crime who may fall into our hands, including the people who only obeyed orders by carrying out the butcheries, should be put to death after their association with the murders has been proved."

This was magnificent oratory. Few readers of that statement generations hence will stop to ponder the fact that one of the main reasons Churchill and FDR had completely failed to openly express any such condemnation of Hitler earlier is that both leaders had feared that if Hitler was chastised openly, earlier, he could call upon both high-minded leaders to accept millions of European Jews, sent by Hitler, as refugees.

Churchill and Roosevelt – as well as leaders of Canada and Australia and India and other lesser powers – dared not openly express any willingness to save Jews from the ovens for political and/or economic reasons based on self-interest. The *Vrba-Wetzler Report* was circulated from May of 1944 onwards but it would not be formally received by the U.S. government until November, by which time it was clear Nazi Germany would be defeated.

With the winds of war changing in favor of the Allies, the Pope decided it would be prudent for the Vatican to end the war on the winning side. He, too, therefore, decided to send a written protest to Admiral Horthy after receiving the news of systemic genocide in the *Vrba-Wetzler Report.* But according to John Cornwall's *Hitler's Pope: The Secret History of Pius XII,* the Pope's missive sent to the Hungarian leader Horthy to stop the Nazi-managed schedule of trains to Auschwitz somehow managed to avoid mentioning the dreadful word "Jews" entirely. It was one thing to express one's horror of genocide; it was quite another to divulge any overt support for Jews.

In the 21st century, it's now acknowledged that without the reportage provided by Vrba, Wetzler, Mordowicz and Rosin, the Allies would not have pressured Admiral Horthy to halt the trainloads of Hungarian Jews being sent to Auschwitz. But the notion that Horthy was solely persuaded to finally stop sending Jews to Auschwitz on strictly moralistic grounds is simplistic. It helps to know that on June 26, 1944, a member of the Jewish Agency in Geneva, Richard Lichtheim, had sent telegrams from London asking the Allies to place members of Horthy's government on the list of those legally responsible for the mass murders. One of his cables was intercepted and shown to the Hungarian Prime Minister who, in turn, showed it to Horthy. It was therefore Horthy's fear of being charged with war crimes, along with the emergence of the *Vrba-Wetzler Report,* that stopped the trains to Auschwitz.

Regardless, Vrba would remain forever disturbed by the fact that only one-quarter of Hungary's 800,000 Jews were saved. Had Jewish leaders and international powers responded immediately to his reportage, most of Hungary's Jews could have been spared.

In the seldom consulted, unused portions of interviews conducted with filmmaker Claude Lanzmann in 1972, Vrba expressed overt criticism of the Slovak Jewish Council for its handling of his report about Auschwitz.

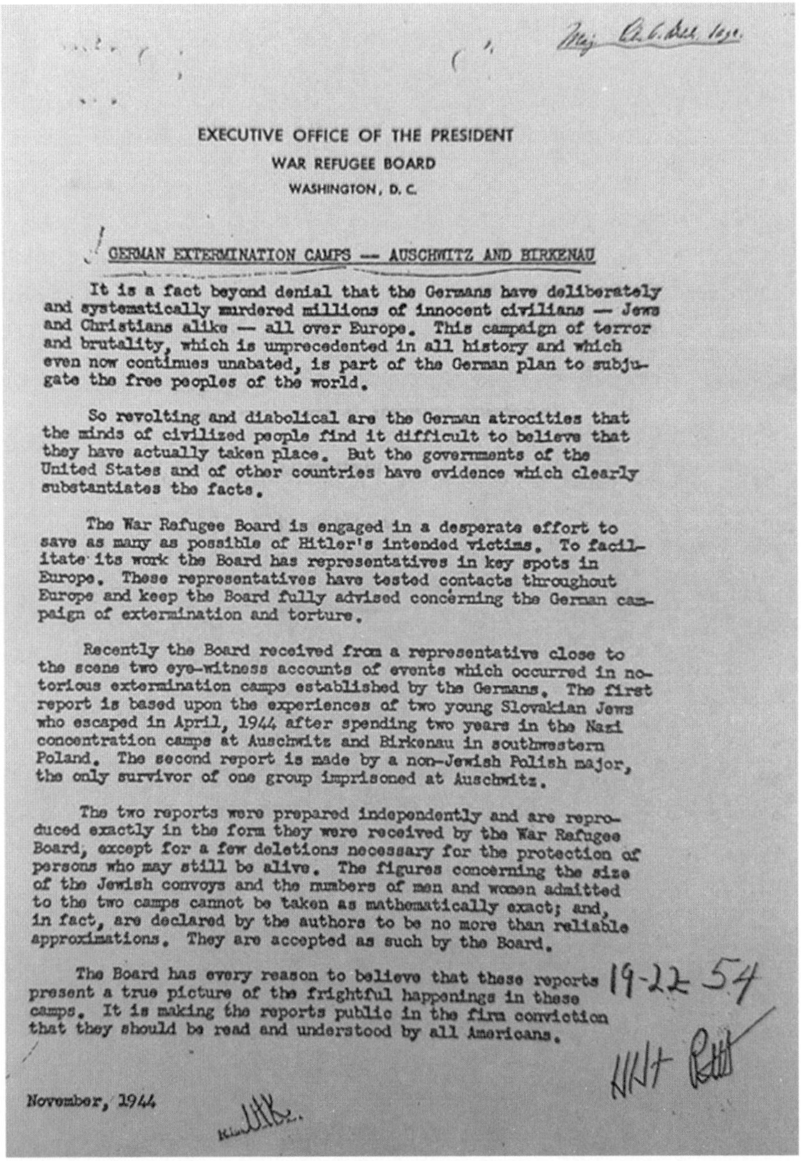

EXECUTIVE OFFICE OF THE PRESIDENT
WAR REFUGEE BOARD
WASHINGTON, D. C.

GERMAN EXTERMINATION CAMPS — AUSCHWITZ AND BIRKENAU

It is a fact beyond denial that the Germans have deliberately and systematically murdered millions of innocent civilians — Jews and Christians alike — all over Europe. This campaign of terror and brutality, which is unprecedented in all history and which even now continues unabated, is part of the German plan to subjugate the free peoples of the world.

So revolting and diabolical are the German atrocities that the minds of civilized people find it difficult to believe that they have actually taken place. But the governments of the United States and of other countries have evidence which clearly substantiates the facts.

The War Refugee Board is engaged in a desperate effort to save as many as possible of Hitler's intended victims. To facilitate its work the Board has representatives in key spots in Europe. These representatives have tested contacts throughout Europe and keep the Board fully advised concerning the German campaign of extermination and torture.

Recently the Board received from a representative close to the scene two eye-witness accounts of events which occurred in notorious extermination camps established by the Germans. The first report is based upon the experiences of two young Slovakian Jews who escaped in April, 1944 after spending two years in the Nazi concentration camps at Auschwitz and Birkenau in southwestern Poland. The second report is made by a non-Jewish Polish major, the only survivor of one group imprisoned at Auschwitz.

The two reports were prepared independently and are reproduced exactly in the form they were received by the War Refugee Board, except for a few deletions necessary for the protection of persons who may still be alive. The figures concerning the size of the Jewish convoys and the numbers of men and women admitted to the two camps cannot be taken as mathematically exact; and, in fact, are declared by the authors to be no more than reliable approximations. They are accepted as such by the Board.

The Board has every reason to believe that these reports present a true picture of the frightful happenings in these camps. It is making the reports public in the firm conviction that they should be read and understood by all Americans.

November, 1944

In November of 1944, the War Refugee Board finally stated the American government had "every reason to believe" the *Vrba-Wetzler Report* "presents a true picture." Much too late.

"The next evening, the (Slovak) Jewish Council arrived with info about me and verified my identity. I was the first Jew who had ever come back. They questioned the truthfulness of our report. My friend Vecla [Wetzler] was upset that they did not really believe us.

"We were questioned separately for about six hours. Finally, they appeared to believe us. I was not yet 21 years old, and there was a law that I could not sign a paper without parental permission. They wasted some days. They should have contacted the Hungarian Jewish Council. We got papers with proof of my Aryan origins for three generations. But they didn't give me shoes.

"The Germans issued a warrant for us. Meanwhile, the first Hungarian transport left for Auschwitz. I felt that I was tricked by the Slovak Jewish Council. I knew I had to find other contacts. We were supposed to talk at a synagogue on a Friday night. Not realizing it was Shabbat, I lit a cigarette as I was hiding near a wall before my talk. A member of the synagogue saw us and ordered us away because we were desecrating the Shabbat. He didn't care what we had to say, he just wanted us away from there. Four months later, he was killed in Auschwitz." [From Tape 4, Side B]

"I turned to the communists for help in Trnava. They thought my story was very sad. The local communist group was helpful. They offered money, documents, a hiding place. They were not helping us as Jews – they did not mention the concentration camps in Russia – but as people who are against the Nazis.

"The communists were not enamored with the Jews because the Jews were all capitalist, and they don't support communism. But the communist group was willing to help us with anything we needed. They would help me get to some unit where, if I wanted to, I can even get to shoot some Germans." [Tape 5, Side A]

~

AFTER PRESENTING THEIR report, Vrba and Wetzler were sent into hiding in the town of Liptovský Svätý Mikuláš, 55 miles east of Žilina. The Jewish leadership were aware that May Day was nearing, and this traditional workers' celebration would be cause for Hlinka guards to search out "Judeo-Bolshevik agitators" in advance of that date. The Nazis at Auschwitz had already issued bulletins to alert central European forces of the Third Reich to be on the lookout for the pair. Therefore, it was propitious for the Auschwitz escapees to leave Žilina and adopt false identities as "pure Aryans" going back three generations. For their efforts and recuperation, they were each supported with 200 Slovak crowns per week, an average salary at the time.

Alfréd Wetzler became Jozef Lánik. Walter Rosenberg became Rudolf Vrba, unaware that an antisemitic Catholic priest in Czechoslovakia with the same name had died about five years earlier. There is no evidence that his would-be protectors felt it might be advantageous to be confused with a pro-Hlinka cleric. Vrba was a fairly common surname in Slovakia, lacking any Germanic traces, whereas he had always disliked the fact that Rosenberg might connote some German heritage. It was primarily important to find a deceased person who did not have any living relatives. Vrba's forged identity document, issued by the Notary Office in Trenčín on May 23, 1944, is preserved at the FDR Presidential Library at Hyde Park in New York.

~

VRBA STATED THE first version of the report was completed by April 27; the Czech historian Miroslav Kárny, who corresponded with Wetzler in 1982, suggests it was completed one day later. Either way, the first version of the document now widely known as the *Vrba-Wetzler Report* was prepared in Slovak and it has never been found or was not preserved. All versions made afterwards are therefore "degenerate," i.e. subsidiaries of the original. Therefore, claims that any institution retains the "original" version of the *Vrba-Wetzler Report* are, strictly speaking, false. As translations were hastily undertaken for a variety of languages, these "copied" transcripts naturally differed in terminology but the numerical estimates made by Vrba and Wetzler were not altered. How and why this April reportage was not officially received in Washington, D.C. by the Director of the War Refugee Board, John Pehle, until October of 1944, approximately six months later, is a complex and disturbing story that cannot be adequately discussed here.

As Rudolf Vrba (at right, with cigarette) returned home as a Partisan hero, the Communists were taking firm control of Czechoslovakia. His valor in Auschwitz and life-saving report were never publicized.

CHAPTER 11

Vrba & the Partisans

THERE IS AN anecdote about Rudolf Vrba wanting to join the Partisans – no doubt promulgated by Vrba himself – in which the recently-escaped, newly-renamed Rudolf Vrba meets with some representatives of the Slovak Resistance forces. "My friends," he tells them. "I need a pistol. Someday a bright SS man is going to see through my false papers." Vrba is initially upset when he is told, "We don't issue pistols to lads like you ..." After a suitable pause, he is then informed, "We issue machine guns!"

Following a period of recuperation, getting accustomed to his new name, reuniting with his teenage friend Gerta, partying with Rosin, Mordowicz and Wetzler, and helping to disseminate the information in the *Vrba-Wetzler Report*, Rudolf Vrba was determined to come out of hiding and fight back by joining a widespread rebel movement towards the end of August, 1944.

Seldom studied by Western historians because there were no Allied troops involved, the military goal of this insurgency, later patriotically dubbed the Slovakian National Uprising, was to open the Carpathian passes, most notably the Dulka Pass, to facilitate the advance of the Red Army.

The battle to gain control of the Dulka Pass connecting Slovakia and Poland would last from September 8 to October 28, enough time and misery for the Nazis to largely crush the hoped-for Slovakian uprising. Some 46,000 Soviet, Czechoslovak and German soldiers perished during the mostly thwarted offensive.

Rebel partisans such as Rudolf Vrba would struggle to survive the winter.

In this tourist brochure photo of the monument near Ladomirová on the Slovak side of the Dukla Pass, a German Pz-IV J tank (left) is overwhelmed by a Soviet T-34-85 tank. A Slovak uprising failed largely because the Soviets took 50 days to fully secure the Dukla Pass.

The report below is the only known record Vrba made in English, at length, about his decorated service with the partisans. At the time, in 1944–45, the heroic resistance to the Nazis in the countryside and mountains of Slovakia was almost entirely associated with Communism, as Vrba makes abundantly clear in his first sentence. As a result, he found it both prudent and necessary to avoid being unfairly tainted as a Communist for the rest of his life. Unlike most political observers in the West, Vrba was aware that some 5,700,000 Russian soldiers were captured in World War II and about 2.5 million died in captivity. According to Martin Gilbert, approximately one million were shot by paramilitary death squads, the *Einsatzgruppen*, and the rest perished in the concentration camps.

Vrba on Being a Partisan

"The Resistance Movement in Czechoslovakia was supported mainly by the Russians. I joined a Czechoslovak insurrection unit which was, at that time, responsible to the Czechoslovakian Government in exile, in London. This was shortly after the 29th August

1944, on which date a proclamation had been issued by the hitherto quisling Slovak Army which changed its allegiance. It proclaimed allegiance to the Czechoslovak Government, and I joined up as a volunteer, immediately. It was commanded by Sgt. Miloš Uher, and I duly swore the oath of allegiance to the London Government and to fight until victory over the Germans or until death. I joined under the name of Rudolf Vrba which had been given to me together with forged papers by the Jewish Authorities four months previously; i.e. Immediately after my escape. This name had been chosen because it was a common name of non Jewish origin.

"These were the only documents I had to present to the Army Authorities, but, of course, it was well-known that they were forged.

"The headquarters of the Army were soon in difficulties and were surrounded by German motorized divisions. We were ordered to stay behind the German lines to disrupt communications and harass the Germans by all possible means. We were quickly isolated, and command of our unit was taken over by partisan headquarters in Kyiv, (Russia); a new commander, Col. Debrov of the Russian Army, was parachuted to us. He was killed in action soon afterwards, and Uher (by then a Captain) resumed command of the unit.

"Capt. Uher was killed in action on 28th February 1945. Lt. Krazicky then took over command of the unit, and his Chief of Staff Placak is the signatory of my discharge papers.

"When the Russian forces arrived on 7th April 1945, we were still actively fighting but severely depleted. At the request of the Russians, we undertook one final military action and then were retired to a military hospital to recuperate before being returned to the front. By that time, I had actively participated in ten battles against SS units in several raids on German artillery posts, in the destruction of railway bridges and supplies, etc.

"I was awarded the Czechoslovak Medal for Bravery, the Order of the Slovak National Insurrection (II Class) and the medal of Honor for Czechoslovak Partisans.

"Capt. Uher was posthumously awarded the title of Hero of the Nation and the Order of the Slovak National Insurrection (I Class).

"The bodies of all members of our unit who had been killed were, after the war, exhumed on orders of the Government and reburied together in a special monument built at the birthplace of Capt. Uher, at Lubina, in Western Slovakia.

"Whilst we were still in hospital, the war ended. Almost immediately after the end of the war, a military commission composed partly of Russian officers and partly of Czechoslovakian officers (who nevertheless came from Russia) suggested that henceforth the unit be renamed 'The Second Stalin Partisan Brigade.' We were all awarded membership of the Communist Party, and everyone signed the collective sheet which took the place of a normal application. I requested a discharge from the Army immediately, as I wished to study chemistry at the university.

"I was discharged as Rudolf Vrba (W. Rosenberg), and I left for Bratislava in May 1945, to commence my studies."

~

LEARNING HOW TO contact the Partisans in order to volunteer was clearly the first step in learning how to join the rebels who were initially fighting back against the Nazi occupation on a rag-tag basis. Jewish elders in Žilina, in particular, Krasňanský, had mentioned there was an underground organization dedicated to protecting Slovak Jewry called The Working Group (*Pracovna Skupina*). It was comprised of Rabbi Michael Dov Weissmandel, Gisi Fleischmann, Andrew Steiner, Dr. Tibor Kovacs, Dr. Oskar Neumann, Avraham Abba Frieder and Wilhelm Fürst. The co-leaders of The Working Group (Weissmandel, Fleischmann, etc.) operated a Jewish school in Bratislava. Consequently, Vrba took a train from their escapees' refuge in Liptovsky Svay Mikulas to Bratislava to find Rabbi Michael Dov Weissmandel. In his private papers, Vrba suggests it was Dov Weissmandel who had asked to meet him. Either way, it is logical that Vrba assumed Dov Weissmandel might know someone who could lead him towards the Partisans.

Later, Vrba would despise Weissmandel as a deluded Nazi puppet. Born in Debrecen, Hungary, in 1903, Weissmandel had grown up in Trnava,

Slovakia and moved to Nitra where he married the daughter of Rabbi Shmuel Dovid Ungar, his teacher, in 1937, and become an Orthodox rabbi of the Oberlander Jews (non-Hasidic). Hence, it is possible they could have set eyes on one another, knowingly or unknowingly, when Vrba was a ward of his grandfather in Nitra.

Weissmandel was studying ancient manuscripts at the Bodleian Library in Oxford and volunteered to return to Europe on September 1, 1939 as an agent of World Agudath Israel. Subsequently, in early May of 1944, Weissmandel became the first European Jewish leader to append a copy of the *Vrba-Wetzler Report* to a plea for the Allies to bomb the railway tracks to Auschwitz, a request delivered via Jewish organizations in Switzerland, Turkey and Eretz, Israel.

Coincidentally, Weissmandel's cousin, Gisi Fleischmann, was perhaps the greatest female saviour of Jews during the Holocaust. Born in Bratislava into an Orthodox Jewish family in 1894, she was the founder of the Slovakian chapter of the Women's International Zionist Organization. She had been sent to London and Paris in 1939 to try and persuade foreign governments to help Jews, only to discover that foreign governments were not at all interested in helping Jews escape from the Nazis.

In keeping with a proposal instigated by Weissmandel and Rudolf Kasztner – a proposal that Rudolf Vrba would scathingly dismiss as "hare-brained" – Gisi Fleischmann was also sent to meet with Jewish leaders in Hungary on a mission to stop transports of Jews to concentration camps in return for ransom payments of between one and two million dollars. As a co-director of The Working Group, Fleischmann, too, had been made privy to the contents of the *Vrba-Wetzler Report* in the spring of 1944. She was probably the first woman to read it aside from typists.

Fleischmann had previously succeeded in smuggling many Slovakian Jewish children into Hungary when it was still a safe haven, and she and Weissmandel had succeeded in paying a $50,000 bribe to the Nazi official Dieter Wisliceny ostensibly to halt the deportation of Jews from Slovakia. No further Jews were deported from Slovakia from the autumn of 1942 until October of 1944. Nonetheless, Gisi Fleischmann would be part of the last deportation of Jews from Slovakia to the gas chambers where she was murdered in October of 1944. After the war, as a prosecutor at the trial of Adolf Eichmann in 1961, Gideon Hausner said, "Fleischmann's name deserves to be immortalized in the annals of our people, and her memory should be bequeathed to further generations as a radiant example of heroism and of boundless devotion."

When Vrba went to visit Weissmandel at his school with Ceslav Mordowicz [according to a letter Vrba sent to Claude Lanzmann, December 27, 1978], Vrba was surprised to enter a room and find zealous young men studying the Talmud. Weissmandel switched from Hebrew to Slovak – a rarity for this devout Jew – and he took care to address the much younger Vrba as "the Ambassador of 1,760,000." This was a flattering way to let Vrba know that he had read and fully digested the *Vrba-Wetzler Report*.

Unfortunately, Weissmandel also confirmed what Vrba most feared – trains transporting Jews to Auschwitz were continuing to leave Budapest on a daily basis.

Later, Vrba would conclude the Nazis were only cynically allowing Weissmandel's school to exist right under their noses in much the same manner as they had established Theresienstadt, the Jewish ghetto in the Czech city of Terezín, to fool the Red Cross. Vrba wrote: "The visibility of Yeshiva life in the center of Bratislava, less than 150 miles south of Auschwitz, was in my eyes a typical piece of Goebbels-inspired activity and brazen Nazi humor. There, before the eyes of the world, the pupils of Rabbi Weissmandel could study the rules of Jewish ethics while their own sisters and mothers were being murdered and burned in Birkenau. At that time, only two months and 150 miles away from an Auschwitz working at highest capacity, the Yeshiva struck me as merely a circus with Rabbi Weissmandel as its main, albeit tragicomic, clown." Vrba's viewpoint is supported by the perspective of Sir Martin Gilbert who wrote, "Deception was a feature of the Nazi intention at every phase of the destruction of European Jewry."

Vrba was nonetheless pleased to learn from Weissmandel that he, too, believed "active resistance" was moral and necessary. Vrba's antipathy would not dissuade him from adding the following footnote to *I Cannot Forgive*. "In August 1944, some months after I met him, Rabbi Michael Dov Weissmandel was captured by the SS and put on a train for Auschwitz. In a piece of stale bread, he concealed a coil of emery thread which could cut through steel. That night he cut a hole in the sealed car and leaped to freedom in the darkness. Later he resumed his clandestine work. After the war he went to New York where he founded a Rabbinical school. He continued to live an austere life and died there in 1958."

After the war, when rival historians Erich Kulka and Miroslav Kárný tried to spread the misinformation that Vrba and Wetzler had known nothing about the preparations for the mass murder of Hungarian Jews prior to the escape by Mordowicz and Rosin, Vrba was able to write to historian Randolph L. Braham on January 17, 1994 and enclose a letter sent by Weissmandel (signed M.B. for Michael Ber Weissmandel) and Gizi Fleischmann (signed G.F.) from Bratislava to Hechaluz, Geneva one month after Vrba's arrival in Slovakia and prior to the arrival of Mordowicz and Rosin in Slovakia on June 6, 1944. This letter forewarned about the mass-murder of Hungarian Jews as forewarned by Vrba and Wetzler.

Significantly, the final paragraph of this letter from Vrba to Braham makes clear, "the Rabbi was well informed about events in Hungary, although he lived in Bratislava. This means that the Jewish leadership in Bratislava and Budapest was well connected and channels for rapid exchange of information from distant parts of Hungary were available (in Bratislava and vice versa in Budapest) before and during the deportation of Hungarian Jews in spring of 1944."

~

IN AUGUST, RUDOLF Vrba went to a village in Western Slovakia, near Nové Mesto, near where Laco Fischer lived, and reported to Sergeant [later Captain] Miloš Uher, later revered as the Hero of the Insurrection. Rudolf Vrba's three co-escapees were much less keen on armed revenge; only Wetzler would eventually follow suit, approximately five months later.

After receiving only 24 hours of training, Vrba joined an attack force of 120 partisans to make a nighttime attack on some 700 SS men temporarily lodged inside a schoolhouse at a town called Stará Turá. The following night, led by Uher, the partisans stealthily surrounded the sleeping Nazi forces that had been sent to Slovakia to quash all local resistance.

"Silently, foot by foot," Vrba recalled, "we edged towards it. Then Sergeant Uher shouted, and we hurled ourselves at its walls and windows. A flash of fire came from a doorway. A dozen flashes answered it. Two men fell beside me, but I scarcely noticed them. I was running now, and tears of happiness were coursing down my cheeks. I was running forward, not backward."

It was a rout. The seemingly invincible Nazis died and screamed just like the ordinary victims at Auschwitz. Vrba recalled the words of his Russian escape mentor, Captain Dmitri Volkov: "Don't be afraid of the Germans. There are many of them but each of them is small. Here in Auschwitz they try to break your mind and body. They try to convince you that they're supermen, invincible. But I know they can die just as quickly as anybody else because I've killed enough of them in my day."

After the partisans withdrew from Stará Turá, the so-called Slovak National Uprising was in full swing. This armed resistance movement in Slovakia was comprised of two distinct branches. According to historian Vanda Raican of Northwestern University, "The Civic Bloc was composed of supporters of banned parties and associations, including Jozef Lettrich, Ján Ursíni, and Matej Joško, who tended to favor the restoration of a democratic Czechoslovakia. They had some connections with former Czechoslovak government officials, who were in exile in London, and cooperated with some illegal groups in the Protectorate.

"The Communist Bloc, represented by Gustáv Husák, Ladislav Novomeský, and Karol Šmidke, on the other hand, advocated for a pan-Slovak organization and a very strong connection with Moscow after the war. They did not recognize prewar Czechoslovakia and had no intention of reunification."

The force with which Rudolf Vrba served was unusually bipartisan. Its Russian leader, Medvedev, and its Slovakian leader, Miloš Uher, represented both the Communist Bloc and the Civic Bloc within a tandem unit. Like Vrba, Captain Miloš Uher had first tried to escape through Hungary to Yugoslavia. After being arrested and imprisoned in Budapest, Uher made it back to Slovakia where he worked in Stará Turá and in Myjava.

In preparation for the declaration of the Slovak National Uprising on August 29, 1944, Uher had organized and armed his own partisan detachment named Hurban, in Lubina, and became its commander. Two days later, on September 1, 1944, Uher co-founded a Soviet-Czechoslovak partisan group with Vladimir Medvedev, leader of Stalin's 2nd Czechoslovak Partisan Brigade in Western Slovakia.

Miloš Uher was killed on February 27, 1945, in Cetuna, just north of Stará Turá, along with at least 14 other partisans, when they were attacked by *Abwehrgruppe* 218-Edelweiss and POHG [Slovak paramilitary adjuncts of the Hlinka Guard, in Slovakian: *Pohotovostné oddiely Hlinkovej gardy*]. Reputedly, 100 fascists were killed after a day's fighting, then Uher was shot from behind during an ambush, in a barn near a pub called *U Gašparýkov* in Cetuna, by a traitor within their own ranks. Uher was posthumously awarded the Order of the Slovak National Uprising I class (1945), the Order of the Red Star (1969) and the Štefánik Order of the 4th degree on May 8, 1992. He was buried with his comrades on Roh Hill, near his birthplace, now the site of a major war memorial.

~

VRBA ARRIVED IN Bratislava in May 1945 to commence his studies: "First, I had to pass my university entrance examination and, accordingly, went to a special school for ex-servicemen to take an intensive preparation course. I was there from May to October 1945. When I passed the university entrance examination, I enrolled on 20th October into the Department of Chemical Technology at the Czech Technical University in Prague. When I left the army, I applied to legalize my new name, Rudolf Vrba. For this, special permission of the Minister of Interior was needed, and valid reasons had to be given. The reasons were that after my experiences of the Germans, I did not wish to have a German sounding name, and this new name was the one under which I had fought actively against the Nazis. My request was granted in August 1945 in sufficient time for me to qualify for university in my new name."

Rudolf Vrba's closest friend in the Partisans was his tent mate, Dr. Ladislav [Laco] Minarik (1916–1997). Vancouver physician Joseph Ragaz knew both men and has verified the importance of their rapport. "At one of my first encounters with Rudi, he told me that after the Auschwitz escape, he had joined with Slovak partisans. Then Rudi found out I knew Laco Minarik. He almost embraced me, saying how happy he was to meet

This rare, personal photo of Vrba's Partisan unit marching in the snow evidently includes Laco Minarik but Vrba's handwriting on the back does not indicate where Minarik is in the entourage.

somebody who knew Laco. Rudi told me he was never as impressed by anybody more than by Laco Minarik! When I asked why, he said that Laco was the most courageous individual he had ever met.

"As a physician, Laco would frequently run out of his tent to treat injured guys. He'd run through the trenches and hills, under a shower of bullets, picking up the wounded. If necessary, he would do the first aid surgery right on the spot, even if there were bullets overhead. And he continued his work in the makeshift tents, whatever they had, with the partisans, to save lives.

"Even though I had known Laco Minarik, he had never mentioned that he was with partisans. Even though his courage clearly bordered on heroism, he never received any medals. Even though he was a chief of a TB sanatorium, and a recognized professor, Laco was always quiet, totally modest, bordering on being shy. He asked questions but seldom talked about himself.

"At first, I did not know much about Rudi being with the partisans.

But when he spoke about Laco Minarik, he became totally alive and full of energy and emotions. He really liked and respected Laco. Suddenly, Rudi was mentioning multiple situations of danger, and the fights he had endured, all after Auschwitz."

Reputedly, an estimated 18,000 partisans fought fascism during the so-called Slovak National Uprising (SNP) that began on August 29, 1944. According to contemporary Slovak sources, some 8,400 foreign participants representing 32 nationalities joined the fray. These numbers are likely exaggerations as European countries continue to reevaluate their degrees of resistance to, and collusion with, occupying Nazi regimes.

~

ROBIN VRBA VISITED numerous historic sites with Rudolf Vrba dedicated to honoring partisan fighters in Slovakia. He never wrote about this period of his life when he was exclusively a soldier.

ALAN: We need to talk about Rudi with the partisans. It's the part of his story the world knows nothing about.

ROBIN: Well, I can tell you that most of the partisans thought the Jews were wimps. Most of them were antisemites. So, Rudi had to prove himself. He was on guard duty and one of the Slovak soldiers was taunting him. He was saying Rudi couldn't be a good guard, things like that. At first, Rudi wasn't going to do anything. Then Rudi turned on him and almost killed the guy. The guy backed off. After that, he didn't have any problems anymore. The Slovaks respected him. They figured he wasn't a normal Jew. Everyone knew Rudi wasn't a wimp. Word went around that he was a killer.

ALAN: And he executed someone.

ROBIN: He did. They had caught this German soldier, and he knew he had to be executed. That's just how it was. In that situation, if it had been reversed, Rudi would have been executed.

ALAN: So, somebody [in the partisans] had to execute this German soldier. There was no Red Cross in the Slovakian countryside ...

ROBIN: That's how the partisans worked. They both knew. Rudi had won the battle. The German soldier said, "I know you have to execute me, but could you please send my dog tags back to my family?" Rudi said yes, okay. He granted this guy's dying wish.

There were two Russian guys with shovels. I guess they must have written down the guy's address or something. Rudi shot the guy, and they buried him. Of course, Rudi didn't send back the dog tags. That was impossible. He just tossed them into the grave.

ALAN: No local post office handy.

ROBIN: Exactly. Considering what the Germans were doing to the Jews, and what Rudi had gone through [in Auschwitz], I thought that was a compassionate way to handle it. The fact that he said yes and didn't just come back with something really nasty to the guy. When he told me that story, I thought it was a story of compassion. You might read it differently.

ALAN: I'm picturing them in the mountains and the bushes, just traveling around, mostly hiding.

ROBIN: I've been in the area. Twice. That's where they were mostly fighting. It's mostly rolling hills and forest and farmland. They call it Katowice [northeast of Bratislava]. They used to have an annual parade there, going up to a place called Hippopotamus Hill.

ALAN: The main memorial for the partisans?

ROBIN: Yes, they have two big statues up there, with all the names of people who were killed during the Partisan period, and there are large stones surrounding it with the names of all the towns they were fighting in. Mainly they have commemorations for the Stalin Brigade, but one of those stones has a plaque of Rudi and Wetzler. It was put on after Rudi died. That time they invited me and Zuza. Freddy Wetzler's wife was there, too. Eta. I didn't really want to shake hands with her. I avoided her. I didn't know what to do because I knew that Rudi was not really very happy with who she was.

ALAN: And you'd been there once before that.

ROBIN: With Rudi. He was being honored. This was before there was the plaque.

ALAN: What was that like?

ROBIN: He was treated very well. Rudi was very social and they were speaking in Slovak, which I didn't really understand a word of. They had a parade. Rudi was not in great shape but we hiked up the hill. It must have been in the 2000s. As we're walking in the parade, arm in arm, he reminisced about the time the partisans had met up with the Soviet regiment and they had joined forces. He told me there was an officer, and he was Jewish, and Rudi said that somebody came up behind him and shot the officer and killed him, in the line. Rudi was there and he saw it. Imagine walking in a brigade with all the Soviets and somebody comes along and just shoots one of your commanders.

One of the generals in the resistance was called Brunovski. He was still alive when we were in that parade because I met him. I think he was a Jew as well. I remember the mayor of the town, [Milan] Ostroski, was very nice. In fact, I met him again later on the Vrba-Wetzler March [Trek]. He had a father about Rudi's age who was complaining about a Jewish partisan who was here in town and he was ruining the purity of the town. [Laughter] He was an antisemite! Rudi met with the father and the father started to talk to him about the Jews. The mayor had to pull his father away. Rudi just thought it was kind of funny. He knew Slovakia was still full of antisemites. Antisemites didn't faze him. As long as they weren't murdering him, or torturing him, he didn't mind them much.

ALAN: Was Rudi happy to be recognized?

ROBIN: He was really proud. I could see it.

ALAN: If people think of Rudi Vrba at all, they don't think about how important this period was to him – fighting back. Freedland's book offers precious little about it.

ROBIN: That's true. He didn't do much original research.

ALAN: There's an article I found that mentions three downed airmen, an American guy and two Canadians, who were looked after by the partisans. And the American wrote down that there was only person in the partisans who could translate for them ... and that saved their lives.

ROBIN: That was likely Rudi. Rudi was very good at that. He was always giving me lists of what to do here and what to give there. I told you he was very nurturing. He was like that with a lot of people. He was very compassionate. It was one of the things I really liked about him. He liked to help people. And he'd learned English as a child.

ALAN: I wish I could have spoken to that downed Canadian airman.

ROBIN: I met him, He went back to Slovakia, once. But I think he was kind of self-absorbed. I don't remember him being very dynamic.

ALAN: If you believe that American's narrative, you quickly come to realize how brutal the conditions were. Up in the mountains. In the snow.

ROBIN: Rudi had a dream once, about being in the partisans. It was 1989 because the Berlin Wall had just fallen. At the time Rudi said it was not a good sign – which turns out to be right in a way. Shortly after that, he had a dream. This is before he went back to visit Czechoslovakia or any of the eastern Bloc countries. In this dream, Uher was there, the commander [of the Partisans], and Rudi loved Uher. Rudi was on the top of this mountain, or on top of a hill, and there was a hut there. A warming hut. And he and Uher were up there. Rudi said, "Look what's happening." And Uher said, "Yup, we're going to have to do the whole thing over again." When Rudi went back to Slovakia, the first time, on his own, he went to the place he'd dreamed about. The hut was actually there. He'd had some sort of prophetic dream. A visionary dream. Rudi said there was still a lot of antisemitism when he was with the partisans. You could feel it everywhere.

ALAN: We assume Rudi would only be haunted by Auschwitz, but that dream harkens back to the time when Uher and his men had teamed up with the Russians, late '44.

ROBIN: I guess so. Around then they heard the Jews from Bratislava were being deported, Rudi was really depressed. He loved his mother. And his commander [Uher] understood it. He commiserated with him. Uher had a wife and a child. And I think he knew that they were dead. He said, "Never mind. The war will be over and you'll marry and you'll have your own family and you'll be able to bond with your own children." I think Rudi's mother had been deported, and she was in Theresienstadt at that time. There was grief when he thought his mother had died. Later, he joked about it.

ALAN: What did he say?

ROBIN: He said she had to lose some weight anyway.

ALAN: That sounds like Rudi. He was a machine gunner, correct?

ROBIN: I don't know. All the partisans have gone now [died]. The last partisan was living in Germany and his name was Dim [pronounced Deem]. Rudi had kept in touch with him. That brigade was famous in Czechoslovakia. Because Rudi's unit fought alongside the Russians, being a partisan probably saved Rudi's life, later on, during the Communist purges.

ALAN: How so?

ROBIN: He did something stupid when he was in Prague.

ALAN: Which was?

ROBIN: It's a bit complicated. You know there were two other Jews who shared a tent with Rudi? Well, one was the doctor for the brigade, Minarek, and Minarek and Rudi were sort of partners with their own tent. Then they added Kominitsky who slept on the floor. Minarek and Rudi would end up in Prague, but Kominitsky became some sort of diplomat in Romania.

Minarek was one of these old-fashioned doctors. He was really dedicated to his patients. He pulled people off the field under fire to bring them into safety. Rudi said that he was the kind of doctor that if the dead were on the battlefront, he would still pull them off the battlefield. He [Rudolf] didn't like that. He thought if the guy is still alive, you pull him off, but you don't pull him off if he's dead. He was angry with Minarek because he was so fastidious on that level.

ALAN: In the current crisis [in Gaza], if one of the captives is killed, they still want to get that body back. It's part of the Jewish tradition.

ROBIN: Yes, that's what Rudi told me. One of the biggest affronts that the Jews had with the Nazis was that they were burning the bodies. Because once the bodies are burned, you can't be resurrected when the Messiah comes. Rudi thought that was nonsense, but he did tell me that. In the Jewish religion, the body is sacred even after death. Rudi and Minarek were educated as very religious Jews, as children. So, they had that in their DNA. They were educated that way. Despite this one disagreement, Rudi admired Minarek and they remained friends for a long time. In fact, I met Minarek when we went to Slovakia in '91.

ALAN: Okay, so now go back to that stupid thing that Rudi did.

ROBIN: After the war, when Minarek got his new papers, he was absolutely livid. This was about 1950 or so. He brought the papers to Rudi. He said, "Look at what they put on the paper. They have put Israel as my middle name." That's what the Germans would do. They had fought with partisans to get rid of that. It was blatant antisemitism. So, Rudi took that document from Minarek, and he went straight to the Central Committee building to complain. I know where it is because he showed me in Prague. He showed me when he told me this story.

ALAN: Letting them know he and Minarek had fought with the partisans?

ROBIN: Yes, I suppose. So, he marched right in there and he got a meeting. He sat down with two officials. "What are you doing here!" he said. "I thought we got rid of this antisemitism when we got rid of the Germans!" That was a crazy thing to do because it was Stalinist Czechoslovakia. But the two guys just looked at each other and said, "Well, we ran out of paper, so we had to use the old paper." They just patted him on the back and told him not to worry. Just go home and do your studies.

Afterwards, Rudi realized he had made a huge mistake. He could have ended up in prison for that. He was lucky. But I think it was also because people really liked him ... He had a charisma ... and he had that background with the partisans ... and that's probably why they let him do what he did.

ALAN: Would they have known he was a decorated soldier?

ROBIN: Are you kidding? The Communist Party knew everything. They would have known he was living with Gerta, for instance. They had a social credit system. Neighbors spied on one another. Without computers, they had everything in his file.

ALAN: Whatever happened to the other guy, Kominitsky?

ROBIN: Kominitsky became something in the diplomatic corps after the war. In Romania. His wife and Gerta [Vrba's first wife] were medical students and friends together. During the purges, when they were purging all the Jews, in the Fifties, under Stalin, they were going to arrest Kominitsky because he was a Slovak. The police had grabbed him, and they were driving him back to Slovakia [from Prague], but Kominitsky got this idea [to save himself]. As they were driving, he said, "You know, my very good friend's mother is in Bratislava and she makes fantastic schnitzel. If we stop on the way, on the way to the prison, she'll make us schnitzel dinner."

They stopped there at Helena's home, and she [Helena] contacted Rudi; she told him what was happening. She got the point. She knew what was going on. She's smart. Somehow, Rudi managed to put pressure on some connection that he had, and they got Kominitsky out of there, so Kominitsky was also one of the few Jews who survived those purges. Maybe Rudi succeeded in convincing someone "higher up" that Kominitsky had also served bravely with the partisans. Kominitsky made up a different story later on about how he had survived the purges.

ALAN: Once again, Rudi saved somebody.

ROBIN: Later on, in Prague, in '94, Rudi was in contact with one of their colleagues, Dr. Zemin, and Zemin told Rudi the story that Kominitsky had made up. Rudi looked at him and said, "That's not how it happened." People had a false opinion of how great this guy [Kominitsky] was.

ALAN: That level of intrigue is far less common in Canada.

ROBIN: Politics are simpler in Canada. You have not had totalitarian regimes for so many years. You just have bits of it. You don't have the whole nine yards.

ALAN: You've characterized Rudi as a fighter, a warrior. If Rudi heard you say that, would he agree with your assessment?

ROBIN: I think so.

ALAN: He was a dapper dresser. Maybe that's connected [to a soldier mentality]?

ROBIN: Yes. He liked zippers on everything! That was his military style. It was all cocky. It was all zippers ... Do you remember there was this button store in Vancouver, in Gastown? They had fantastic buttons, and I had this outfit and I wanted to change the buttons on it. So, Rudi was marching around outside, while I was in the button store, and finally he was getting a little annoyed. He came into the button store. The proprietor said, "Oh, would you like to see the buttons your wife picked for her outfit?" He said, "No, actually I'm a zipper man, myself." [Laughter]

ALAN: Did it ever strike you that his soldier mentality was inappropriate?

ROBIN: No. He observed things. He told me, "Look, don't play the intellectual. It doesn't come out right when you do that. But if you treat everybody like they're a customer, that's perfect for you." It wasn't a compliment. But he was right.

ALAN: It was an assessment.

ROBIN: But it was good advice. It was advice that helped me.

ALAN: You trusted his judgement about things.

ROBIN: I did. A good soldier has to make assessments as well. His idea was that life was a war. And you're a soldier in this life. That was his approach. And I think I had a bit of that approach as a child because it was always important for me to be strong. Like, if I went to the doctor, I had to be strong, I wouldn't cry. That kind of thing. So, that approach [of Rudi's] probably resonated with me.

When he was in Auschwitz, he looked at himself as a soldier. I think that gave him a lot of strength. To think he was a soldier against Nazis. He already had that. He was a partisan in Auschwitz. Remember, when he was 17, or even 16, he wanted to escape to England, he wanted to join the English army. His whole idea was that he was going to fight Nazis. He was already mentally a soldier.

ALAN: At age 17, he was already thinking, "Okay, I am going to go away somewhere so I can get a gun and fight."

ROBIN: Absolutely.

ALAN: When you fell in love with him, do you think you understood all that immediately?

ROBIN: No, I didn't get it all. It's only now, in reflection backwards, that I can see it.

ALAN: You were not smitten with a war hero.

ROBIN: No, it took a while. At a certain point, I got it. But I think he also told me. He explained it to me [who he was].

ALAN: A soldier mentality is antithetical to our Canadian niceness.

ROBIN: It depends on who you are associating with.

ALAN: We say "sorry" all the time.

ROBIN: It depends where you are.

ALAN: Mild-mannered Vancouver is totally divorced from a soldierly attitude. In fact, that's a pretty good definition for what it tries to be.

ROBIN: But being a soldier is not being un-nice. It has nothing to do with being nice or not nice. It has to do with whether you are strong or not strong. You must be clear in your job. In whatever job it is you have, at any particular point of time, you can have a nice façade and still be a soldier. I think you could be looking at a soldier as being negative.

ALAN: That's true. I was raised in a non-soldierly world.

ROBIN: I think a lot of people who are very competitive can still have a soldierly approach. In Canada, that competitiveness is just hidden a bit more. If it comes across as assertive, you hide it. But it's still there. I am sort of competitive, but when I first moved to Canada it took me a while to figure out I had to add a lot of words to whatever I said so that

The three downed airmen who relied on Vrba as a translator among the Partisans.

I didn't come across as abrupt. When I moved back to New York, they all thought I was Canadian! [Laughter] I have the same fight in me; it's just a different façade.

ALAN: You are disobeying Rudi now. You are sounding very intellectual.

[Laughter]

ROBIN: Well, I know! And that's what he told me not to do!

[Laughter]

ALAN: Just be my arm candy, and I'll be your soldier, and everything will be all right.

[Laughter]

ROBIN: Except he didn't want me to rely on him as my soldier. He wanted me to be my own soldier. He wanted me to have my own strength.

There is no extensive documentation of Vrba's time with the Partisans in his own hand. Keeping a diary would likely not have been permitted. Evidence of the partisan brigade has been found, however, in records pertaining to three downed airman who were sheltered by Uher's rebels.

Robin Vrba remembers Rudolf Vrba telling her about the airmen for whom Vrba served as a translator:

"Rudi had studied English as a young person. When he was in the partisans, Rudi spoke English. There was a Canadian airman that the partisans found, and Rudi was the translator. It was either Canadian or American. But I think it was a Canadian. There is some kind of record of this in one of the military museums in Slovakia ..." [She is likely describing a museum in Modrovka, curated by Bohuslav Ferianec.]

The best description of living conditions within Rudolf Vrba's partisan unit has been provided by one of the downed airmen, Edwin Burkhardt an American who survived the winter of 1944–45 in the forests and mountains of Slovakia alongside the downed Canadian aviators Stuart May and Jack Ritch. His story makes clear that all three men could not have survived without the assistance of "a Slovak who could speak fairly good English."

Ed Burkhardt was a nose gunner who took refuge with the partisans after his B-24 bomber plane known as *TenMenBak* was downed in the Slovakian countryside between the villages of Omšenie and Trenčianske Teplice. This plane had been on a mission to bomb an oil refinery. The crew was largely inexperienced but managed to parachute to the ground. One crewmember died; eight others were captured.

Burkhardt describes at length how he and two Canadian airmen survived mainly due to the guidance from "a man who could speak fairly good English." He continues, "The group was headed by a Slovak captain ... I also met two Canadians in this group, Lt. Stuart May of Weston, Ontario, and Lt. Jack Ritch of Edmonton, Alberta. The Canadians had been with the Partisan group since October 17, 1944 when they had crash-landed in a Mosquito."

Ed Burkhardt's 2,400-word memoir was published under the title "My First Mission" in the June 2004 edition of *The Liberaider*. Born on April 14, 1923 in Pikes Creek, Luzerne County, Pennsylvania, Edwin A. Burkhardt had served as the nose gunner on B-24 *Tenmenbak* of the 764th Bomber Squadron, 461th Bomber Group, 15th Air Force based out of Torretta Airbase in Italy.

The Missing Aircraft Report (MACR) 10683 indicates that on December 17, 1944, Burkhart's ill-fated plane was sent on a mission to bomb the oil refineries in Odental, Germany. After the bombing run, the bomber *Tenmenbak* had an engine problem and dropped out of formation and was shot down by enemy fighters. The plane crashed, killing one crewmember. Eight crewmembers were taken prisoner, and one was able to evade capture with the help of Uher's Partisans in Slovakia. A memorial in Trenčianske Teplice, Slovakia includes parts of the plane wreckage.

Burkhardt returned to duty via Crimea and North Africa. He died at age 87 on April 4, 2011, in Silver Spring, Maryland and was buried in the Arlington National Cemetery.

A documentary film made in 2000 by Rick Carr follows surviving crewmembers to the countryside of Slovakia where they discover the remains of their B-24 bomber, giving rise to a book by Dr. Zuzanna Janacova, published in 2001, as *Tenmenbak*.

CHAPTER 12

Alfréd and Eta Wetzler

Alfréd and Eta Wetzler, both Auschwitz survivors, were married after the war in 1948.

VRBA AND ALFRÉD Wetzler were divided by politics and geography after World War II and they respectfully drifted apart. The regrettable estrangement that ensued between Vrba and Wetzler over the years is partially attributable to the fact that Vrba knew his friend's wife had been a Block Leader inside the Auschwitz women's camp.

Constrained by the Communist government, Wetzler worked as a journalist/editor from 1945 to 1950, moved to Bratislava (1950–1955) and worked on a farm (1955–1970) until he was sidelined by failing health. He died in Bratislava on February 8, 1988, and was buried in the Orthodox Jewish Cemetery.

After his birth in the Slovakian town of Trnava on May 10, 1918, Alfréd Wetzler was partially raised in the backyard of a synagogue with his three brothers. After high school, he worked as a laborer until he was called up for compulsory military service in 1940. According to the Polish historian Henryk Świebocki, Wetzler was arrested in 1941 after he had attempted to sabotage the operations of a brick factory. Repeatedly interrogated during four months in a Bratislava prison, Wetzler was finally released; soon afterwards the Hlinka Guard came to his parents' home to escort him to the transit camp at Sereď, Slovakia – where he was soon robbed. To escape the precariousness of life in the Sereď camp, Wetzler volunteered, with 1,000 others, to do "farm work" at Auschwitz, a little-known place not far from the Czechoslovakian-Polish border.

Wetzler arrived at Auschwitz I on April 13, 1942 and became prisoner #29162. He was transferred the next day to Sector BIb of the men's camp at Auschwitz II (Birkenau) when it still had only three main buildings. For approximately three months he was a construction laborer along with 200 other Jews, helping to erect an armaments plant. Świebocki, a senior historian at the Auschwitz-Birkenau State Museum (Państwowe Muzeum Auschwitz-Birkenau), has noted that Wetzler made an aborted escape attempt in 1942. Having noticed there was a sewer pipe that went from the men's camp in Section BIb to outside the fenced compound, Wetzler undertook reconnaissance by entering the sewer system through a manhole near Barrack 7. The transit through the pipe was surprisingly easy. He was certain he had gone beyond the perimeter of the camp only to discover there was an iron grate at the end of his journey, barring the way. He was only able to crawl backwards to captivity with great difficulty.

Having benefited from the advice of senior prisoner #7699, Pawel Gulba, Wetzler was able to obtain the coveted job of *Schreiber* [scribe] in section Blb of Auschwitz-Birkenau, the so-called French Block, before switching to a similar position at the Block 7 "hospital" where he proceeded to record more than 50,000 deaths. He was transferred to the camp mortuary to keep track of prisoners who supposedly had died of natural causes as of January 1943. This job of tallying daily death tolls beyond the crematoria also entailed keeping track of how much gold was extracted from the teeth of the corpses. Despite the obvious problems with hygiene, the job of corpse-counter was one of the best jobs in the camp because Wetzler had a small office and avoided hard labor.

The collectors of corpses were able to visit most sectors of the camp and therefore could provide Wetzler with up-to-date reports on current events. Wetzler's advisor Pawel Gulba, referenced as Pavel in Wetzler's novel, was born in Bobryk, Poland and survived the war. He was registered at the Ebensee Displaced Persons camp in Austria on April 20, 1945.

In June of 1943, Wetzler was transferred to serve as a clerk for Block Bld where the blockleader was a fellow Slovakian, Arnošt Rosin. Wetzler later claimed he had himself transferred to a similar position at Block 9, approximately two months before he would undertake his escape with Rudolf Vrba, thereby attempting to safeguard Rosin from any subsequent interrogation, but it remains questionable if plans were hatched for Wetzler and Vrba's participation (as the preferred "guinea pigs") that far in advance (in February) when we now know the preceding escape from the woodpile hideout (by Cytryn, Balaban, Abramovicz and Eisenbach) had only just occurred in early March.

Because Vrba was consistently an outspoken and penetrating critic of those who were complicit with Nazi operations, including Jews and prominent figures in Israel, there have been efforts to discredit Vrba by elevating Wetzler as the senior, and therefore more sober, reporter of events. As well, because Wetzler lived most of his adult life after the war behind the Iron Curtain, many of the historians from Eastern European countries have tended to favor the older figure of Wetzler as being the escape leader, diminishing Vrba as a much younger hothead in the process. As a "star" in Lanzmann's *Shoah*, Vrba had also succeeded in leading a seemingly comfortable life in the West as an exemplary scientist who selflessly served as an anti-Nazi courtroom expert witness – complete with a beautiful wife – so there was much to envy from afar.

Vrba became a decorated war hero after fighting for the partisans under Captain Uher. It is much less known that Wetzler was also briefly associated with Uher's partisan outfit. Through no fault of his own, Wetzler was unable to save 20 badly wounded partisans under his supervision, when they were overwhelmed by German troops. Wetzler, with his Auschwitz tattoo, was somehow spared but he underwent interrogation, the nature of which has not been recorded. His life was saved by the advance of Russian troops.

In a letter to Kazimierz Smoleń of the Auschwitz Museum on December 18, 1989, in response to Smoleń's letter to him on November 24, 1989, Vrba notes that Wetzler was "a soldier of the Czechoslovak Army in the *Partyzan* Unit of Captain Miloš Uher" until the end of the war and "Wetzler joined me there in February 1945 and was with us until March 1945, when he fell again into the hands of Germans. He was liberated in March 1945 by a surprise artillery shelling of the prison by the advancing Russians."

The Soviet regime dominated Czechoslovakia for the ensuing decades. Wetzler and his wife were required to embrace communism. They were poor, with minimal material comforts. Rudolf and Robin Vrba sent several gifts of money, in the forms of bonds via Switzerland.

In Communist Czechoslovakia where the Holocaust was rarely discussed openly, and where antisemitism resurfaced in the 1950s, Wetzler persevered as a modest, calm person and his heroism was not divulged. Far too much of Slovakian society had supported the Nazis. He wore long-sleeved shirts and a jacket to conceal his tattoo and was restricted to low-paying jobs.

Articulate and well-read, he worked as an editor for the humor magazine *Roháč*, then as a civil servant and a tourist guide. As a retiree, from 1979 onward, he helped in the library on Šalviová Street, in the town of Ružinov, as a part-time, disabled pensioner. A co-worker, Darina Horkáová, fondly recalled him bringing snacks to work, as well as a slice of bread and a piece of sausage or bacon. He always used a small pocketknife to eat.

Wetzler once asked if Horkáová had read *What Dante Did Not See*. She said she had read it and admired it. Known to her fondly as Uncle Fred, he proceeded to borrow his own book from the library without letting her know he was its author, Lánik. Only later did he reveal that Jozef Lánik and Alfréd Wetzler were the same person.

"My father did not expect gratitude," his daughter later wrote in the preface to a reissued version of the novel.

Wetzler and his wife had an apartment on Križna Street. As a chronic smoker with a weak heart, he stopped coming to help at the library in the fall of 1987. He died on February 8, 1988, and was buried in the Jewish cemetery on Žižková Street in Bratislava.

Although he had testified at the Frankfurt Auschwitz trials and supplied a deposition for the Eichmann trial, he was never accorded credit as a war hero or a public figure in his homeland until after his death. Posthumously, he was awarded the Order of Ludovit Stur II Class in 1997 and the Cross of Milan Rastislav Stefanik in 2007. A park has been named after him in Ruzinov in front of the Pan-European University. The Bratislava-born, Slovakian President Zusana Čaputová visited his grave on the national Victims of Holocaust and Racial Violence Day. His daughter, Tatiana Kernova, a pediatrician, died in 2012.

~

THE EXTENT TO which Wetzler's novel about his time in Auschwitz is not reliable as a truthful account becomes clear to anyone who takes the time to read it carefully. Living under the yoke of Soviet occupation, Wetzler fashioned his tale to suit Soviet authorities. For instance, he claims the escape hideout was located "in the 'Mexico' area, where they intend, in the shortest possible time, to complete a vast camp for ten thousand Soviet prisoners, whom allegedly they are already holding elsewhere." The notion that the Nazis were intending to transform their murder factory into a penal colony to accommodate 10,000 already-captured Soviet POWs is seemingly a propagandist misinterpretation. Mexico was being erected for the anticipated massive influx of up to 800,000 Hungarian Jews, not all of whom would be gassed immediately.

Although Wetzler distorts the truth to please Soviet authorities, much of Wetzler's prose is compelling. His omniscient narrator asks: "How many have they tortured to death, shot, hanged, poisoned, killed with phenol, killed with injections of cancer, typhus, malaria, by electric current or asphyxiation? Altogether three million, possibly more."

This is an estimate in keeping with Vrba's calculation of 2.5 million murdered, plus or minus 10 percent, which he formally submitted within his sworn affidavit at the trial of Adolf Eichmann in 1961. The overall death-toll estimate initially made by the most famous Auschwitz commander, Rudolf Höss, exceeded 3 million, but then he reduced that estimate to 2.5 million at his hearing in Nuremberg. (Bizarrely, Vrba would subsequently be asked by Höss' publisher to supply an expert, insider reader's report on the manuscript of Höss' autobiography, later published in Polish in 1951 and in German in 1956.)

These estimates by Vrba, Wetzler and Höss were undercut by the incredulous Jewish elders who placed themselves in the position of arbiters in April and May of 1944. Consequently, erring on the side of caution, the

Initially, Wetzler was a role model for Vrba as a ladies' man.

Vrba-Wetzler Report claims the Nazis accumulated an overall death toll of 1.76 million at Auschwitz between April 1942 and April 1944. Since then, Holocaust deniers, academics and major institutions have combined their disbelief and caution to whittle that figure down to around 1.2 million overall, and now the Auschwitz murder toll has been reduced to 1.1 million by the Auschwitz Museum. As European nations seek to reduce their varying degrees of Holocaust culpability and the "fate" of the Jews becomes the preserve of academics, the viewpoints of Höss and Vrba are dismissed as anachronistic. They were merely there.

It is now seldom mentioned that the most notorious torturer at Auschwitz, Technical Sergeant Wilhelm Boger, estimated in 1945 that the murder toll in Auschwitz exceeded four million; in 1945, testifying at a trial as a witness and not as a defendant, Pery Broad, a member of the Political Department at Auschwitz, stated between 2.5 million and three million were executed. Also, according to Hermann Langbein in *People of Auschwitz*, the SS physician Friedrich Entress initially testified at Gmunden, Austria, on July 30, 1945 that 2 to 2.5 million were murdered; when pressed, he agreed the overall murder toll could be five million.

The Political Department and its admissions division was the only office permitted to maintain a tally of those who were gassed. As head of that division, Maximilian Grabner, aka "Lord God of Auschwitz," testified at a trial in his birthplace of Vienna on September 16, 1945, saying, "During my term as head of the Political Department it was at least three million." Grabner was only at Auschwitz from May of 1940 to December of 1943. In 1945, using his wartime alias Jozef [Jožo] Lánik, Wetzler assembled a pamphlet about the war crimes committed by the Nazi regime, with an emphasis on Slovakia, entitled *Nemecké a gardistické zverstvá* (*German and Guards' Atrocities*). Again under his assumed name Jozef Lánik, Wetzler published a booklet in 1946 entitled *Oswiecim, hrobka štyroch miliónov ľudí. Krátka história a život v oswiecimskom pekle* (*Auschwitz, The Tomb of Four Million People. A short history and life in the hell of Auschwitz in the years 1942–1945*). The publisher is listed as Košice: Povereníctvo SNR pre informácie. Although this volume is a composite of the knowledge gained by all four escapees who met in Bratislava, the other three informants are not credited. Both publications stress the need for reparations and trials.

Wetzler's semi-fictional work about Auschwitz was first published in Slovak as *Co Dante nevidel* in 1964. It had evolved from a fictional short story called *Death Lies on the Other Side*, in which the narrator references Wetzler's actual tattoo number. That story had been written in the third person for a literary competition in 1958. According to researcher Nikola Zimring, co-editor of the 2020 version of Rudolf Vrba's *I Escaped from Auschwitz*, one of the judges who rejected Wetzler's submission was Auschwitz survivor Erich Kulka whose own book *Night and Fog* addressed the same subject matter. Presumably, Kulka wanted the Auschwitz literary territory for his own.

In his introduction to an English version of Wetzler's amalgam of fact and fiction, retitled *Escape from Hell* and first published in 2006, Robert Rozett, Director of the Yad Vashem Libraries, states *Escape from Hell* "straddles the line between memoir and literature, in many ways like Eli Wiesel's much heralded *Night*." It doesn't help the reader to be convinced that Wetzler's hodge-podge is somehow in a class with the most venerated work by Elie Wiesel if, in that process of making the compliment, Wiesel's first name has been misspelled as Eli. In 2006, one of Yad Vashem's chief historians Yehuda Bauer was still adversarial to Vrba's outspokenness and welcomed Wetzler's alternative voice.

As a mishmash of imagination and truth, Wetzler's only novel often reads like a haphazard first draft, poorly edited. On one page the author states "One thousand two hundred SS men have poured out of their barracks for the hunt." Ten pages later, a Nazi commander is angry "at one thousand seven hundred trained elite soldiers who cannot find two hungry and half-alive scumbags." The number could be 1,200 or 1,700 – not both.

The lead Auschwitz escapee character named Karol, based on Wetzler, is repeatedly superior to his younger, feckless cohort, Val, a deviant substitute for the character of Vrba. Wetzler was aware his escape partner had gained some notoriety in the West. *Escape from Hell* is therefore a work of jealousy and even revenge. Later we read that "Karol" (Wetzler) encourages "Val" (Vrba) to speak in the basement of the old people's home in Žilina, as if Vrba was someone reticent to speak his mind. Skim-reading historians and filmmakers have nonetheless continued to mine this work as a counterpart to Vrba's memoir.

What Dante Did Not See was republished as a non-fiction book in English through the efforts of a Hungarian scientist Péter Várnai, living in Cambridge, England, whose father's family came from what is now Slovakia. While researching his family roots, Várnai discovered his family name had been changed from Wetzler. He consequently went to Bratislava where he met and befriended Wetzler's widow, Eta Wetzlerová, and they jointly agreed he was likely a relative of her deceased husband. Várnai set about securing a publisher for an English edition and acquiring the services of a translator, Ewald Osers, who completed the task in 2006 and who has "asserted his moral rights as the translator." Wetzler's novel was then renamed and remarketed in English as *Escape from Hell: The True Story of the Auschwitz Protocol* (Berghahn Books 2007). A paperback version was issued in 2020.

In the original Slovak version, the character who clearly represented the older and therefore wiser escapee, Wetzler, is named Karol; the character that clearly represented the younger and less reliable character, Vrba, goes by the name of Valér. In the English version, these names are Karol and Val. This novel was republished in Slovak shortly after Wetzler's death in 1988. A fourth edition crediting Wetzler as its author instead of Jozef Lánik, appeared in 2009. This new edition contained the first, complete Slovak version of the Auschwitz Report (*Auschwitz Protocols*). Hence, it took 65 years before Slovakians could read the most influential and important document of World War II, heroically prepared by two native sons, in their own language.

To gain favor with the Communist authorities, Wetzler claimed the two escapees were headed for the Soviet Union. His account nonetheless served as the basis for a Slovakian feature film made in 2021 and viewed globally, *The Auschwitz Report*, in which the roles of the real-life characters are reversed. It is now difficult to ascertain which depiction of the Vrba-Wetzler escape is more unreliable – Wetzler's original fictional version or the Slovakian feature film.

~

In an interview conducted at his home in 2022, the Czech-born novelist Jan Drabek shared a very important story about Alfréd Wetzler that Drabek heard from his father.

> "My father was in Auschwitz. In 1947, he went back to Poland with a group of Czechoslovaks to give testimony for the trial of the Auschwitz commandant Höss and that trial lasted from March 11 to March 29. During that time their hosts took them on a trip around Auschwitz environs. Among the former Czechoslovak prisoners

that day was also a certain Alfréd Wetzler. When they were passing a small cottage, Wetzler suddenly cried out, 'Stop! Please stop!'

"Wetzler proceeded to knock on the door of the cottage. An old lady opened it. He took her in his arms and kissed her. Greatly moved, Wetzler came back to the car and asked his colleagues to give him all the money they had. He gave it all, along with his watch, to the surprised lady. His eyes were filled with tears.

"Wetzler explained to her that when he and Rudi were escaping from Auschwitz, in desperation, against all advice, they had knocked on her door and asked for help. This was the same woman who had given them food and clothing and valuable directions. This was the woman who had saved their lives."

This anecdote about Wetzler's return to Auschwitz is vital because it illustrates the extent to which Wetzler's novelized memoir about the escape is indeed fiction. In Chapter 12 of his book *Escape from Hell,* Wetzler, instead, goes to great lengths, for most of the chapter, to describe the pair's meeting in a forest with a young mother and her young boy named Wladek. The dislikable character of Val [Vrba] castigates the more admirable character of Karol [Wetzler] for not being sufficiently wary.

"You trust the first person we've met," Val says reproachfully, whereupon the more noble character in the novel, Karol, replies, "If you want to live, you've got to trust."

The first person that Vrba and Wetzler actually met as they were heading towards the Beskid Mountains was clearly the woman in the cottage, the same person to whom Wetzler so eagerly provided money and his watch. This person who actually took pity on them is absent from Wetzler's version of events.

Rudolf Vrba has written: "We chose a house more or less at random. As we made our way round to the yard at the back, chickens darted around our feet and somewhere a goose honked indignantly. An old woman, dressed in the voluminous black frock and white head scarf of a Polish peasant, came to the door and behind her we could see the worried face of a girl about eighteen. In our best Polish, we greeted her in traditional fashion: 'Praise be to the name of Christ.'"

In Vrba's version, the pair are told by the old woman that they still have a long way to go to reach the mountains. They slept in her house, chopped wood for her the following day, and were replenished by potato soup. Later, this old woman woke them at 3 a.m. and gave them several cups of coffee. They refused her offer of money ("four marks, about a pound") before recommencing their trek at night.

Vrba writes, "For two reasons I did not want to take her money. In the first place, I felt I owed her much more than she did us. Secondly, I was thinking of Volkov's cardinal rule – take no money or you'll be tempted to spend it – and was determined not to break it."

It would take the pair two more days to reach the halfway point of their journey, the town of Porebka "where Sandor Eisenbach and his three friends had been captured." Wetzler never references the preceding escape attempt by the foursome who had been involved in the construction of the hideout in Mexico.

~

THE ESTRANGEMENT THAT ensued between Vrba and Wetzler over the years is partially attributable to the fact that Vrba knew his friend's wife had been a Block Leader with a damaging reputation inside the Auschwitz women's camp. This fact is essential for understanding why the two escapees did not remain close friends. Vrba never publicly "outed" his friend's wife.

Katya Singer was an assimilated Czech Jew who served as a *Rapportschreiberin* in Auschwitz from September 1942 until her deportation to Stutthof in 1944. [A *Rapportschreiberin* was a registration clerk who received reports on the number of prisoners in the camp.] She gave a recorded interview on July 21, 1991, at the Prague Intercontinental Hotel. The interviewer Susan Cernyak-Spatz, a camp survivor, suggested that "ordinary prisoners in average commandos have said in biographies and other books that the *blockovás*, especially the Slovakian ones, were beating the prisoners and stealing parts of their rations."

KATYA SINGER: That is not quite true. Only two were known to beat prisoners, the two youngest. It is always like that. Among a thousand people there are always ten who are evil. But I did not select the *blockovás*. Every matron had been assigned a block and they had decided who would be a block worker and who would be the *blocková* … The *blockovás* would beat a prisoner who was dirty and did not have to be dirty; who was caught stealing and did not have to steal.

SUSAN CERNYAK-SPATZ: From my own experience in an *Aussencommando* block, I know that it is not easy to keep clean there.

KATYA SINGER: I know that Eta Wetzler was one that beat the prisoners. She was *blocková* on Block 25 [the death block]; that was terrible.

Wetzler met his wife-to-be in Auschwitz where she was Block Leader in the women's barracks at Birkenau. She was born in Slovakia and grew up in a poor, non-religious Jewish family with two brothers. Her father was an electrician who mostly made money as a traveling salesman for electrical appliances. She once described him as politically naïve and "a warm person, but completely unsuitable for trading."

Poverty was Eta's main burden. Only later in life did she realize that she was being sent to the other side of town to visit a rich aunt so that she could be fed lunch. She was humiliated when she had to deliver a "testimony of poetry" in order for her fees to be waived at the German grammar school where she was an outstanding student. When she saw hateful signs condemning Jews, she was not greatly concerned. Her family was seemingly assimilated.

At age 16, in August of 1941, Eta sewed a yellow star onto her clothing. She was on that first train of young women who were sent to Auschwitz and arrived March 26, 1942. Her ability to speak German so well elevated her quickly in the camp hierarchy.

According to a Slovakian *SME* article by Marek Horvatovic in 2007:

"Her two brothers and mother managed to hide in Liptov throughout the war, her father spent a critical time in Bratislava … Eta did not like to talk about what she experienced in the camp, but sometimes she made a remark that shocked. She was direct, so she blurted out something about the piles of corpses by the ovens and the piece of bread that one of them was holding in her hand, and she, after typhoid, grabbed that skive to survive. And she went on. Or she plebeianly mentioned how fitting it was that she came from modest means. It was an advantage in the Auschwitz jungle and, paradoxically, also the fact that she had been there since 1942. She was among those who kept the camp running, there was no choice, she was responsible for one block in the camp ...

"The story of Fred's escape also became Eta's story. She stood by him in these ungrateful years, urged him to capture the escape from the Polish Auschwitz to Slovakia, so that a book could be made of it. She was proud of Fred and spoke of him with love even when she seemed to complain. Mr. Alfréd Wetzler died in 1988. In America or Britain, such a rare person would have at least a street, if not a square, in every major city. Slovakia is not yet ready for real heroes.

"Eta was a journalist, in Prác and Roľnícky noviny. In 1968, after the Soviet invasion, she took the 'wrong position' and was definitively expelled from the party. It was difficult for her to fight through, she 'fell down' for a while, but the strong dynamo that always drove her started after a while. Daughter Táňa was here, a miracle that she came into the world after the concentration camp.

"November 1989 was redemption for Eta ... She could go directly to Vienna. She was very happy about her freedom. She translated from German, sometimes gave lessons. She had a raspy, smoked voice and strong arms, in which many in her apartment on Bratislava's Krížna Street liked to lose themselves in order to immediately immerse themselves in great debates ... [But] For Eta, Judaism was not a topic ..."

~

As a *Blockführerin* (female *Blockführer*), Eta Wetzler had been in charge of the often-brutal *kapos* whose job it was to persecute, intimidate and punish prisoners. Put simply, she had enormous influence on who lived and who died.

Eta was able to end her internment in Ravensbrück where her reputation was largely unknown. From there, she was first taken to Denmark with other liberated, female prisoners, en route to Sweden. She once recalled, "They took us on trucks to Denmark and the Danish mothers spread white tablecloths for us in a large meadow, put bread and butter on it ... and the thousand hungry ladies ran to the tables, and in one second, there was nothing on them. No tablecloths, no kettles, no plates. Those golden Danish mothers told us that we don't have to hide anything anymore, that we will have everything."

She remained in Sweden for further recovery, then she was able to return on a train to Prague at Christmas in 1945. She become an ardent Communist, but later became disenchanted. She said Auschwitz made it clear to her that human beings are animals. For most of her long life, she was bitter about the lack of recognition accorded to her husband while they lived behind the Iron Curtain in Communist-controlled Czechoslovakia.

Simultaneously, she resented any prominence Vrba received in the West. She probably influenced her husband to take a similar position. At the same time, Eta Wetzlerová knew that Vrba had the wherewithal to expose her for being complicit with the murderous Nazi agenda in Auschwitz. It would have been easy for him to do so. He never did.

She died in May of 2007.

Corroborative evidence to support Rudolf Vrba's low opinion of his escape partner's wife can be found in Hermann Langbein's study *People in Auschwitz*. "In the women's camp," Langbein recalls, "inmates from Slovakia with low numbers rose to the status of a kind of aristocracy." By August of 1944, most of the female block elders were Slovakian Jews. Lucie Begow, who arrived in Auschwitz in the spring of 1944, recalls how these Slovak women, who had arrived in Auschwitz as teenagers, were referred to as the "camp generation" because they had learned to adapt to the Nazi dictates from the construction phase onward. "With one exception," she told Langbein, "their behavior was more German than that of the Germans."

There is no reason to believe that Eta Wetzler was that lone exception. Grete Salus did not mince words describing the temperament of her block elder in the fall of 1944. "The pressure of this position turned almost all of these women into utterly merciless monsters and veritable hyenas." Another Slovakian block elder in the women's camp was renowned for giving beatings even when there was no Nazi prison official present. Having arrived in Auschwitz as a tall, blonde beauty, the Slovakian Sara Meisels was overheard by Sura Zofia Herson-Nowak saying, "I have lost so many relatives here that I know no pity."

Ana Novac has concluded that the Slovakian women were menacing block elders because they resented having endured the crudest years of Auschwitz while relatively recent arrivals had been living comfortably at home with bread and butter. Novac's description of one such Slovakian block elder begins, "She is alive only when she is giving a beating. Then she comes to life like a tennis player who fell asleep during his training and finally starts a match. Her chin juts out and her beautiful, languid lips are pinched. For an instant she motionlessly eyes her victim. Then there flashes around her mouth that peculiar, somewhat evil, and a bit intoxicated smile that brightens her in the truest sense of the word. She swings her whip backward, only to make it whiz down with all her strength the next moment."

This section of Langbein's book is especially sobering when one simultaneously views photos of the untainted, Slovakian teenage girls before they boarded that first train of Jews sent to Auschwitz and subsequently obtained positions of authority. "Some of them," he writes, "but not all, definitely were amoral persons by nature. The majority of them had been made that [way] by the terrible, enervating life that gnawed away at a human being like a running sore ... They had become inured to human suffering because they had suffered too much themselves."

~

Joseph Neumann was born in Eastern Slovakia in 1916. He worked as a lumberjack and managed to evade capture until April of 1942, at which time he was sent by train to Auschwitz I. After processing, he was sent to Auschwitz II where, with a high temperature due to typhus, he was taken to the hospital by a friendly *kapo.* The next day he was further weakened when a Dr. May from Warsaw was required to extract blood from Neumann for transfusion purposes. Increasingly, Neumann no longer cared whether he lived or died. It was in this deflated state that Neumann met Alfréd Wetzler, who had arrived in Auschwitz only a short time before him.

"I offered him my bread because I couldn't eat," Neumann recalled in 1988, "but he wouldn't take it. He said, 'Keep it, you will need it.' I was already resigned on life [prepared to die] but he [Wetzler] had some kind of connection there [in Auschwitz]. I decided I wanted to die with him."

Neumann was able to survive with relative security after he was

Auschwitz survivors Erich Kulka (later an adversary), Joseph Neumann and Rudolf Vrba. Photo from Vrba's personal archives, date and location unknown.

accorded the relatively easy job of collecting the tattoo numbers of camp suicides, working in association with Wetzler who oversaw the camp morgue for non-gassed, non-executed camp prisoners. Neumann was not an intellectual. He never wrote a book. But these men naturally bonded for self-protection because they were all Slovakians.

Neumann cites the importance of Vrba and Wetzler's escape in the interview that was conducted by the Holocaust Memorial Foundation of Illinois (now the Illinois Holocaust Museum and Education Center) on August 21, 1988 [Accession Number: 1989.346.51 | RG Number: RG-50.031.0051]. But this section is absent from a transcript that was made after the oral interview had been sent to the United States Holocaust Memorial Museum Oral History branch on December 12, 1989. Ruth Linn has continuously alleged that Vrba has been made invisible by major Holocaust institutions, and this is yet another example. She has alleged that even though Yad Vashem had collected one of the most foremost collections of literature pertaining to the Holocaust, it had no English or Hebrew version of the *Vrba-Wetzler Report* as of 2004. As well, its Hungarian version was held within the archives for and about Rudolf Kasztner.

Oddly, in a rough transcription of the Neumann interview made available online by the USHMM, Vrba's name is not mentioned, whereas the USHMM account does cite some of the details of the Mordowicz and Rosin escape. One must listen to the original, hard-to-hear Illinois version of the audio to learn how Neumann and Vrba also crossed paths in Auschwitz. The seldom-cited and never-heralded Neumann was in no way exemplary as a character, but he was nonetheless a witness to various events regarding three major figures in Auschwitz history – Lederer, Vrba and Wetzler.

As previously outlined, on the night of March 8–9, 1944, when 3,792 members of the so-called Czech Family Camp were murdered (including Vrba's lover Alice Munk), the exceptionally beautiful Renée Neumann and her mother Eda were spared (along with approximately 60 others) due largely to the interventions of SS-*Unterscharführer* guard Victor Pestek who then arranged for Renée's mother to have a relatively secure job in the infirmary. "I want to do something to forget the smell of burning human flesh and feel a little cleaner," Pestek supposedly said. Pestek had been so well-liked as a supervisor of the Czech Family Camp that he had been accorded the nickname *miláček* – Czech for "darling" or "doll" – and Vrba would later describe Pestek as "the only honorable SS man I ever met … who saw the vileness that lay beneath those smart, green uniforms and had the courage to strike against it."

It was pure coincidence that Joseph Neumann just happened to share the same surname with Renée Neumann. His recollections of Pestek are contained in Kulka's *The Death Factory* and within his Illinois interview during which Neumann claims he was asked by Victor Pestek to join him for his audacious escape attempt. In the interview he does not indicate as to whether or not he was aware that Rudolf Vrba and Wetzler had already both been asked by Pestek to participate in the same scheme. When Neumann conferred with his friend Wetzler and asked his opinion of the escape plan, Wetzler advised him to never trust the word of a Nazi. Vrba and Wetzler were aware that, recently, an SS man named Dobrovolný had offered to help a Jewish childhood friend to escape from Auschwitz, only to turn him in for a pay bonus, whereupon the would-be escapee was brutally executed.

When, eventually, Siegfried Lederer, a Jew born in Pilsen, Sudetenland in 1904, agreed to the plan of the Romanian-born Pestek, he was a prudent choice. Previously apprehended by the Nazis for his covert activities, Lederer had been active in Plzeňák 28, a Czech resistance group in Zbraslav (so named because it had 28 members). This background information serves to explain how and why Lederer deserves to be credited as the first Jew to successfully escape from Auschwitz only a few days before Vrba and Wetzler would begin their escape on April 7.

When the besotted Pestek returned to Auschwitz on May 25, 1944, and somehow managed to establish a hiding place for himself in "Mexico," he discovered his damsel in distress, Renée Neumann, was still unwilling to be liberated if it meant endangering the life of her mother. It was at this juncture that the other Neumann, Joseph, received a message via the camp underground saying that Pestek wanted to talk to him. Fortunately, for Neumann, that rendezvous was thwarted, whereupon Pestek was recognized and taken to Block Eleven, the punishment block, for prolonged torture. Pestek was tried by an SS and Police Court at the Katowice branch and shot to death. We know this because the scribe named *Unterscharführer* Mertens, who was present at the trial, also attended the execution on October 8, 1944, at the Miedzybrodzie Bialskie subcamp of Auschwitz.

~

ONLY NEAR THE end of Neumann's two-hour interview do we learn about a beating that Wetzler endured after he was caught by the Nazis persuading a new transport of doomed Jews, trapped inside a train car, to give him their valuables, having told them they were all destined to die anyway.

"In June of 1942," he says, "Jews from a large vicinity were brought in and were put in isolation. Nobody was supposed to go in or out. Fred Wetzler went in and asked the new arrivals to leave their jewels behind so they could be used by the living. The SS caught Wexler [sic] ("Wetzler") and beat him. A friend of Wexler ["Wetzler"] named Miller [sic] got involved and was sentenced to death. Somehow, he [Wetzler] survived with a suitcase from the new inmates."

Neumann clearly liked and admired Wetzler. He had no reason not to be telling the truth. He recalls how Wetzler was helpful and kind to him. Therefore, there is no logical explanation as to why Neumann might choose to invent such a story about someone who apparently had helped him to survive.

Wetzler's attempt to acquire precious gems and currency from doomed Jews was not extraordinary but the outcome of this incident is peculiar. Vrba told stories about how the Nazis frequently enforced heinous punishments for the attempted theft of seemingly minor items. Wetzler was not yet a camp fixture; he was expendable in 1942. Therefore, the beating that Wetzler endured would likely have been prolonged and extreme.

Possibly, after Wetzler was almost certainly nearly beaten to death for his audacity, Wetzler was subsequently motivated to risk his life and leave one of the most secure jobs in the prison hierarchy, a position in which he had his own private sleeping arrangements and a fortifying food supply, as an act of desperation and revenge.

As previously explained, the original plan was for the pair to test the security of the hideout for three full days and then allow two of the builders of the hideout into the chamber. We have since learned that psychologically and physically, as their distressing situation worsened, Wetzler was unable to remain calm. Wetzler told Vrba he could not bear to remain another three days and nights within the frigid woodpile. Therefore, Vrba responded to the elder Wetzler's sense of desperation and agreed to essentially double-cross the builders of the hideout. The two other would-be escapees, when they learned they could not enter the hideout as planned, then took their revenge by adding more lumber atop the woodpile, making it seemingly impossible for Vrba and Wetzler to escape.

This nightmarish scenario – as later outlined to Robin Vrba and corroborated by two others – put the already fragile and weakened Wetzler over the edge of sanity. Once they had exhausted themselves in removing the added lumber over their heads, the pair started to run through the darkness but Wetzler's extremely agitated state made him a liability. This explains why Vrba told his wife he had to strike Wetzler to bring him to his senses, to keep him quiet, to get him to crawl and run to safety with him – to save his life.

Rudolf Vrba never said or wrote anything derogatory or demeaning about his elder escape partner. He also omitted mentioning that Wetzler had taken some money or gold with him during their escape, thereby contravening the advice of their Russian escape mentor, and that Wetzler had made an attempt to go into a village to buy food. This foolhardy decision resulted in a shower of bullets that almost got them killed.

Wetzler's post-war life never amounted to much, possibly because he was still suffering mentally. Certainly, within the repressive Communist and antisemitic society of post-war Slovakia, with a wife who was reviled by other Auschwitz survivors as an oppressive *kapo*, Wetzler was hugely disadvantaged. Rudolf Vrba not only knew this and sometimes sent money; he also chose not to make the life of his escape partner more difficult by describing in print Wetzler's moments of weakness during the escape. He did mention Wetzler's frailties privately, however, to Robin, his wife.

Wetzler is not known to have written about the humiliations and suffering he endured at the hands of the Nazis; whereas Rudolf Vrba wrote at length about his various physical privations and tended to take pride in overcoming them.

CHAPTER 13

Vrba vs. Kasztner

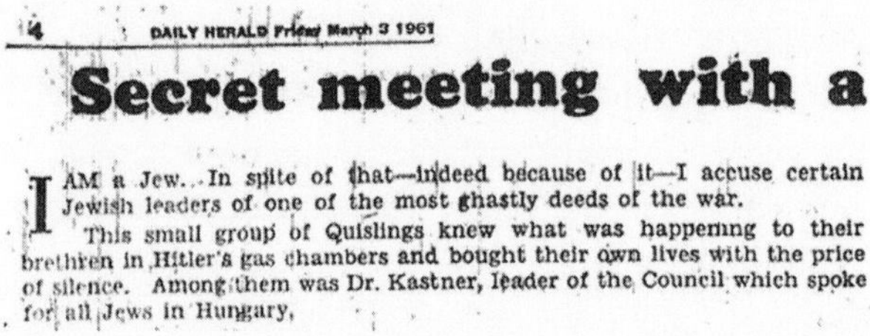

4 DAILY HERALD Friday March 3 1961

Secret meeting with a

I AM a Jew...In spite of that—indeed because of it—I accuse certain Jewish leaders of one of the most ghastly deeds of the war.

This small group of Quislings knew what was happening to their brethren in Hitler's gas chambers and bought their own lives with the price of silence. Among them was Dr. Kastner, leader of the Council which spoke for all Jews in Hungary,

RUDOLF VRBA BEGAN his fifth and final article for the *Daily Herald* in 1961 with these words: "I am a Jew. In spite of that – indeed because of it – I accuse certain Jewish leaders of one of the most ghastly deeds of the war."

After referencing "Quislings" who knew about Hitler's gas chambers and had bought their own lives with the price of silence, he takes aim at one alleged Jewish turncoat in particular, the self-confident lawyer Rudolf Kasztner (spelled phonetically for British readers as Kastner], "leader of the Council that spoke for all Jews in Hungary."

A controversy persists to this day as to the extent prominent Jewish and Zionist leaders should be held accountable for a myriad of failures to adequately inform Jews about the lethal dangers of boarding the trains. For the rest of his days, Vrba would chiefly lay the blame for the failure to adequately inform approximately 800,000 Jews in Hungary about the Holocaust on Kasztner, the Zionist leader from northern Transylvania.

Having settled in Budapest after his native land was acquired by Hungary in 1940, Rudolf Kasztner was the first non-Slovakian official to receive a copy of the *Vrba-Wetzler Report*. After Vrba and Wetzler had dictated the contents, Oskar Krasňanský, a chemical engineer who was also president of the Zionist Organization of Czechoslovakia, had given the original report to typist, Gisi Farkas, who made several copies. Krasňanský hastily traveled to Bratislava from Žilina to meet Kasztner and give him a copy on April 28, 1944. Krasňanský verified in a post-war statement that he delivered the document to Kasztner directly, by hand.

Subsequently, Kasztner met with the Jewish Council of Budapest at their headquarters on Sip Street. As one of the Vice-Chairmen of the Relief and Rescue Committee in Budapest, it was primarily Kasztner who chose not to publicize the contents of the *Vrba-Wetzler Report* to Jews at large while he was engaging in private negotiations with Adolf Eichmann, the Nazi primarily responsible for transporting Hungary's Jews to the world's most infamous death camp. Kasztner did, however, pass along a copy to Geza Soos, who led a Hungarian resistance group, who gave it to Joszef Elias, who ran a Protestant missionary organization, who had his secretary translate it into Hungarian and make six copies. The Council president, Samu Stern, was incredulous, as were others who feared they would be arrested if they dared circulate its contents. Essentially, these Jewish Council leaders resolved to not circulate the contents of the *Vrba-Wetzler Report* in order to save their own skin.

Kasztner's first meeting with Eichmann occurred on April 25, 1944, with a second meeting around the same period when he was made privy to the contents of the *Vrba-Wetzler Report.* "By then," Vrba later wrote, "Kasztner and his colleagues in the Zionist leadership in Hungary were already committed to their negotiations with Eichmann and to the dispatch of their colleague, Joel Brand, to Istanbul. They therefore gave no publicity whatsoever to the facts about Auschwitz which were now in their possession."

A few days later, still feeling burdened by what he knew, Kasztner went to the opulent home of the Swiss vice-consul in Budapest, Carl Lutz, a man who would soon be responsible for saving far more Jews than the much better-known Swedish diplomat Raoul Wallenberg. Galvanized by what he read, Lutz drove in his car with Kasztner to immediately make contact with the head of the Hungarian Zionist Organization, Otto Komoly, who wanted to spread the news and initiate a self-defence initiative.

But Kasztner urged caution. As both friends and rivals, Rudolf Kasztner and Joel Brand were establishing themselves as leading figures in Vaadah, the Budapest Relief and Rescue Committee that was established in 1943. To complicate matters, Brand's wife Hansi happened to be Kasztner's lover – and quite possibly she was smarter than both of them. It was this trio who became the self-elected brain trust who tried to develop the best strategy for saving the Jews of Hungary.

As Randolph L. Braham makes clear in *The Politics of Genocide*, "The SS preferred to negotiate with the Vaadah rather than with the Jewish Council leadership, as they valued the international contacts and foreign currency sources of the Zionists."

The Vaadah leaders had established contacts with SS occupation forces in consort with Rabbi Michael Dov Weissmandel of Bratislava. Much to Vrba's lasting disdain, it was Weissmandel who believed he had successfully halted the deportation of Jews from Slovakia in June of 1942 by bribing the Nazi administrator Dieter Wisliceny. Hence, the Vaadah leadership in Hungary believed it was reasonable to attempt to rescue Hungarian Jews through financial dealings with the SS. In fact, by the autumn of 1944, it would become tragically apparent that the Nazis had only suspended the deportations of Slovakian Jews and that the bribes paid to Wizliceny were not sufficient to stop mass murder.

On April 5, 1944, the first day that Hungarian Jews were forced to wear the Star of David, Kasztner and Brand had their first meeting with Wisliceny who gave them assurances that Hungarian Jews would not be ghettoized or deported.

Naively unaware that the SS still didn't have the manpower in Budapest necessary to implement large-scale roundups of Jews, and that Wisliceny and Eichmann had no independent power concerning the Final Solution and were subject to the dictates of Himmler and the Nazi regime in Berlin, the Vaadah leadership agreed to pay $2 million dollars [roughly 6.5 million in *pengő*] to Wisliceny as proof of Zionist good will and liquidity.

Kasztner was the bag man. He had delivered the first instalment of 2.5 million *pengő* on April 21. As compensation, as ghettoization was well underway, the SS freed some prominent Jews and began to pose the possibility of special emigration opportunities for selected Jews, with transit to either the United States or a neutral country that would accept them.

By April 25, the genocide genius Eichmann had met with Vaadah's Joel Brand, and they discussed bartering the safety of one million Jews in exchanges for goods that would support the German war efforts. To implement this grandiose scheme, Brand would gain the personal freedom to travel abroad and seek the financial backing of world Jewry. Meanwhile, Kasztner entered into his own backroom dealings with Eichmann to implement his own scheme to save his relatives and friends.

While retaining his own freedom of movement and not being required to wear the yellow star, Kasztner was able to organize and finance safe passage out of Hungary – ideally to Spain or Portugal – for a trainload of approximately 1,684 Jews, many of whom were of Kasztner's own choosing, including wealthy Jews who would pay enormous sums for safe passage out of Hungary. The exact financial figures remain unknown, but it is generally believed that the Nazis received approximately $1,000 for every Jew on the so-called Kasztner train. As a catalyst for this arrangement, Kasztner would agree to keep the contents of the *Vrba-Wetzler Report* under wraps.

Vrba believed Kasztner had shown the *Vrba-Wetzler Report* to Eichmann as soon as possible as a bargaining chip. Eichmann was a superior poker player. Instead of allowing the privileged trainload of Jews that left Budapest on June 30 to reach Switzerland as envisioned, because, by this time, Spain and Portugal were no longer feasible as destinations, Eichmann had all the passengers disembark at the Bergen-Belsen concentration camp on July 8.

While Hungarian Jews were continuously sent to Auschwitz from Budapest, Kasztner and the other Jews who managed affairs in Budapest had to keep their mouths shut while the privileged Jews who had paid huge sums to escape remained in limbo in Bergen-Belsen. Passengers on the Kasztner train would not make it to Switzerland until December of 1944, after more than 400,000 Hungarian Jews had been efficiently incinerated. Himmler eventually authorized their departure, not Eichmann.

It is generally assumed that Kasztner won a victory in the long run, but the truth is more complex. David S. Wyman's *The Abandonment of the Jews,* first published in 1984, provides a fascinating summary of the extent to which 62-year-old Saly Mayer, the Joint Distribution Committee's representative in Switzerland, was the ingenious negotiator who successfully convinced the Nazis that he controlled a fund of at least five million Swiss francs that was up for grabs.

Groundwork for the mass murder of Jews from Hungary was laid when Hungarian leader Admiral Miklós (Nicholas) Horthy took this joyride with Hitler in Berlin in August 1938.

According to Wyman, it was Mayer who succeeded in bringing out 318 Hungarian Jews held in Bergen-Belsen in August of 1944, and he was again crucial in the eventual transport of 1,368 Jews (from the original transport) to Switzerland in December by insisting that their continued internment was impeding discussions for cash. "Mayer's endeavors," Wyman concludes, "touched on the heroic." All this was accomplished despite the War Refugee Board's insistence that no ransom arrangements would be permitted, and Mayer could only act as a Swiss Jewish leader, never as a representative of any American organization, including the WRB.

In Randolph L. Braham's *The Politics of Genocide: The Holocaust in Hungary*, we learn that most Hungarian Jews, although subjected to harsh discriminatory practices since 1938, had continued to believe that Miklós Horthy would protect them until the war was over.

"Influenced by their leaders," Braham writes, "Hungarian Jews never believed they would befall the same fate as Polish Jews after four years of relative security during World War II. They knew Allied forces were advancing towards Hungary. Soon Hungary would be liberated from the yoke of

Nazi constraints. Hungary would never be made *Judenrein* [Nazi term for "cleansed" of Jews]. Everything would soon revert to normal again."

Even when German occupation led to the ghettoization and deportation of Jews from parts of northern and eastern Hungary, Jews in Budapest believed that such catastrophic events in the countryside would never be replicated in the much more sophisticated arena of the capital "in full view of foreign diplomats." The large contingent of Jews in Budapest was reassured by Adolf Eichmann, who promised that nobody would be harmed unless they were foolish enough to support, or join, the partisan rebels or Tito's units.

Meanwhile, Soviet troops were approaching the Carpathians. It was only a matter of time before the relatively small contingent of Nazi soldiers in Budapest would be forced to flee. A cabinet minister in Horthy's administration assured the public they would never consent to planning "the extirpation, destruction, or torment of the Jews" when the liberation of Hungary was imminent. It would not make sense militarily for the Nazis to divert their outnumbered troops from counteracting the Russians and partisans in order to rid Budapest of its many thousands of Jews.

The chilling truth became decipherable only when gendarmes were suddenly patrolling the civilized streets of Budapest. Jewish leadership completely failed to anticipate that the Nazis would choose to redouble their efforts to win their campaign against the Jews when they knew they would be simultaneously unable to vanquish the advancing Soviets.

Kasztner was far from alone in his belief that negotiation was far more prudent than confrontation. Braham recounts the fate of a young Budapest physician, Dr. Imre Varga, who led a delegation of leftist and resistance-oriented Jews. In early June, as soon as the Nazis exhibited signs of shifting their repression of Jews from rural parts of Hungary to "Zone III, in Trianon, Hungary proper" where urban Jews would be rounded up, Varge pleaded with the Jewish Council to discontinue its policies of conciliation and passivity in order to obviate complete annihilation. Varge was told that Jewish resistance would be futile, and failure to comply with Nazi directives would "unimaginably aggravate the situation of others." In despair, Varga committed suicide the following day.

For the rest of his life, Rudolf Vrba claimed Kasztner's duplicity included giving Eichmann knowledge of the *Vrba-Wetzler Report*. "As soon as he received our reports," Vrba said, "Kasztner had shown them to Adolf Eichmann in Budapest, and Eichmann, who was responsible for getting the Hungarian Jews into Auschwitz ovens without undue fuss, knew that the whole operation was in jeopardy while we were alive and at liberty."

Vrba believed Kasztner had used his *Vrba-Wetzler Report* as a bargaining chip in his private negotiations with Eichmann. He first raised this matter in print, in English, in the *Daily Herald*, advising readers he had supplied "Hungarian Zionist leaders" three weeks notice that Eichmann was planning "to send a million of their Jews to his gas chambers ... Kasztner went to Eichmann and told him, 'I know of your plans; spare some Jews of my choice and I shall keep quiet.'" "Eichmann not only agreed," Vrba exaggerated, "but dressed Kasztner up in an SS uniform and took him to Belsen to trace some of his friends."

This allegation was true. In his memoir, Vrba would not relent. He wrote, "It is my contention that a small group of informed people, by their silence, deprived others of the possibility or privilege of making their own decisions in the face of mortal danger. In the fifth year of the war, there were some Kasztners who were thinking that the Nazis could be negotiated with. Only an idiot would believe that – or else a traitor covering up something ...

"While I was prisoner number 44070 at Auschwitz, the number is still on my arm, I compiled careful statistics of the exterminations ... I took these terrible statistics with me when I escaped in 1944 and I was able to give Hungarian Zionist leaders three weeks notice that Eichmann planned to send a million of their Jews to his gas chambers ...

"Kasztner paid Eichmann several thousand dollars. With this little fortune, Eichmann was able to buy his way to freedom when Germany collapsed, to set himself up in the Argentine."

These various accusations from Vrba go a long way to explain why the Israeli historian Yehuda Bauer, in particular, sought to limit awareness of Rudolf Vrba in Israel. Having been able to flee from Europe with his parents just prior to the outbreak of World War II, Bauer was highly sensitive to Vrba's accusations that privileged Jews "in the know" were able to avoid tragedy at the expense of the unwary and uninformed. While Bauer admitted Vrba was "one of the Heroes of the Holocaust," he consistently sought to denigrate Vrba by casting him as a "bitter Auschwitz survivor." Although not a psychiatrist, Bauer disparaged Vrba by writing, "the trauma of the Holocaust had a severe effect on the internal intra-Jewish discourse, in the form of baseless accusations whose origin lay in the despair and anger over the loss of so many."

But Vrba's accusations were far from "baseless." Over the decades, as the truth behind the so-called "Blood for Goods" or "Blood for Trucks" negotiations with Eichmann has come to light, it's obvious that Vrba was justified in suggesting some Jewish leaders had bargained for the safety of a few at the expense of the majority. The psychiatrist Robert Krell once personally confronted Bauer about his anti-Vrba bias, face to face, but Bauer would not relent.

Rudolf Vrba's memoir was consequently kept from the Israeli / Hebrew-reading public for decades. Coincidentally, the country where Vrba eventually found safe haven also ignored his heroic role in World War II. Canada's now thoroughly discredited "None Is Too Many" approach to would-be Jewish immigrants during World War II has made future governments in Canada reticent to recognize a firebrand such as Vrba who could "speak truth to power." Canada's failure to appropriately acknowledge Vrba as a truth-teller has played into the hands of Holocaust deniers.

In 1992, historian Martin Gilbert teamed with one of Canada's foremost human rights lawyers, Irwin Cotler (subsequently Canada's Justice Minister and Attorney General, as well as a primary force behind the Wallenberg Centre for Human Rights in Montreal), to support a formal nomination for Rudolf Vrba to receive the Order of Canada, the country's top honor for a private citizen, but their efforts fell short. At the time, Cotler wrote to Gilbert, "I fully concur with you that Vrba is a 'real hero.' Indeed, there are few more deserving of the Order of Canada than Vrba, and few, anywhere, who have exhibited his moral courage. Canada will honor itself – and redeem itself somewhat – by awarding him the Order of Canada." Another initiative fronted by Gilbert's Canadian-born, second wife also failed.

Any argument that Kasztner's decision not to help spread awareness of the content of the *Vrba-Wetzler Report* was inconsequential has been squelched by the renowned scientist Georg Klein who said, "It is in no small part due to Rudolf Vrba that I am alive today."

At age 18, while serving as an assistant to Dr. Zoltán Kohn, a member of the Jewish Council in Budapest, Klein was able see a copy of the

Vrba-Wetzler Report in May of 1944. Upon reading it, he was immediately convinced he must either flee from Budapest or go into hiding.

"I still remember the feeling of nausea and intellectual satisfaction I felt when I first read what later became known as *The Auschwitz Protocols*," Klein recalled. "Nausea because I realized that I was reading about the fate of my beloved grandmother, my uncles, and many other relatives and friends who had already been deported from my father's village in the north-east. I also knew I was reading about my own probable fate. The paradoxical but very distinct intellectual satisfaction stemmed from the fact that this was first text that made sense. Nothing else that we were told or were telling each other made any sense whatsoever. The dry, nearly scientific language of the report made a stronger impact than a thousand emotional outbursts. It was this report that prompted me to escape. The definite knowledge of what was waiting at the other end of the railway line overcame my fear of being caught and shot. I tried to warn all my relatives and friends, but no one believed me."

Klein fled Budapest and eventually became a prominent scholar in the field of cell biology in Sweden. For decades after the Holocaust, Klein (1925–2016) assumed Rudolf Vrba must be dead. Then, in 1987, the Karolinska Institute professor and Nobel Prize committee member saw Claude Lanzmann's *Shoah* and realized that Vrba was still alive. He promptly bought a plane ticket from Stockholm to Vancouver to meet the man who he credited with saving his life.

"I first 'met' him on the cinema screen in *Shoah*," Klein recalled. "When he spoke about his escape from Auschwitz with his friend Wetzler and of the report he had written to warn Hungarian Jews as the first authentic eyewitness account from the largest death camp … I immediately realized that this was the report I had been shown by one of the members of the Jewish Council in Budapest in greatest secrecy, only a few weeks after it has been written.

"The *Vrba-Wetzler Report* significantly and perhaps decisively contributed to the survival of approximately 200,000 Hungarian Jews (out of 800,000), representing most of the Jewish population of the capital, Budapest. The information conveyed by that report both directly and indirectly contributed to the veto of the continued deportations by the Hungarian head of state, Horthy, in the first week of July 1944."

When the Swedish-Hungarian scientist came to British Columbia and asked Vrba how he could manage to live in such a docile place like Vancouver, where hardly anyone knew about his heroism, Vrba told him about a colleague who, after seeing him featured in Claude Lanzmann's film *Shoah*, had asked if the story was true. "I do not know," Vrba had told him. "I was only an actor reciting my lines." Missing the sarcasm, the man replied, "I didn't know you were an actor. Why did they say that film was made without any actors?"

Klein continued: "Only then did I understand that this was the same man who lay quiet and motionless for three days in the hollow pile of lumber while Auschwitz was on maximum alert, only a few yards from the armed SS men and their dogs combing the area so thoroughly. If he could do that, then he certainly could also don the mask of a professor and manage everyday conversation with his colleagues in Vancouver, Canada, that paradise land that is never fully appreciated by its own citizens, a people without the slightest notion of the planet Auschwitz." [This information is excerpted from an essay by Georg Klein written in Swedish, translated by Peter Stenberg and Lena Karlsröm, in *Contemporary Jewish Writing in Sweden* (University of Nebraska Press, 2004).]

There are two polarities when examining the legal and moral case against Rudolf Kasztner. On the one hand, the German-born, Israeli judge Benjamin Halevi concluded, "He didn't sell his soul to the devil; he was the devil." On the other hand, the Budapest-born, publisher/author Anna Porter wrote, "If you're in hell, who do you negotiate with but the devil?"

Born in 1906 in Kolozsvár (later known as Cluj or Cluj-Napoca), Rudolf Kasztner grew up in Transylvania when it was still part of Romania. In 1924, when Rudolf was 18, his older brother Gyula, an ardent Zionist, went to live on a kibbutz in Palestine. This left Kasztner, a lawyer/journalist, as the male head of a well-to-do family at age 22 when his father died while reading the Torah at the synagogue on the seventh day of Passover.

Definitely exceptional, Kasztner learned to speak five languages – Hungarian, Romanian, French, German and Latin – and he was undoubtedly arrogant. "He had no sense of other people's sensitivities," a fellow law student observed, "or he didn't care whether he alienated his friends."

As a law school graduate, Kasztner became the assistant of one of the wealthiest Jewish citizens of Kolozsvár, Dr. Jozef Fischer. He then married

Hoping to clear his name for a bid to enter politics, Rudolf Kasztner brought his own story into the headlines by launching a defamation case against a little-known pamphleteer who had vilified him in print by claiming Kasztner had secretly bargained with Adolf Eichmann to garner special treatment for wealthy Jews and his family. Kasztner, in essence, objected to the truth.

his employer's fragile, 18-year-old daughter, Elizabeth (nicknamed Flower Bud), in 1934, when he was 28. She admired him unconditionally. She was therefore pliant when he moved to Budapest in the spring of 1941 and began a war-long affair with his intellectual equal, Hansi Brand, a mother of two and the wife of the Zionist activist Joel Brand.

It is from this point onward that Kasztner turned into a Faustian figure. The U.S. Holocaust Memorial Museum has provided a succinct summary of Kasztner's rise in influence and his ultimate fall from grace.

> "Beginning in April 1944, Kasztner and Joel Brand entered into negotiations with Dieter Wisliceny and Adolf Eichmann of the SS in the hope of suspending deportations of Jews from Hungary. In late April 1944, Adolf Eichmann proposed 'selling' 10,000 Jews in exchange for trucks delivered to the Nazis. Brand traveled to Turkey to present the proposal to the Allies and representatives of

the Yishuv (the Jewish community in Palestine). After Brand failed to return from Istanbul, Kasztner took over negotiations with Eichmann and Kurt Becher, even as the mass deportation of Hungarian Jews began in May 1944.

"In June 1944, Kasztner convinced Eichmann to allow nearly 1,700 Hungarian Jews to escape Hungary and the deportations to Auschwitz. A small committee headed by Otto Komoly, chairman of the Relief and Rescue Committee, Kasztner and other Hungarian Jewish leaders selected the passengers for the rescue transport.

"The list of nearly 1,700 Jews slated for release included wealthy Jews, Zionist leaders, prominent rabbis (including the Satmar Rebbe, Joel Teitelbaum), and perhaps most controversially, Kasztner's own friends and family members. Kasztner would later argue that he had insisted on the inclusion of his own family to convince others of the safety of the convoy. There were 338 Jews from Kasztner's home city of Cluj. Other passengers on the 'Kasztner train' represented a cross-section of Hungarian Jewry: journalists, teachers, artists, nurses, housewives with small children, peasant farmers, and small businessmen.

"On June 30, 1944, the 'Kasztner train' left Budapest, carrying 1,684 individuals in exchange for an unknown sum of money – some reports indicate perhaps $1,000 per person paid in currency, gold, jewels, and shares of stock collected by the Jewish committee. Despite a promise from Adolf Eichmann that the train would travel directly to Switzerland, the transport reached Bergen-Belsen on July 8, 1944. The passengers were held in the camp for several months in the *Ungarnlager* (Hungarian camp).

"In late August 1944, 318 Jews from the Kasztner train were released from Bergen-Belsen and transported to Switzerland. On December 7, 1944, the remaining 1,368 Jews from the transport reached Switzerland. Kasztner traveled to Switzerland in late November 1944.

"After the war, Kasztner intervened on behalf of Kurt Becher, Dieter Wisliceny and Herman Krumey with whom he had negotiated in Hungary. He declared to the International Military Tribunal in Nuremberg that Becher in particular was one of the few SS leaders who had the courage to resist the Nazi plan for annihilation of the Jews and that he had, in fact, attempted to rescue Jews. Thanks in part to Kasztner's statement, Becher was not prosecuted as a war criminal.

"Kasztner moved to Israel after the war and continued his active role in Labor Zionist politics, becoming a spokesman for the Ministry of Trade and Industry in 1952.

"Kasztner's controversial role in negotiating with the SS became prominent news in 1953 when Malkiel Gruenwald published a leaflet accusing Kasztner of having collaborated with the Nazis. Gruenwald was a Hungarian Jew who had lost dozens of relatives in the Holocaust. He charged that through the negotiations with Eichmann and Becher, Kasztner had participated in the destruction of Hungarian Jewry. He also charged that Kasztner had personally benefited from his negotiations with the SS while failing to warn Hungarian Jews of the impending deportations, even though he was among the first to receive a copy of the *Vrba-Wetzler Report*, from Slovakian Jewish leaders in late April 1944.

"Gruenwald sought to expose what he saw as Kasztner's crimes. A member of Ha-Mizrahi (the religious Zionist party), Gruenwald also hoped to denounce Mapai (the Labor Zionist governing party) and force the government to appoint a commission that would investigate the events leading to the destruction of Hungarian Jewry.

"Kasztner subsequently sued Gruenwald for libel. Because of his position as a government official, Kasztner was represented at trial by Haim Cohen, Israel's attorney general. The trial of Gruenwald for libel would become known as the 'Kasztner Trial.' Gruenwald's defense attorney, Shmuel Tamir, succeeded in turning what was supposed to be a libel trial against Gruenwald into an indictment of Kasztner and the ruling Mapai Party.

"Four key charges against Kasztner were outlined in Gruenwald's pamphlet:

- Collaboration with the Nazis.
- Paving the way for the murder of Hungarian Jewry.

- Partnership with a Nazi war criminal [Kurt Becher] in acts of thievery.
- Saving a war criminal from punishment after the war [Kurt Becher].

"In his judgment on June 22, 1955, Judge Halevi accepted most of Gruenwald's accusations against Kasztner. He ruled that by saving the Jews on the Kasztner train while failing to warn others that their resettlement was in fact deportation to the gas chambers, Kasztner had sacrificed the majority of Hungarian Jewry for a chosen few. It also had become clear during the trial that Kasztner had indeed submitted testimony on behalf of Becher after the war, a fact he had earlier denied. The verdict triggered the fall of the Israeli Cabinet after the government sought to appeal on Kasztner's behalf.

"The Supreme Court of Israel overturned most of the judgement in January 1958, stating that the lower court had 'erred seriously' in its decision. Before the highest court returned this verdict, however, Kasztner was assassinated near his home in Tel Aviv on the night of March 4, 1957, by three veterans of the right-wing pre-state militia group Lehi, once a splinter group of the Irgun. He died of his injuries twelve days later."

The culpability of Rudolf Kasztner as an agent of the Holocaust remains a divisive issue for modern Jewry to this day. That is why, when the highly placed Canadian publishing executive Anna Porter of Toronto approached Budapest-born Peter Munk for support for a biography project, the Toronto-based president and founder of the world's largest gold mining company, Barrick Gold, encouraged her to instead write *Kasztner's Train* (Douglas & McIntyre, 2007), subtitled *The True Story of Rezső Kasztner, Unknown Hero of the Holocaust.*

While employing invented conversations in the style of a novel ("[I] have allowed myself the leeway to reconstruct scenes and dialogue …" Porter writes), *Kasztner's Train* could be cynically interpreted as being as much of an effort to serve Peter Munk as an attempt to exclusively serve the truth. It doesn't help that in the first paragraph of her Introduction she states, "Munk's energy and charm are legendary as are his successful business ventures."

Similarly, it does not help that *Kasztner's Train* does not make it abundantly clear from the outset that 16-year-old Peter Munk was one of 14 Munk family members on the Kasztner Train that enabled 1,684 mostly wealthy Jews to flee from the mass murder agenda of Adolf Eichmann. Due to bribes of gold, jewelry, gems and currency, the young scion arrived in Switzerland, where, according to a *Canadian Jewish News* obituary, "Peter pursued a life of partying, ski trips and chasing girls."

Kasztner is described as an "unknown" hero in the subtitle. This is bizarre. The Romanian-born Jewish lawyer and journalist was, and remains, easily one of the most notorious Jews of the Holocaust, having been famously trounced and denounced as a scoundrel by the American screenwriter Ben Hecht in his well-known 1961 book *Perfidy*, banned in Israel for many years even though about half of its text consists of verbatim transcripts from the first, famous trial in Israel involving Kasztner, overseen by Judge Benjamin Halevi.

Kasztner's alleged duplicity during World War II has been examined for decades, by historians and lay readers alike.

It is simply a fact that Rudolf Kasztner was the first person from outside Žilina, Slovakia to have received a copy of the *Vrba-Wetzler Report* and it is simply a fact that in order to enable rich people to flee Hungary, Kasztner preferred to keep most of the other Jews of Hungary in the dark about the cattle cars. It is therefore fairly easy to conclude that while he collected large sums of money and precious gems from those who were able to buy their way to freedom, poorer Jews were doomed.

It is simply a fact that Kasztner was granted permission from the Nazis to travel unescorted to his hometown of Cluj to arrange to take his own relatives to safety. The fact that the Nazis could trust Kasztner to travel alone to Cluj and not widely spread the news about the true nature of the Holocaust, after he had read the *Vrba-Wetzler Report*, speaks volumes as to why Kasztner was loathed by Vrba.

In a compelling essay on Kasztner entitled *The Devil's Advocate*, Francisco Gil-White has pointed out, as Ben Hecht had done, that there were only 20 Hungarian gendarmes and a lone SS officer to guard the 20,000 Jews of Cluj [Kolozsvár] when Kasztner returned there, and that during this period Jews were no longer being killed on the other side of the Romanian border, less than three miles away because Romanian soldiers were diverted by the approach of Soviet soldiers, but Kasztner nonetheless saw fit not to encourage the Jews of Cluj to consider their options by making them aware of the contents of the *Vrba-Wetzler Report.*

"If Kasztner breathes a single word of this truth to a single condemned Jew in Cluj" writes Hecht in *Perfidy*, "the entire Final Solution will be wrecked."

During a world-famous libel trial in Jerusalem in 1954, initially welcomed by Kasztner, the following exchange occurred between defense lawyer Shmuel Tamir and Kasztner on the witness stand.

TAMIR: Did your Budapest committee contact other towns on the telephone?

KASZTNER: I didn't personally. But there was a special subcommittee which dealt with these matters.

TAMIR: Did the members of your subcommittee telephone to the other towns of Hungary?

KASZTNER: I don't know.

(...)

TAMIR: I put it to you, Dr. Kasztner, that you could have used the telephone to call the towns and villages of Hungary.

KASZTNER: Yes.

TAMIR: Did you talk to any other town than Cluj?

KASZTNER: I? No, I didn't manage to. I couldn't do everything myself. So I concentrated on Cluj, for obvious reasons.

TAMIR: Dr. Kasztner, you could have phoned the other towns, just as you phoned Cluj?

KASZTNER: Yes, that's right.

TAMIR: Then why didn't you contact the Jews of all these towns on the phone to warn them?

KASZTNER: I didn't because I didn't have time enough.

TAMIR: If you were so busy with your political activities, why didn't you assign the task to another Rescue worker less busy than yourself?

KASZTNER: That was impossible.

TAMIR: Let us sum it all up. You had the opportunity of communicating with all the towns of Hungary.

KASZTNER: Yes.

TAMIR: And you, Rudolf Kasztner, head of the Hungarian Jewish Agency Rescue Committee, do not know if any of your assistants tried to warn the Jews of Hungary?

KASZTNER: (wildly) I can't remember.

Written not just to excuse or exonerate Kasztner, but seemingly to also celebrate him – something that would doubtless please Peter Munk – *Kasztner's Train* nonetheless provides a trail of clues as to the character of its protagonist. We learn:

> "Kasztner often dismissed people as stupid."
>
> "Kasztner was outspoken, brash, unafraid."
>
> "He was too smart to be much loved even by those he had helped."
>
> "He was intolerant of his critics."
>
> "Kasztner was not the sort of man who recognizes anyone as his superior."
>
> "He knew whom to bribe and how much to offer, whom to flatter and how."
>
> "Not only was Kasztner smarter and better read than others, but he also let everyone know that he was superior in wit and knowledge."

This was the man that Rudolf Vrba despised. This was the man who believed he could outsmart the Nazis in general, and Eichmann in particular; this was the man who encouraged Jews to cooperate with Eichmann when he had less than 200 Nazis at his disposal in Budapest.

Coincidental with Kasztner's rise to prominence in Cluj, the father of the now-famous billionaire George Soros was also surviving by his wits as a lawyer in Cluj (now Cluj-Napoca). Having acquired false documents to disguise his Jewish family as Christians, Tivadar Soros – who had been born into an orthodox Jewish family as Theodor Schwartz in 1893 – later wrote a memoir in Esperanto that was subsequently translated into English as *Maskerado: Dancing Around Death* (2000).

In his private papers, Rudolf Vrba kept notes pertaining to Soros Sr.'s book describing how the privileged likes of Kasztner and the local Jewish Council did all the organizational work for Eichmann.

"When systematic persecution of the Jews began [in Cluj]," George Soros's father recalled, "it was carried out not by the Germans, nor by their Hungarian lackeys, but, most astonishingly, by the Jews themselves. One of the first things the Germans did was to form a so-called Jewish Council, consisting of the leaders of the Jewish community. Council members were made personally responsible for the implementation of the various German measures relating to the Jewish population. As a reward, they, their families and those who worked for them were exempted, at least at the beginning, from these restrictions.

"The Germans invented this brilliant scheme at the beginning of World War II. It had already been used in other occupied countries with conspicuous success. The Jewish Council carried out German wishes more conscientiously than the Germans could themselves. There was nothing the Germans could not request that they were not ready, without a second's thought, to provide. Of course, their own skins were at risk; if they did not comply, they would be the first to be punished; if they did, they would be safe – or so they thought. They appealed to the Jewish community earnestly, almost desperately, to follow orders ...

"Nothing could have suited the Germans better; they saved themselves the trouble and expense of having to enforce their own orders. It was a masterstroke."

In return for his own freedom to travel almost as he pleased without having to wear the yellow star, the cocksure Kasztner was able to develop friendships and respectful agreements with other top Nazi officials, most notably the Nazi fixer Lieutenant Colonel Kurt Becher, a duplicitous character who gained legal rights to the assets of the wealthy Chorin-Weiss-Kornfeld-Mauthner families. As part of a private deal negotiated with Ferenc Chorin, Jewish members of these families were able to gain safe refuge in Spain or Portugal as of May 18, 1944 in exchange for ceding control of the Weiss Manfréd Works to the SS.

Becher had been sent to Hungary by *Reichsführer*-SS Himmler, and he reported to Himmler, so he was therefore not beholden to Eichmann. Becher responded to bribes, whereas Eichmann would not; hence the two top Nazis in Budapest (Eichmann and Becher) disliked one another. Kasztner and Becher, two dashing figures, went to nightclubs and casinos together and worked cooperatively while large sums of money, in the form of bribes, were exchanged without, of course, any paper trail.

As Chief of the Economic Department of the SS Command in Hungary, Becher was eventually appointed by Himmler as Special Reich Commission for all concentration camps. When he and Kasztner schemed and partied together, Becher was renowned for traveling with six large suitcases full of booty that became known as the Becher Deposit.

After the war, Becher was arrested in May of 1945, but he never faced trial due to Kasztner's interventions. Becher was merely imprisoned during the Nuremberg Trials and served as a prosecution witness. *Kasztner's Train* would have the reader believe it was Kasztner's outstanding moral character – a friend standing up for a friend – that enabled Becker to live freely as one of the wealthiest men in Germany and ultimately the world's most successful Nazi until he died in 1995. But if Becher had been forced to provide details in court of his activities in Hungary, his testimonies would have provided evidence for the prosecution of Kasztner.

Interviewed in Tel Aviv in the 1970s, Kasztner's wartime lover Hansi Brand offered another explanation as to why Kasztner had protected Becher from prosecution. She claimed Kasztner had been smitten with Becher's countess-lover Hermine, the widowed Countess von Platen, who had begged him to speak on behalf of Becher. She stayed in Nuremberg during the time that Kasztner was preventing Becher from being prosecuted. "Rezső [Rudolf] could never resist a pretty woman," Hansi Brand said.

Whereas Rudolf Vrba risked his life and gained zero benefit for sounding the alarm that ultimately saved at least 200,000 others, the likes of those who saved only themselves by riding on Kasztner's train, for a price, were not inclined to be boastful about their good fortune, giving rise to Porter's novelistic account in which she invents conversations in order to paint a sympathetic portrait of Kasztner while managing to mention Rudolf Vrba only twice in passing.

The deep divide between Jews who owed their lives to the privileged passage on Kasztner's train and those who had relatives who instead rode in boxcars to Auschwitz can never be healed or forgotten. As much as anyone, as much as Adolf Hitler and Adolf Eichmann, it was perhaps the monied egotist Rudolf Kasztner who had inspired the original title of Vrba's memoir, *I Cannot Forgive.*

~

As the Director of the Institute for Holocaust and Genocide Studies and associate professor of communication sciences at Babeş-Bolyai University in Cluj, Romania, Dr. Zoltán Tibori Szabó has made a remarkable contribution to Holocaust research into the *Vrba-Wetzler Report* by compiling a chronological list of 61 people who, between April and June of 1944, had been made aware of the content of the report. He did so in his academic paper, *The Auschwitz Reports: Who Got Them, and When? The Auschwitz Reports and the Holocaust in Hungary.*

Here is the complete list that Szabó has compiled. Notably, it includes Adolf Eichmann as one of the first people to have access to the *Vrba-Wetzler Report.* Eichmann's relative pre-eminence in this list explains why Rudolf Vrba maintained a lifelong aversion to the first two people named in this chronology of events.

APRIL 1944

1. Rezső Kasztner, Vaada deputy head, on April 28, 1944.
2. Rabbi Michael Ber Dov Weissmandel, one of the leaders of the working group (Pracovna Skupina) in Bratislava, on April 28, 1944.
3. Samu Stern and the members of the Jewish Council in Budapest, on April 29, 1944.

MAY 1944

4. Adolf Eichmann, SS-*Obersturmbannführer*, one of the officers in charge of the deportations in Hungary, at the end of April or the beginning of May 1944.
5. Géza Soós, counselor of the Hungarian Ministry of Foreign Affairs, one of the leaders of the resistance group called the Hungarian Independence Movement, at the end of April or the beginning of May 1944.
6. Reverend József Éliás, leader of the Good Shepherd Committee of the Hungarian protestant churches, at the end of April or the beginning of May 1944.
7. The Istanbul branch of the Jewish Agency, at the beginning of May 1944.
8. Giuseppe Burzio, the representative of the Vatican, delegated to the independent Slovakian state, at the beginning of May 1944.

9. Fülöp Freudiger, president of the Budapest Autonomous Orthodox Israelite Community, at the beginning of May 1944.
10. Carl Lutz, Swiss vice-consul in Budapest, at the beginning of May 1944.
11. Carl Ivan Danielsson, Swedish Minister in Budapest, at the beginning of May 1944.
12. Per Anger, secretary of the Swedish legation in Budapest, at the beginning of May 1944.
13. Ottó Komoly, president of the Hungarian Zionist Organization, at the beginning of May 1944.
14. Miklós (Moshe) Krausz, head of the Palestine Office in Budapest, at the beginning of May 1944.
15. Mária Székely, later Mrs. László Küllői-Rhorer, the Hungarian translator of the *Vrba- Wetzler Report*, at the very beginning of May 1944.
16. József Cavallier, the head of the Holy Cross Society, at the beginning of May 1944.
17. Miklós Esty, secular papal chamberlain, vice president of the Actio Catholica, at the beginning of May 1944.
18. Lajos Reményi-Schneller, Hungarian Finance Minister, at the beginning of May 1944.
19. Jean de Bavier, the delegate of the International Red Cross in Budapest, no later than May 13, 1944.
20. Nathan Schwalb, the head of the Jewish Agency and of the Hehalutz office in Geneva, on May 17, 1944.
21. Abraham Silberschein, the delegate of the Jewish World Congress, no later than May 17, 1944.
22. Zeev (Vanya) Pomerantz, Jewish Agency emissary in Istanbul, on May 19, 1944.
23. Angelo Rotta, Papal Nuncio in Budapest, at the beginning of May 1944.
24. Gennaro Verolino, Vatican counselor *uditore* in Budapest, at the beginning of May 1944.
25. Jusztinián Cardinal Serédi, Prince Primate of Hungary on May 10, 1944, but no later than May 20, at least one copy.
26. András Zakar, Cardinal Serédi's secretary, at the end of May 1944.
27. Reverend Albert Bereczky, Reformed priest in Budapest, at the beginning of May.

28. Bishop László Ravasz, president of the Reformed (Calvinist) Church General Synod, on May 12–14, 1944.
29. Lajos Kemény, Lutheran dean from Budapest, at the beginning of May 1944.
30. Bishop Sándor Raffay, leader of the Lutheran (Evangelical) Church in Hungary, on May 10–14, 1944.
31. Judge Géza Kárpáti (Kárpáty), at the beginning of May, 1944.
32. Sándor Török, writer and acting member of the Committee of Christian Jewish Alliance in Hungary, middle of May 1944.
33. Rabbi Solomon Schönfeld, in the second part of May 1944.
34. Countess Ilona Edelsheim Gyulai, the widow of István Horthy, at the end of May or the beginning of June 1944.

JUNE 1944

35. Mrs. Miklós Horthy, at the end of May or beginning of June, 1944
36. Miklós Horthy Jr., the son of the Regent, in June, 1944.
37. Regent Miklós Horthy, a copy sent through Sándor Török at the end of May or the beginning of June; a copy sent by Ernő Pető through Miklós Horthy, Jr., the Regent's son, in June 1944. The Regent also received copies from Cardinal Serédi and Bishop Ravasz, most probably sometime in the middle of May.
38. Rabbi Fábián Herskovits, in the first part of June, 1944.
39. Elizabeth Wiskemann, British representative in Bern, on June 13, 1944.
40. Leland Harrison, American Minister in Bern, on June 13, 1944.
41. Richard Lichtheim, the head of the Jewish Agency office in Geneva, in the middle of June 1944.
42. Lea Komoly Fürst, in the middle of June 1944.
43. Sára Friedländer, in the middle of June 1944.
44. Monsignor Mario Martilotti, Vatican legate in Switzerland, in the middle of June 1944.
45. József Reisinger, a Turkish consulate employee of Jewish origin, in Budapest, in the middle of June 1944.
46. Florian E. Manoliu, Romanian diplomat and attaché of the Romanian consulate in Bern, on June 18, 1944.
47. Jaromír Kopeczký, Swiss representative of the Czechoslovakian Government in Exile, on June 19 or 20, 1944.

48. George Mantello (György Mandel), businessman from Beszterce, Northern Transylvania, first secretary of the Consulate of El Salvador in Geneva, on June 21, 1944.
49. Chaim Pozner, representative of the Palestine Office in Switzerland, in the second part of June 1944.
50. Saly Mayer, Swiss representative of the Joint organization, no later than June, 1944.
51. Mihály Bányai, head of the Swiss Aid for Hungarian Jews (*Schweitzerisches Hilfskomitee für die Juden in Ungarn*), on June 24, 1944.
52. Walter Garett, a British Exchange Telegraph-Independent News Agency correspondent in Zürich, on June 24, 1944.
53. Pope Pius XII probably found out about the situation of the Hungarian Jews from Angelo Rotta by the beginning of May 1944, but no later than June 25, via Switzerland.
54. President Franklin D. Roosevelt, no later than June 25, 1944.
55. King Gustav V of Sweden, in the second part of June 1944.
56. General F. M. West, British military attaché, in the second part of June 1944.
57. Allen W. Dulles, American OSS representative in Switzerland, in the second part of June 1944.
58. Max Kimche, Swiss lawyer and businessman, in the second part of June 1944.
59. Winston Churchill, British Prime Minister, at the end of June 1944.
60. Robert Anthony Eden, British Foreign Minister, at the end of June 1944.
61. Leaders of Swiss International Red Cross Committee, no later than end of June 1944.

~

RUDOLF VRBA REMAINED firm in his admonishments for the role played by Kasztner. In support of some analysis of the Eichmann trial provided by Hannah Arendt, Vrba first went public with his disdain for Kasztner in 1961, followed by this letter to the editor of the Sunday edition of the English newspaper *Observer*, printed on September 22, 1963.

"With my friend Fred Wetzler from Slovakia, I managed to escape from Auschwitz on April 7, 1944, and we headed straight for the Zionist leaders. In April 1944, we handed to a high representative of the Zionist movement, Dr. Oskar Neumann, a 60-page detailed report on the fact that extermination of 1,760,000 Jews had taken place in Auschwitz and that preparations were complete for the annihilation of one million Jewish Hungarians during the very next weeks.

"Did the *Judenrat* (or *Judenverrat*) in Hungary tell their Jews what was waiting them? No, they remained silent and for this silence some of their leaders – for instance, Dr. R. Kasztner – bartered their own lives and the lives of 1,684 other 'prominent' Jews directly from Eichmann. They were not 'helpless and benumbed hostages' but clever diplomats who knew what their silence was worth.

"The 1,684 Jews whom they bought from Eichmann included not only various prominent Zionists, not only relatives of Kasztner, etc., but also such Jews who were able to pay with millions, like the family of Manfred Weiss. At the same time, they silently watched as more than 400,000 Hungarian Jews, unaware of their fate, were tricked into Auschwitz, where thousands of their children were not even gassed but merely thrown into the pyre alive."

~

THE CHARISMATIC MANNER in which Vrba could convincingly make his case about Kasztner rendered him *persona non grata* at Yad Vashem. This antipathy could only finally subside with the 2024 death of the potentate of Jewish history, Yehuda Bauer, who was intimidated by Vrba's first-hand knowledge of the Holocaust and his rational claims that some Jews were complicit. As a global awareness of Vrba is coming to the fore, it is conceivable that Bauer's influence will wane and Rudolf Kasztner, the fixer of sanctuary for the rich, will be condemned in perpetuity on the basis of these simple words from the Holocaust's most widely recognized survivor:

> "Nobody cared enough to tell us, 'Don't go.'"
> – *Elie Wiesel*

Martin Gilbert and Rudolf Vrba in Vancouver

CHAPTER 14

Reflections

He was a good friend to me, and I always gained immensely from his wise advice. As you know, he did not suffer fools gladly, so we tried not to be a fool! He led me along several rich historical paths, and I shall always treasure his vigorous, informative letters ... He, Wetzler, Rosin and Mordowicz, all four of them Jews, did as much as anyone could – or did – in actually saving Jews. – SIR MARTIN GILBERT

Rudolf Vrba saved his own life. Of all the witnesses, he is the one whose demeanor, whose frank, ironic smile, whose precise, organized speech, would lend support to the theory that some people, given the circumstances, are innate survivors.

He was immortal to me. He still is ... He fascinated: beneath his somewhat Mephistophelian appearance and the sweet Slovak music of his English, there was a man of steel, of boundless valor, audacity, hardness, purity. His black and sardonic humor was the sign of the most brilliant intelligence, the most penetrating thought, virtues that allowed him to survive for two years, first in Maidanek [sic], then in Auschwitz, before succeeding the impossible escape. To survive had meant to receive 47 blows on the buttocks from a frightful caning, to escape the phenol injection in fever, struck by the epidemic of exanthematous [sic] typhus, but struggling with all his might to remain upright and hide from the scrutinizing gaze of the SS selectors his swollen and blued legs which would have condemned him to immediate death. By his courage, his intelligence, his loyalty, his vital force, Vrba, at 18 or 19 years of age, was already considered to be a veteran, which in Auschwitz was a title to respect and admire … the story of his escape make it one of the most devastating reads ever.

– **Claude Lanzmann**, *Shoah* director

He ranks up there with the giants of Jewish history.

– **Arnold Ages**, Canada's first synagogue scholar-in-residence, Beth Tzedec Congregation

Few, anywhere, have exhibited his moral courage.

– **Irwin Cotler**, Nobel Prize nominee

He's a rare person. He totally enriched my life.

– **Robert Krell**, leading Holocaust educator

Rudolf Vrba did not correspond to the image that people usually have of a person from Auschwitz. His face shows relatively few wrinkles, and his hair shows no trace of gray. In any case, he looks younger than his thirty-nine years, and his eyes reflect humor rather than tragic experience. His appearance really matches who he is, which is a mix of world citizen, intellectual and scientist. – **Alan Bestic**, Rudolf Vrba's co-author

Vrba said, from the moment he arrived, that he was going to be an optimist.

– **Otto Pressburger**, fellow Auschwitz survivor

It was not just tobacco and gasoline that saved Vrba's life. It was also saved because Vrba admired knowledge. He was a scholar who knew its power and believed that the deportees should have been given that power, too. He felt that many lives would have been saved if they had known the fate that awaited them in Auschwitz. He promised himself to bring them that knowledge, and he kept his promise. – **Ruth Linn**, *The Guardian*, 2006

I was posted to the Swedish embassy in Budapest during the war time, and in the spring of 1944 Dr. Vrba – who had managed to escape from Auschwitz – gave the Embassy an authentic report about the Nazi extermination of the Jewish people. This report was forwarded to the Swedish government, who in their turn passed it on to the Allies. I thus strongly recommend Dr. Vrba to receive a Canadian award for bravery and contribution to the knowledge about Auschwitz. – **Per Anger**

After his escape from Auschwitz, he convinced his sister — my mother — to run away with me somewhere into the woods. And that is why I am able to stand here in front of you as a sexagenarian. – **Stefan Horny** (nephew)

Rudi was a man of towering, uncompromising intellectual honesty.
– **Christopher Friedrichs**, UBC professor and friend

Few other survivors have been able to present their experiences in a manner which enjoys wide respect and authority among his university colleagues and has been so helpful to the general public's understanding of these events … Vrba's belief was and is that the information about Auschwitz was suppressed in order that leading members of the Slovakian and Hungarian Jewish Council, and its off-shoot the Relief and Rescue Committee, could do a deal with Eichmann and his henchmen. In return for their silence, these men purchased survival for themselves, their relatives, a coterie of Zionists, and a number of wealthy Jewish entrepreneurs. In June 1944 these fortunate individuals boarded a train which eventually carried them to freedom in Switzerland. Many went on, subsequently, to hold prominent positions in the newly established state of Israel. They were also responsible for the formulation of the heroic myth of Zionist resistance and rescue from their Nazi persecutors. Official Israeli historiography had no place for alternative interpretations of what had happened in Hungary, or for any slander of the *Judenrat* for their collaboration with the Nazis.
– **John Conway**, UBC history professor and friend

Where do I begin on Rudi? Suffice to say, he was the bravest man I have ever known, and that includes several acts of bravery I have witnessed … We visited Rudi in hospital after an operation. The surgeon removed a lump from his chest the size of a tennis ball. Rudi explained that a lump had formed in his chest after the beating he received in Camp Kanada, which had calcified … Overriding Rudi's seriousness was a joviality that we both enjoyed. Especially over good food and the inevitable slivovitz!!! He always considered himself to be the best schnitzel maker ever.

– **Stanley Medicks**, commander in Mahal (Volunteers from Abroad) during the Israeli War of Independence

In the 1950s he once attended a commemoration of Auschwitz victims where not a word was said about any Jews. The talk was about Communist heroes. Some man next to him asked him if he noticed that the stage is "lousy with Jews." Rudi did not respond because it was the time of the antisemitic Slansky trial, and he did not want to "provoke his own fate." But he never attended another meeting of the anti-fascist fighters … When the neo-Nazi Ernst Zundel was tried in Toronto in 1985, his lawyer, Doug Christie, asked Rudi about watching the long lines of Jews, waiting for their demise in front of the gas chambers. "You watched them come in and watched them not coming out," Christie said, insinuating that Vrba therefore could not prove any allegations of mass murder. "Yes," Rudi replied, unperturbed. "A quarter of a million people went in, and I never saw one civilian come out. So, it is possible that they are still there, or that there is a tunnel and they are now in China. Otherwise, they were gassed."

– **Jan Drabek**, Czech-born novelist

What I remember most was him saying that one of the strongest motivations for the Shoah, in addition to antisemitism, was plunder. He compared this to the burning of the witches in Europe when all their assets went to the Church after their death. Once the law changed and the family inherited instead of the Church, the burning stopped.

– **Pnina Granirer**, Vancouver artist from Romania

Vrba's proudest boast is objectivity.

– **Eric M. Breindel**, *Harvard Crimson* (1974)

Biochemistry, as a subject, can be intimidating, but I never remember it being that way with him. It is interesting that with his having the experience that he did, his past life was completely unknown to us as students. I'm sure we would have been in awe of him had we known what he accomplished. He must have been very humble and private about his difficult past.

– **Dr. Gary Jackson**, UBC student in 1975–76

The first time I encountered Dr. Vrba was in 1980 as a second-year UBC medical student. I was late for the first of a series of pharmacology lectures given by this vigorous, thickly accented professor of unknown origins. I was immediately struck by how unusual it was for someone to have risen to the level of teaching faculty in this otherwise waspy and notoriously bureaucratic Canadian medical school when his mastery of English, and perhaps also his academic accomplishments, seemed relatively recent achievements. But his commanding presence and personal dignity garnered great respect – even some intimidation – amongst my medical school classmates ... It was only many years later that I learned of his determination and heroism.

– **Jeffrey Claman**, MD FRCPC, Clinical Associate Professor,
UBC Department of Psychiatry

It's striking how much Vrba and Wetzler got right about the layout of the camps, the mechanics of mass extermination and even down to the name of individual prisoners.

– **Nikolaus Wachsmann**, author of *KL: A History of the Nazi Concentration Camps*

Rudolf Vrba embodied the tension between action and words, reason and emotion, that is at the heart of Holocaust studies. He and others have given us powerful models of how to combine scholarly rigor and human engagement in pursuit of truth.

– **Doris L. Bergen**, Chancellor Rose; Ray Wolfe, Professor of
Holocaust Studies in the Department of History; Anne
Tanenbaum Centre for Jewish Studies at the University of Toronto

In contrast to the trickling news items available, the [Vrba-Wetzler] report revealed the total and terrible reality of the extermination of human beings, organized methodically and pedantically, planned as a crime of massive proportions ... This report is exempt from feeling; the text is dry, as if the authors simply wrote about how one should bake bread.

– **Maria Szekely**, translator of the report in Budapest in 1944

Vrba's experiences ... [on the arrivals ramp at Auschwitz] were key to the report having the authority that it did. His story was breathtaking. He had what's described as a photographic memory. He was able to give eyewitness testimony that was unshakable and he played a key role in the [Ernst] Zundel conviction. He was able to tell the story with such clarity that people were able to understand the Holocaust. He remembered the languages that prisoners spoke, and he knew how many could be crammed into a railroad car.

– **Bernie M. Farber,** CEO, Canadian Jewish Congress, 2006

There were probably no other two prisoners who knew the workings of Auschwitz-Birkenau as well as Vrba and Wetzler did. This information they felt they had to reveal to the free world – somehow, someway – despite the impossibility. They believed that the world would listen to their eyewitness testimony that the Nazis were gassing and burning Jews by the tens of thousands daily and that if the Jews knew what fate awaited them in Auschwitz, they would rebel and refuse to board the deportation trains.

– **Rabbi Hanoch Teller,** a senior docent in Yad Vashem (2019)

Rudi was wonderful. He was very open. He didn't talk down to kids. He wasn't dismissive as a lot of adults were in those days.

– **Richard Bestic** (son of Alan Bestic)

Rudi was gorgeous and totally charismatic. And he was funny. With his cherub smile and his eyes wrinkled. Sometimes it was gallows humor. I remember we were in Auschwitz for a Canadian Broadcasting Corporation documentary. The producers were Canadian, but we had a Polish film crew. They were great. We were traveling with them in this old Polish bus that was always breaking down. We were doing the film inside the camp. Then it was about 5:30, and it was time to leave. We were trying to get out. The gate had been locked. It was really muddy. Everybody started to really fret. Increasingly, they were quite upset. To be locked inside Birkenau. How are we going to get out? Rudi was cheerful. "Never mind," Rudi said loudly so everyone could hear, "I know another way out!" – **Robin Vrba**

CHAPTER 15

Why Isn't Rudolf Vrba Already Famous?

In Plato's *Apology,* Socrates compares himself to a gadfly sent by the gods to rouse the city of Athens which he likens to a large and sluggish horse. Rudolf Vrba was a charismatic gadfly whose truth-telling was anathema to the Jewish establishment. Just as Athenians did not take kindly to being likened to a sluggish horse, many Jews have not appreciated Vrba's clear-eyed verdict that some Jews streamlined the mass murder of at least six million people by serving on *Judenrat* councils while facilitating the unprecedented theft of all Jewish properties, possessions and wealth.

Having met at least 100 trains arriving on the platform at Auschwitz, having watched Mengele for his countless selections, having worked in the Kanada warehouse for the stockpiling of stolen goods and having escaped in order to write the *Vrba-Wetzler Report,* Vrba, like Socrates, was a hard man to dismiss, but establishment historians under the influence of Yehuda Bauer succeeded for decades in marginalizing Vrba.

Rudolf Vrba was an unwelcome individualist who told the truth. Even the *Shoah* filmmaker Claude Lanzmann was taken aback by Vrba's candor and objectivity. In Israel for two years, Vrba had felt he did not belong. It has taken academics seven decades to ultimately concede that Vrba and his escape partner must be credited with saving 200,000 lives.

Finally, here's a biography. In the words of the 3rd-century skeptic philosopher Sextus Empiricus (recrafted by Henry Wadsworth Longfellow), "The mills of the gods grind slowly, but they grind exceedingly fine."

Rudolf Vrba's Letter to the Auschwitz Museum, 1989

THE UNIVERSITY OF BRITISH COLUMBIA

COPY

Department of Pharmacology &
Therapeutics
Faculty of Medicine
2176 Health Sciences Mall
Vancouver, B.C. Canada V6T 1W5

Telephone (604) 228-2575
Fax (604) 228-6012

18 December 1989.

Mgr. Kazimierz Smolen,
Panstwove Museum Oswiecim Brzezinka,
32-603 Oswiecim-5,
POLAND.

Dear Mgr. Smolen:

Re: Your Letter Wyd. 571/30/3468/89 - November 24, 1989

I thank you for your letter. Please find below my comments.

1. I am very surprised by the content of your above letter. You are saying that another letter was sent to me on 1 March 1989, which I never received. This latter-mentioned letter (the copy of which I received only from you now) was addressed to my address in Vancouver, but obviously not sent to me, but to the United States Holocaust Memorial Council. It was never submitted to me from there.

   I cannot understand why a letter addressed to me was sent by your office to a different address in a different country. I live in Canada, not in the U.S.A. In any case, it is deplorable that your letter to me was not forwarded to me, although my address was on it.

2. I enclose an article written by myself, entitled "Footnote to the Auschwitz Report". After reading this article, you might understand that I am not very popular with all of the members of the U.S. Holocaust Memorial Council, which might perhaps explain why your letter was never submitted to me. There they might be more interested to have you print their version of events relevant to the Vrba-Wetzler Report, rather than my version. The fact that I remember and see things in a different light might perhaps not fit exactly their views and wishes.

3. I enclose two articles of J. S. Conway, Professor of History at this University (both German and English versions), which analyze the origin and further fate of the Vrba-Wetzler Report. In my opinion, Conway's articles are as close to the truth as possible.

4. The statistics in the Vrba-Wetzler Report are based mainly on the fact that, until June 8, 1943, I was in the "Rollwagenkommando" (i.e., that part of Aufräumungskommando (' "Kanada" -) which "worked" on the old Ramp. Thus, I was present at the arrival of each transport and in good position to prepare the statistics by memorization. Neither I nor Wetzler carried any papers when we escaped from Birkenau. As I was for the rest of my time in Auschwitz a Blockschreiber in the Quarantine Camp in

.../2

Mgr. Kazimierz Smolen,
Panstwove Museum Oswiecim Brzezinka,
Page 2

Birkenau (B-II-a), I could continue to keep up my statistics by speaking to the "Zugangs", who knew from where their transports came, and how many persons were in their transport before "selection" for the gas chambers. I also kept up contacts with the"Rollwagen kommando" (after I became Blockschreiber in B-II-a), and I could double-check my figures.

5. As far as my legal name is concerned, my first free act on leaving the Auschwitz complex was to de-germanize my name and I wrote the Report as Rudolf Vrba. Should you have published the Report under any other name, I refuse to accept the author's honorarium which you mentioned in your letter of 24 November 1989.

   I find it improper that instead of using my legal name (Vrba) you refer to me by a formerly used German name (Walter Rosenberg), which I (for obvious reasons) did not use after my escape from Auschwitz. All of my papers published after 7 April 1944 (including more than 50 scientific papers) until this day were published under my legal name Vrba. This oversight on your part plays into the hands of those with the mentality of the Nazi press (which always referred to the USSR-minister Litvinov only as Finkelstein), and also of the Communist "judges" during the purges (who referred to Zinovev as Apfelstein and Slansky as Salzer). All this is grist for the mill of the Neonazis and also some other demagogues. It was not very kind of you not to let me see your draft before publication and I trust that you understand my reflections.

6. From reading the Vrba-Wetzler Report, obviously my statements therein start with paragraph 2 of the Report - description of Auschwitz I. I was in Auschwitz I from 30 June 1942 (as 44070) until 15 January 1943 (when "Aufraumungskommando" was transferred to Birkenau). Thus, I knew well the geographical situation and habits of "order" in Auschwitz I (whereas Wetzler was there only for 1 day and was immediately transferred to Birkenau). It would be, of course, difficult to decide now which part of the Report stems from Wetzler and which from me, and it is right to consider it as a result of the efforts of both of us - to the best of our knowledge and abilities.

7. As for the question 4 in your letter of 24 November 1989: Yes, it is true that I served (as Rudolf Vrba) as a soldier of the Czechoslovak Army in the Partyzan Unit of Captain Milan Uher ("Hero of the Slovak National Uprising" in memoriam) from 16 September 1944 until the end of the War. I was awarded the Czechoslovak Medal for Bravery, Order of Slovak National Insurrection (Class 2) and Medal of Honour of Czechoslovak Partyzan. Wetzler joined me there in February, 1945 and was with us until March, 1945, when he fell again into the hands of Germans. He was liberated in March, 1945 by a surprise artillery shelling of the prison by the advancing Russians.

.../3

Mgr. Kazimierz Smolen,
Panstwove Museum Oswiecim Brzezinka,
Page 3

Finally, I wish to add the following remarks:

(a) The purpose of our escape from Auschwitz, and of our Report, we to warn the remainder of the Jewish population of Europe which still survived, particularly in Hungary, of ther imminent fate. It was our belief that the widest possible publicity should be given to the Nazi policy of total annihilation, so that the earmarked victims would be alerted in time, and would then take all possible action to avoid the fate of the rest of European Jews, in particular by resisting the efforts of the Nazis to segregate, concentrate and to deport them. Our report was placed in the hands of Hungarian Judenrates in April, 1944. At that time we still had good reasons to believe that the Judenrates in Hungary were not yet aware of the true nature of the "resettlement" and of the existence and purpose of the Auschwitz-Birkenau complex.

Our warning, however, never reached the general Jewish population of Hungary. Instead, more than 400,000 of them passively boarded the trains, and more than 99% of them arrived in Auschwitz believing that their families are moved to "resettlement areas". As we well know, all these masses of people from Hungary died in Auschwitz in May and June, 1944. This was possible only because of the deliberate suppression of our Report by the Jewish Councils, in the interest of the so-called "negotiations" with the Nazis undertaken by the Jewish leaders in Hungary. By failing to inform the deportees in Hungary about the true objectives of "resettlement", these leaders bear a heavy burden for the subsequent tragedy, which in loss of human life was equivalent to that of at least three Hiroshimas. The post-war attempts to white-wash the activities of this group, as for example, in the book by A. Bliss, "A Million Jews to Save", has seriously distorted the history of these events, and attempted to give a varnish of respectability to what I call in my enclosed articles "Kastnerism". What is my understanding of this word, you might gather from my enclosed article, as published in Jewish Currents ("Footnote to Auschwitz Report"). Probably you can gather my attitude to this problem: the cornerstone of the Nazi annihilation policy consisted in keeping secret the true objectives of the "resettlement"; disinformation of victims (or withholding of vital information) was the cornerstone of the successful mass-murder, "negotiations" with Eichmann were only an alibiism, and a cover for treason and collaboration with Nazis, who spared the lives of some of the prominent Jews and at the same time swept hundreds of thousands others into the Auschwitz death factory.

(b) My escape (and Wetzler's) from Auschwitz was planned and carried out without the help of any organization, especially not some legendary "Jewish resistance group" operating from Slovakia or from anywhere else. It appears to me that such a group was formed only recently in Jerusalem in order to improve not only the Jewish future, but also the Jewish past.

...4

Mgr. Kazimierz Smolen,
Panstwove Museum Oswiecim Brzezinka,
Page 4

As a result, attempts are being now made so that the actual events are being replaced by a fantastic Hagadah-type story about some connection of a "Jewish working group in Slovakia" with Auschwitz and some completely invented "Jewish resistance organization" which enabled me and Wetzler to collect statistical data in Auschwitz and "smuggled me out". My system of collecting and memorizing all the data contained in the Vrba-Wetzler Report would require some detailed explanation which is far beyond the scope of this letter and can be understood only within the frame of a detailed knowledge of the administrative system imposed by the Nazis in their Auschwitz-Birkenau complex during the years 1942-1944, as well as a knowledge of my mnemotechnical methodology. In view of the technicalities involved in carrying out the escape, it is ridiculous to assume that I (or Wetzler) carried any papers, plans, or gas-cannister labels with us, as claimed by instigation of Otto Kulka and Yehuda Bauer from Jerusalem. All statistics, maps, and other information contained in the Vrba-Wetzler Report were carried from Auschwitz exclusively by memorization and recorded on paper in Slovakia on 25 April 1944.

Yours sincerely,

Rudolf Vrba

Dr. Ing. Rudolf Vrba, C.Sc. (Prague),
Associate Professor,
Department of Pharmacology &
Therapeutics.

RV/elj

Enclosures

CHAPTER 16

Robin Vrba Interviews

Robin and Rudolf Vrba as newlyweds in Boston, 1974.

RUDOLF VRBA'S AMERICAN-BORN wife, Robin, knew him best and longest. They lived together in Vancouver, Canada, from 1975 to 2006. Here is the first half of a two-part sequence of interviews between the author and Robin undertaken in 2023 and 2024. More interview segments will appear in Volume II. [A few segments have been inserted, for context, into preceding portions of this volume.]

Meeting Rudi

ALAN: When did you meet Rudi?
ROBIN: It was '74.

ALAN: And the date?

ROBIN: It was around Stefan's birthday [Stefan Horny, Vrba's nephew]. I think his birthday was in April. So, probably April '74.

ALAN: The same month as the escape – exactly 30 years before.

ROBIN: We were married more than a year after that.

ALAN: What was the date you got married?

ROBIN: September 13, '75. First, we had to go down to the main Boston Courthouse to validate that Rudi was divorced. That was difficult because we only had this one piece of paper from Gerta. It was a Czech-to-Swedish-to-English translation of the divorce agreement that she had used to get herself married in England. We were very lucky to find this very friendly judge. I guess he liked us, or maybe he took pity on us.

Either way, he designated a clerk to spend five hours in the law library stacks looking for some kind of legal ruling or precedent that would allow him to proceed. Finally, they got something. Because I had driven a delivery van for one of my jobs, we registered as a Scientist and a Truck Driver. Rudi really liked that. We were married by a rabbi in my parents' backyard.

ALAN: But when you met Rudi, you had just taken a job as a recreation director, at a nursing home, correct?

ROBIN: Yes. I met Rudi when I was working in Norwich, Massachusetts [100 miles west of Boston]. I had a friend in Norwood [Greater Boston, a half hour drive from Norwich] who invited me to a party in Boston. Her name was Judy Goldberg. She was probably about ten years older than me. She was a divorced lady who was kind of mentoring me. She was looking to meet somebody. She was invited to this party, not me. I almost didn't go. She pushed me into going.

ALAN: She wanted a companion so she wouldn't have to go alone?

ROBIN: Not really. She was motherly. I think she was trying to help me out. A lot of women nurtured me. I guess they saw something I needed. Rudi was the same thing. Towards me, he was very nurturing.

ALAN: So, your friend basically says, "Hey, you're not getting out and about enough."

ROBIN: Yeah. I did have boyfriends. But I guess she thought I should meet someone who was more interesting.

ALAN: More on your level?

ROBIN: [Self-disparaging] No, not on my level.

ALAN: But she must have had a high opinion of you ... in order to take you to this party.

ROBIN: Well, I don't know about that. I didn't want to go and she really pushed me into it. That's the gist of it. This was a private party. It was in somebody's apartment across from Mass General Hospital where Rudi had his position.

ALAN: So, you're going there with no expectations.

ROBIN: Exactly.

ALAN: How many people?

ROBIN: Maybe 30 to 35 people. It was a pretty crowded apartment.

ALAN: If Judy was much older than you, I'm guessing you were likely one of the youngest people at that party.

ROBIN: That's why Rudi gravitated towards me. Because I was the youngest one there.

ALAN: Explain *gravitated*.

ROBIN: Well, when he came into the room, everybody kind of focused on him. He had that sense of presence. When he came into a room, everybody looked. He was being introduced to everyone. And then he got introduced to me – and that was that.

ALAN: How long before he asked you on that first date to the opera?

ROBIN: A short time after. The next week.

ALAN: That meant you would have to drive back to Boston. Was that the following weekend?

ROBIN: Something like that.

ALAN: Do you remember the name of the opera?

ROBIN: It was *War and Peace*. We had box seats. Somebody must have given him those tickets, right? He was at Mass General Hospital, and they all had connections to the arts ... Rudi *loved* the opera. When he went to New York, he always went to the opera. But I'd never been to an opera before. It was quite impressive! And I was being treated like a princess. It was really nice.

ALAN: It sounds like you felt you were in an Audrey Hepburn movie.

ROBIN: Something like that. It was the Seventies. It was fun. But once we went to New York, to see the opera, and New York was pretty dangerous. I didn't really understand what was going on. I didn't realize how dangerous it was. We went to the opera in Lincoln Center. Afterwards it was so cold. The whole crowd was going in a certain direction, and I kind of pushed us in a different direction. Then it became obvious that nobody was going where we were walking. These two young guys were coming towards us; they had brass knuckles. Rudi saw what was going on. He knew body language. He pushed me away and those two guys did a 180-degree turn and those two guys walked away. It was amazing. I don't know how he did it. It was like some sort of military maneuver. It was pretty scary, actually. His reaction was to show them that he was going to fight. It chased them off. He was mad at me afterwards because I had made us not follow the crowd.

ALAN: Was he that way in other situations?

ROBIN: Oh, yeah. [Laughter] He was always aware that we couldn't get trapped. Always.

ALAN: I've heard stories of people who, after traumatic experiences, will only sit in a restaurant if they see the front door.

ROBIN: He wasn't like that. But he read the signs. He knew things. He knew what people could do.

ALAN: Do you remember any other dates with him?

ROBIN: We were sitting in this formal restaurant. We were near a man with a very long beard. Rudi could see I was quite intrigued by that guy. So, Rudi talked to the guy. He was from Montreal. But he just *looked* interesting. There was nothing interesting about him at all! But mainly I remember Rudi was kind of shocked when I ordered a Coke instead of a glass of wine.

ALAN: How was his English by this time? Because by then he had lived in England.

ROBIN: He was more articulate than most people I know. He had a heavy accent. It was part of his sex appeal. But you have to remember that Rudi had already studied English as a young person. When he was in the partisans [1944–45], Rudi spoke English. I think there was a Canadian airman that the partisans found and Rudi was the translator. It was either Canadian or American. There is some kind of record of this in one of the military museums in Slovakia.

ALAN: He went out of his way to learn languages.

ROBIN: He did. He told me once that he was thinking of becoming a linguist. He learned English first as a child. He had a cousin about ten or fifteen years older than him. Lily Just. Her father had been some sort of diplomat in Yugoslavia. They were Jewish. I met her in Vienna. She was Viennese. She was educated, and she said to me that when Rudi was about 10, and he came to visit their family in Vienna, they were sitting under a tree, and she was teaching him English. She was fluent. She ended up working for the Americans after the war as a translator. She said to me she was really impressed by how smart that child was. She was studying English at the time, and she said he was picking it up faster than her.

ALAN: Would they be conversing in Slovakian?

ROBIN: No, that would be in German. She spoke German, Hungarian and English. But she might have spoken Slovak, come to think of it, because she was a confidante of Rudi's mother. Her mother's sister was Rudi's mother. She helped Rudi's mother, Helena [aka Ilonka], all the time. Rudi's mother kind of terrorized her and manipulated her quite a lot.

ALAN: So, Lily was Jewish and living in Vienna?

ROBIN: Uh-huh. It was interesting because they had another cousin in Vienna whose name was Max Schneider. That was another first cousin. And that was the cousin who Rudi's grandfather thought was better than Rudi. Max Schneider was a member of the Communist Party of Austria. So, when Rudi met some of the underground people in Auschwitz, his "calling card," so to speak, was that Max Schneider was his cousin.

ALAN: Was Max Schneider in Auschwitz?

ROBIN: No. He survived the war. He wrote a few things. He was a member of the Communist Party until the Communist Party kind of kicked him out. He was a naive communist; you know, he really believed it. When Lily, his first cousin, went to work for the Americans, they had to stay separate from one another because the Americans would have been very concerned if they knew her first cousin was a communist. He didn't want to have anything to do with the Americans. They only began to be friendly and see each other again in the Eighties [1980s].

ALAN: So, did this Lily Just person first meet Rudi when he was about 10?

ROBIN: No, she probably knew him when he was born. Because she was the one who told me that Rudi's mother was having a lot of trouble getting pregnant. It took about ten years to get pregnant before Rudi was born. So, of course, Rudi was a very special person in Rudi's mother's life. Lily was a confidante of Rudi's mother.

ALAN: We're somehow getting a long way from Massachusetts …

ROBIN: It's much more interesting! [Laughter]

ALAN: More than dating and sex? [Laughter]

ROBIN: When Rudi left Vancouver to go to Boston, he had to take out a loan to do it. He told his bank manager he was also going to sell his car. The bank manager said, "What are you going to do for a car in Boston?" Rudi said, "Well, I'll meet a girl and she'll have a car." I guess that was part of my sex appeal. [Laughter] I had a yellow Pinto.

ALAN: So, one day, if we ever wanted to make money off your memoirs, the title would have to be …

ROBIN: *My Yellow Pinto*. [Laughter]

ALAN: Except nowadays people would think it's about a pony.

ROBIN: When we came back to Vancouver, we met the bank manager for another loan. He said to Rudi, "Oh, I see you have your asset!" [Laughter] Then a few years later, I'm sitting on a couch with this couple in East Vancouver, pitching for getting a [real estate] listing, and I look up and there was this picture of our bank manager on the wall. That was *really* bizarre. The woman was his daughter.

ALAN: Back to that party in Boston. We know Rudi was charismatic and intelligent, but I can also easily see him at this party, seeing you, and seeing a yellow Pinto in his future.

ROBIN: [Laughter] Most of the girls at that party had a car. It wasn't an unusual thing to have a car. I just remember going to the party with all the people there, and I remember Rudi coming into the room, and I'm thinking, "Oh, my God. That guy is adorable." He was being introduced to everybody and I think he stopped at me. I was probably at the end of the introductions.

ALAN: So, you don't remember any particular conversation? Was he interested in you or was he just interested in Rudi?

ROBIN: He was very interested in people. You know. He talked to you in the same way.

ALAN: No, when we met, he mainly talked about himself. I was being Mr. Polite Interviewer.

ROBIN: But he knew the situation with you. He found out what was going on.

ALAN: No, not at all. I didn't mention anything about my brain tumor for about two hours. I tried to say as little as possible; that way he would say as much as possible. It was more like a monologue. Once he knew he had a very receptive audience, I nodded in all the right places. When my brain tumor came up, we talked about it for about 20 seconds. [Laughter] He was happy to perform for me. It wasn't 50/50 after all … I just kept asking all the right questions. He asked where the tumor was. I pointed to my head. He just said, "Oh, you'll be fine." Looking back, I can see now that was the smartest way to handle it.

ROBIN: Rudi usually didn't want me to tell people how we met. It had nothing to do with where we met. He just thought it was none of their business. An invasion of privacy. He gave me different ways of handling it. One way was to say, "Well, it's an interesting question." People assumed I must be a student, but of course, I was actually a college dropout. He didn't mind them thinking I was his student as long as they didn't know the whole story.

One time he was at the beach, and some guy pigeonholed him and started to ask him really personal questions. Rudi said to him, "Are you an immigration officer?" And the guy pulled out his sheriff's badge! [Laughter] Another time, I remember this guy was standing there, pumping me on this. It was in Vancouver, and we were already married. He said, "How did you meet?" And I said, "Oh, that's an interesting question." Then he asked me another way and I just giggled. All of a sudden Rudi comes over, grabs me by the arm and looks the guy straight in the face.

"If you must know," he said. "We were actually predestined by birth!"

ALAN: A good point to end.

ROBIN: Okay. Monday at 9 a.m., your time, and 12-noon, New York time … That can be a standing thing.

ALAN: It works for me.
ROBIN: Ciao.

Saving Rudi's Life

ALAN: I want to talk more about the time you saved Rudi's life.
ROBIN: It's kind of hard for me to retell it.
ALAN: You told me once before – really well – in New York. But we didn't tape it.
ROBIN: I had had a boyfriend before Rudi, but he had got killed in a car crash. I was kind of sensitive to that. Having a boyfriend pass away. I had been going out with Rudi for maybe a month and a half or so. I don't remember why, but I knew Rudi was home, and he wasn't answering the phone. At that time, you could be on the phone and it could just keep ringing and ringing and ringing. I let the phone ring. For some reason, I was worried that there was something wrong. There was some reason at the time, but I can't remember what it was. Maybe I had talked to him before, and he didn't sound right. I had some reason for suspecting there was something wrong. But I was kind of shy. I wasn't very pushy. And I wasn't possessive. I was really subdued ...

He lived in a complex that had security, so I went [drove] to the complex and I talked to the security guard. I talked them into going into the apartment. I was really kind of embarrassed. I was thinking, "What if he's in bed with somebody?" The two security guys let me go in with them. There was a tall man and a short, fat guy. Why, I don't know. I just had this feeling that I had to check this out. So, the three of us are going into the apartment, and there is Rudi passed out in the bed. They had a lot of trouble waking him up. It took a few minutes.

He was very sweet about it afterwards. He tells the story, "There I am, sleeping very nicely, and in comes Tweedle-dee and Tweedle-dum." But he was extremely exhausted afterwards. It took him three or four months after that to actually get his energy back. When he went back to Vancouver, the doctor looked at the cardiogram and said, "You know you had a silent heart attack?" But in those days, they didn't call it silent. He just said, "You had a heart attack. When did that happen?" Of course, it must have been that time.

ALAN: Before, when you told me this story, you mentioned that you had called him more than once.

ROBIN: That's right. I called him once. Then I called him again. That time I just kept letting the phone ring. He never answered. So, I got dressed to go over there.

ALAN: You were expecting him to be home at that time?

ROBIN: Yes. For some reason, I knew. This was during the day; it wasn't at night. And it's interesting because when I told you this story the first time, I never thought I had saved his life. It was only when I first told you, for the first time, that it dawned on me. He might have been going into a coma.

ALAN: The doctor corroborated that later. There's no other interpretation you can give it. You said they couldn't wake him up for several minutes ...

ROBIN: It's still a conjecture, I would say.

ALAN: I like your second version better.

ROBIN: Why?

ALAN: Because this time you threw in the bit, "Well, he might have been in bed with somebody."

[Laughter]

ROBIN: Well, that's what I thought. I was a little shy about it. At that age. Oh, my God. I would have been *so* embarrassed.

The Bread Girl

ALAN: What is your date of birth?

ROBIN: I don't want to put a date of birth.

ALAN: You're in your seventies.

ROBIN: Yes.

ALAN: Can we start at the beginning? With your parents?

ROBIN: Sure. My parents were both born in Fall River [Massachusetts] to immigrant parents who all came from eastern Europe, probably from a

Jewish *shetl*. One grandfather was from Romania. My father belonged to the Orthodox synagogue, and my mother belonged to the conservative synagogue, so, growing up, I went to both. We were very family oriented, and I was educated in Jewish traditions. By that I mean we celebrated all the holidays together. We had cousins. It was a very traditional, small-town, Jewish community.

ALAN: And your grandparents' name was Lipshitz?

ROBIN: Yes. My parents were married as Mr. and Mrs. Lipshitz. When I was born, it was still Lipshitz. And then they changed their name. I used to spend a lot of time at my grandmother's house which was next to the elementary school. So, I would leave the elementary school and walk to the house. I remember the house, but I can't remember her. And I was six.

ALAN: So, your father became Robert Lipson. And you were Robin Lipson.

ROBIN: Yes.

ALAN: Your Dad fought in the U.S. Army during World War II, and he was involved in the Jewish War Veterans Association. What was he like?

ROBIN: Well, he was a fairly civic-minded person. He was also a board member of Fall River Jewish Home, a member of Temple Beth El, and president of Adas Israel.

ALAN: You had three siblings, correct?

ROBIN: Yeah. I had two siblings [growing up], and then my sister was born when I was fifteen. I had two younger brothers, Bruce and Gary. Now I own a house with Bruce, and my mother lives there. My brother Gary does a lot of my legal work. We were not very close when we were growing up, but he's become a really nice brother. I terrorized them when I was in a position of strength. Then they got together and tried to beat me up. That was the end of our relationship [laughter] until we grew up.

Then, when I moved back to the States, I had a lot of issues with Rudi's book, legal rights, and my brother is an international property and patent lawyer. He's good at administration, which I'm terrible at, so he helped me sort everything out. Now he does all the negotiations for stuff like book rights. He's such a nice brother! We weren't really that close when we were growing up, but he became a really good friend.

ALAN: So, it was your brother who wrote that excellent letter asking [Jonathan] Freedland to cease and desist in his attempt to sell film rights?

ROBIN: Yes. And I've always been very close to my sister. She's in her fifties now; she's quite bright and she calls me her little sister. [Laughter] We have a good relationship.

ALAN: Your Mom is in her nineties.

ROBIN: Right. Her name is Renée and she's still alive. We have moved to a new city, outside of Fall River, and my mother is now doing artwork. She just got interviewed in the local paper. The article is really funny. People assume she's in her late seventies and she must be hard of hearing. She has to say to them, "Why are you yelling at me?"

ALAN: I am getting the sense that you grew up in a relatively functional family.

ROBIN: Well, I don't know. We grew up in a bakery family. Bertha's Bakery. That, in itself, is a little dysfunctional. Getting up and going to work at two o'clock in the morning everyday ... nobody eats together! We were kind of all pulled into the bakery. I think my business skills came from there. When I went to work in the bakery, my father had this older lady who was very strict, and she took me under her wing. She trained me how to work in the store. So, my business skills stemmed from that, when I was fourteen.

I had a good time. I had a good memory for numbers. I used to add all the prices up in my head. It was kind of fun because people would say, "How did you do that!" It was just a simple trick that I had. They were impressed because I was fourteen years old.

ALAN: So, your parents were not simply involved in the baking and selling. They were also owners or proprietors.

ROBIN: Correct. I think they probably had about 60 employees. It took up a whole city block. They had a huge wholesale business. When the cake decorator quit, my father sent my mother to Boston to study cake decorating, so she did all the cake decorating. She liked the peace and quiet. She would go in at one o'clock in the morning and do all the cakes when nobody was there. The bakers would come in at three. Although my father was the business manager, if somebody didn't show up he'd still have to go in and work on the bench. He didn't know how to make a *challah* [braided bread for ceremonial occasions]. His father was a master baker and told him he didn't know how to make a *challah*. [Laughter]

ALAN: So, this was a specifically Jewish bakery.

ROBIN: It was. We had the inspector from the kosher place come in and check out the goods. They were worse than the health inspectors.

ALAN: So, Bertha's Bakery was an institution probably known through the state.

ROBIN: More like southeastern Massachusetts. When I did a talk in Fall River a number of years ago, it was written up in some newspaper. So, I got a phone call when I was in New York from this man who lives in Florida. He said his mother was in a nursing home, and his mother was in love with the bread from Bertha's Bakery. Because it no longer exists, he wanted me to tell him where he might able to get that kind of bread. [Laughter]

ALAN: So, it was an institution that lasted for seventy years.

ROBIN: Yes. My grandfather started it. He had all the sons and one daughter working in it. My father had a twin brother. The twin brother left. I think they had a couple of bankruptcies. My father bought it out, but he kept everyone from the family who wanted to stay. My uncle, my father's oldest brother, who was born in Europe, he was a master baker. And my grandfather was a master baker.

ALAN: Was the grandfather's wife named Bertha?

ROBIN: Yes. When they started, they called it My Own Quality Bakery. They were in a different location. One of my aunts suggested they should have special wrapping. So, they had a picture of me on the wrapping. The Bread Girl.

Then they changed the name when they bought the store in the middle of Fall River. So, people would say, "Well, go to Bertha's and take a left" or "Go to Bertha's and take a right." The telephone number for Bertha's Bakery was 40721. I said to Rudi, "Did you notice that?" and he said, "Yes, I noticed that." Rudi was very interested in that [tattoo] number on his arm. He saw 44070 on a lot of things.

ALAN: When did Bertha's cease to exist?

ROBIN: About twenty years ago.

ALAN: Would you say your upbringing was middle class?

ROBIN: It was a working business class family. Whatever I wanted, I could get. I thought we were rich but we weren't.

ALAN: You went to B.M.C. Durfee High School.

ROBIN: We called it Durfee. The building's still there. It was modeled after some French city hall. It wasn't a great school, but it was nice architecture.

ALAN: What percentage of the population of the town was Jewish?

ROBIN: The town was about 100,000 people. It was on the Taunton River that connects it to the ocean. So, it was a line between New York City and Fall River. The people who couldn't make it in New York in the garment industry could set up factories in Fall River where it was much cheaper. So, a lot of the earlier Jewish citizens were in the garment industry. Even so, I think only about ten percent of the town was Jewish. 10,000 people. That's my guess. There were two Jewish cemeteries.

My mother knew the history. She used to take people on walking tours. Hard to believe, but it was the textile capital of the world at one time. In the 1920s, there was a very wealthy class. There are a few signs of that in some of the remaining architecture. After the Depression, all the industries moved down south. It never really recovered.

ALAN: Did you have any formal Jewish education?

ROBIN: Two days a week I went to Hebrew school, after school. I suffered through Sunday school on Sunday.

ALAN: What were your ambitions or interests when you were a teenager?

ROBIN: Not a lot. I had a friend who was very smart. She filled out my application for college. I was in a bit of nowhere land. She gave me a bit of direction. But I did eventually drop out of college. I didn't have a lot of energy for study. Rudi said I was not the academic type. That was probably true.

ALAN: But you were socially adept?

ROBIN: Yeah. I was an "introvert-extrovert." I had very good business skills for a young woman. That gave me an extroverted approach. But I think on a social level I'm shy.

ALAN: Would you describe yourself as serious?

ROBIN: Yeah, I think so.

ALAN: Paul Simon always wanted to be a relief pitcher in baseball. What were your dreams?

ROBIN: Well, I wanted to be an actress. I was involved in theater. I was in a lot of plays. Until I got a really bad review, and I lost my interest.

ALAN: I remember you mentioned some sort of harrowing experience before New York. What age were you?

ROBIN: Twenty-two. That's when I quit. My mother had a huge inferiority complex, so I think that she decided she didn't want me to have the same inferiority complex she had. I was the first born. So, when I was three years old, she put me in summer camp. I was very homesick. She had to pick me up after a week. Meanwhile, I used to walk to the store myself at three years old. It was a mile away. And then I'd come home. She thought I was very reliable. So, she put me in drama. At four years old, I was on the stage. My mother told me, the first time I was on the stage, she had a psychotic experience. When the curtain opened, she said everything in the room went black, but I went into a halo light. [Laughter] I didn't have any guidance, so it just kind of petered out.

ALAN: Wasn't there a drama department in high school?

ROBIN: No. I think when I got interested in boys, I lost interest in theater.

ALAN: It can be a detriment to be defined as being exceptionally attractive ... There can be a beauty burden.

ROBIN: I don't think I was considered that attractive. I mean, I was okay.

ALAN: You didn't want to be an astronaut.

ROBIN: [Laughter] When I saw 007 [James Bond], I wanted to be a spy.

ALAN: But you never got a license to kill.

ROBIN: Not exactly. I got a job as a recreational director in a nursing home! I went and volunteered in the nursing home across the street in Fall River. I was twenty-one. The lady there took me under her wing. There were a lot of people who saw a lot of potential in me. She thought I should get out of Fall River. She thought it was a dead end. The nursing home company had five homes. There was a very chic home in Norwood, Massachusetts, outside of Boston. So, she got me that job. She got the girl in Norwood fired to get me that job. It was a great job for me, and I was really good at it. There were 120 patients. I'd get them involved in activities.

Leaving Boston

"He was avoiding traps his whole life."
– *Robin Vrba*

ALAN: What happened after your wedding?

ROBIN: We went to San Diego for a honeymoon. I remember on the plane ride from San Diego to Vancouver, Rudi said to me, "Oh, by the way, it rains a lot in Vancouver." [Laughter] I guess he thought that was something I needed to know. It didn't matter to me. The weather was stunning from the time we arrived until the beginning of October. After that, it rained absolutely every day, until the end of March.

It was gorgeous when we arrived. We stayed at the Faculty Club [University of British Columbia] in the same room that the Queen stayed in. The Queen was registered to stay downtown in the Hotel Vancouver but in reality, for security, they put her up in the Faculty Club. That's what Rudi told me. When I was in the room at the Faculty Club, he met with Sir Eccles downstairs, one of the Nobel Prize winners, and he was mad at me because I wasn't there.

ALAN: I met Rudi there, too.

ROBIN: It was his hangout. He felt comfortable there.

ALAN: Before Vancouver, Rudi's life had been fraught with insecurity ever since he was a teenager. Was it also 1975 when he got tenure?

ROBIN: Probably. Rudi certainly didn't have tenure when he went to Boston, so it must have been when he came back. His work was funded by NRC [National Research Council of Canada], and that was actually a tentative arrangement. It was not permanent. If he survived at Harvard Medical School, maybe it became automatic. I don't even know. There must have been something, a document, that told him he was now on the permanent staff at UBC.

In Harvard, they wanted him to stay. He thought about it, and he decided to go back to Vancouver. They asked him to stay but he would have been on soft money [grant money]. This was above my head at that time. I had so much missing information. But he used to confide in me. We'd have these big discussions. I didn't really know all those colleges that were involved.

ALAN: All his life, ever since the time he was fighting in the partisans, he had no security.

ROBIN: It was crucial for him, that's for sure. He didn't really like Vancouver, but he knew that it was a better choice for him. He didn't like it when he came back. He found it provincial.

ALAN: It is. Compared to MIT. [Massachusetts Institute of Technology]

ROBIN: He was at Harvard. He had such a good time at Boston. He had a very high position. He was really a well-known scientist. And he was famous. The Bostonians knew who he was. Unlike the Vancouverites. They had no clue who he was.

There was a scientist at UBC, a guy from India. He eventually won the Nobel Prize, but not while he was in Vancouver. He was married to a Swedish girl. This was before I came. There was a huge discussion at UBC while he was there as to whether or not they should allow this Indian guy to go into the Faculty Club. He left to go to MIT. Rudi met him in Boston. He was friendly with him. After he won the Nobel Prize, UBC started to promote him as their Nobel Prize winner, right?

ALAN: When they hadn't been sure whether or not he could enter their Faculty Club.

ROBIN: That's how life is.

ALAN: Who was the head of the department when Rudi came back?

ROBIN: Foulkes.

ALAN: Not Tom Perry.

ROBIN: Foulkes. He was also an American. He and [Dr. Tom] Perry were friends. They both left the U.S. due to McCarthyism. Jim Foulkes was a very nice gentleman. He was part of the Communist Party, and he had a beautiful command of the English language. He had a kindness. He was kind to Rudi. Whenever Rudi had to publish a paper, he helped Rudi edit the paper.

ALAN: So, it stands to reason that maybe Foulkes helped Rudi get tenure.

ROBIN: There were people who really liked Rudi. I think the Dean might have helped, too. He realized what was going on. Rudi had a charisma. And if somebody was really on a high level, they actually started to love him. I saw that a few times. I never met that Dean, but I think that Dean had a sense of decency, and there was an attraction to Rudi. He thought that here was a fine professional and he was getting the bad end of the stick.

ALAN: It was like Rudi had two lives: First, he goes through hell and struggles to make ends meet, going from pillar to post, then meets this beautiful woman who is smart enough to know she isn't going to change him. He gets a position of security in a university where he has tenure.

ROBIN: I would not give myself that much credit.

ALAN: Well, it's true. Rudi has been making it up as he goes along. Even though he doesn't like Vancouver, because it certainly wasn't Prague or Vienna, the notion that he could have stability, with an income that isn't going to be taken away by the Nazis, must have changed him.

ROBIN: Yes, I think his wisdom told him that was a good deal. His wisdom told him I was not malicious. He knew I wasn't competing with him, like Gerta was. And he knew that he could educate me. I was moldable. And he was a very nice husband. He really did take care of me. That's what you want in a husband, right?

I don't know if I was smart enough not to change him. I think it might have been the opposite. I was so naïve that I looked at him like he was God. [Chuckles] I like to think it was more my naivete than any smartness [that made the marriage work]. But I think you're right about the security. He knew that security was very important. For sure.

In a way, this goes contrary to a lot of things he taught me. "Look, don't get caught in a bureaucracy. There's no end to getting caught in a bureaucracy. Or a governmental quagmire. Really avoid it." Every time there was a chance that that would happen, he showed me not to do that. He was avoiding traps his whole life. He had a second sense of what were traps. He did. I mean, I'd have to say he did have a trap aversion.

ALAN: And we don't have to be much of a psychiatrist to make some assumptions about that.

ROBIN: And I think you're right. He didn't like Vancouver. People were not very interested in him. But he didn't much care about that. The people weren't really nice to him. But the system protected him. The [tenure] system that was in UBC was good. Once he got into the system, it was hard for any individual in the system to kick him out. So, the *system* protected him, not the individual. And he understood it.

ALAN: He found a bureaucracy where he never had to salute.

[Rudolf Vrba didn't get his tenure fully formalized until he got back to Vancouver. This was the main reason he returned. For the first time, he felt confident he could afford a wife and have the security of knowing he could support his mother and his daughters for whom he had failed to provide adequate emotional or financial support earlier. He was very popular in Boston, and he would have much preferred to go back to London to be near his daughters, but his need for some security won the day.]

Arriving In Canada

ALAN: What were your first impressions of Vancouver?

ROBIN: I thought it was like America. Rudi said no, the atmosphere is different. It's not like America. "It's not the same," he said. "You can't be as friendly as you were in Massachusetts."

ALAN: Do you remember arriving?

ROBIN: I remember we had to rent a car at the airport, and we needed some special form that the new NDP government had implemented. I wasn't even a landed immigrant yet, but I had to rent the car and drive it, instead of Rudi. He said that was typical Communist! [Laughter] Even though Rudi had once been a Communist himself, he was very anti-Communist. The left-leaning NDP had just been in power for the first time. Rudi was a member of the Liberal Party. He would vote Liberal.

ALAN: But overall, how did the city strike you?

ROBIN: People were mostly welcoming. I didn't know the international driving symbols, so I took a left hand turn on Burrard. The police pulled me over. But when they found out I was staying at the Faculty Club, they let me go. They just told me to learn the symbols.

My American passport had expired so I had a special immigration pass.

I was able to apply for my Canadian landed immigrant status through San Francisco. They didn't make me leave Canada. I just had to keep going back to the airport to get it updated until I got my documentation. Every time I went back, the guy would say, "Oh, my favorite client."

But soon after we got there, I was walking around Gastown and there was this policeman on his horse. I thought, "Oh, that's very charming." I tried to stop him, to ask directions, and he almost ran me over. [Laughter] Rudi said, "Well, he probably thought you were a prostitute walking around Gastown."

ALAN: Our manners are different than in the U.S.

ROBIN: Well, it depends where you are in America. The pulse in America has changed since I left. America is more like Canada now, but the pulse in New York City is still special.

ALAN: Generally, I'd say Canadians are more moderate in our behavior.

ROBIN: Maybe so. Rudi was only in Boston for two years and yet he made so many friends. He was like a magnet to people. People were dying to be with him. They just loved his company. In London, he was extremely popular, too. He had so many friends. But in Vancouver, he was kind of isolated. In general, the people weren't that nice to him. It was very, very different.

ALAN: When you walk around the Stanley Park seawall nowadays, you'll hear ten different languages in five minutes. But in the Seventies, he would have sounded very different. Maybe people were standoffish with Rudi because of his accent.

ROBIN: His accent was part of his sex appeal. With me, anyway. And he spoke many languages. In Boston, they knew that he was an educated person. He told me that when he moved to London, before that, he had these fantastic sandals – they were marquee sandals – [laughter] and a doctor friend said to him, "You know, Rudi, with those sandals and your accent, the girls are going to fall in love with you here."

ALAN: And lots of them did.

ROBIN: But, in those days, Vancouver had such a provincial environment. He didn't really like to leave campus. Before I came, he told me if you went downtown everybody wore these baseball caps. It was like the Wild West, really backward.

But when I took him exploring, he said, "Oh, it's more interesting than I thought." I had a very easy time in Vancouver. The whole world was open to me, whatever I wanted to do there. Vancouver was very nice to me.

ALAN: Did you always live on the UBC campus?

ROBIN: Not at first. We stayed at the Faculty Club for a few nights, then we rented something [off-campus], near Jericho Beach, for about six or eight months. Rudi had put his name on a waiting list for MacKenzie House and then we got an apartment there [#1107, on-campus, in 1976]. The house manager liked us so, when we put our name in for the penthouse, we got it when it became available.

ALAN: I think it was Helen Karsai who told me you didn't have your name on the intercom.

ROBIN: I was a little paranoid. I didn't want the names on there.

ALAN: I had assumed it was because Rudi didn't want his name there.

ROBIN: It was me.

ALAN: Were you paranoid because of his background?

ROBIN: I was. There were things going on. I was a little concerned. Like when the Nazis were marching in Skokie, in Illinois. [In March of 1977, the leader of the pro-Nazi National Society Party of America informed Skokie police they intended to march on May 1 through Skokie, a town of 70,000 people. More than half of the residents were Jewish, including thousands who had survived Nazi concentration camps.]

Rudi wrote a letter to [President Jimmy] Carter [concerning a different matter]. And the next thing we knew we had the RCMP investigating Rudi. The police came. I wasn't there but they asked him if he had a gun.

ALAN: And what was his answer?

ROBIN: He didn't.

ALAN: That letter of his to Carter, would it be in the archives in New York?

ROBIN: I don't know. Maybe.

ALAN: I'm going to hire someone to find it. [The letter was found.]

ROBIN: It's probably in his file [with the FBI/CIA] and you could get it with the Freedom of Information Act in the U.S. For that matter, it's probably in his file in Canada, too, because the RCMP was alerted.

THE UNIVERSITY OF BRITISH COLUMBIA
2075 WESBROOK PLACE
VANCOUVER, B.C., CANADA
V6T 1W5

FACULTY OF MEDICINE
DEPARTMENT OF PHARMACOLOGY

6 September 1977.

Mr. James E. Carter,
President of The United States of America,
White House,
Washington, D. C.,
U. S. A.

Sir:

I am writing to you to ask for your help in a matter important to us all. This I am doing in my capacity as a member of the North American academic community, as well as that of Vice-President of Comité International des Camps and that of a former prisoner of Auschwitz (1942-1944, No. 44070).

It has come to my knowledge from very reliable sources that during the period of September 24th to October 31st, 1977, a number of public and other meetings of former members of several SS-Divisions will take place in West Germany.

Public meetings have been scheduled by the members of the following SS-Units:

SS-Panzer Division "Das Reich";

SS-Body Guard Division "Adolf Hitler";

The 4th SS-Police Division;

and other SS-Divisions as outlined in the enclosed papers. The meetings are scheduled in various West German towns, in particular: Nürnberg, Neuenburg, Altensteig, Marktheidenfeld, Biedenkopf, Lenggries, Weilburg, Ebstdorf, Ulm. These meetings can take place only if the mayors and councillors of these towns give their approval.

I would like to reiterate here the following:

1. It has been declared by the Nürnberg Tribunal in 1945 that (with the exception of the SS-Cavalry) all Units of SS, including the so-called Waffen-SS, are criminal organisations. Therefore, the care and fostering of the traditions of these SS-Units amounts to the promotion of criminal organisations.

.../2

Mr. James E. Carter - 2 - 6 September 1977.

2. Under the despotic and tyrannical national-socialist rule in Germany, the SS- and also the Waffen-SS did consider it as their task to annihilate the racial minorities and they did all they could do towards this end.

3. All tasks in the Auschwitz Concentration and Annihilation Camps were performed by members of the Waffen-SS. This I reiterate here not only as an ex-prisoner of Auschwitz, but also as the co-author of the Auschwitz Report which was entrusted to President Franklin Delano Roosevelt in the summer of 1944. Neither President Roosevelt nor numerous historians who have studied this document during the intervening years have found any inaccuracies in my statements. I trust that my present statements will hold true just as well.

4. The nursing and fostering of SS-traditions is not only criminal, but it is also a dangerous example for the young and uninformed people in Germany today.

I wish to recall here the memory of all honest soldiers who sacrificed their lives to save us all from the despotism of the SS and I wish to recall the names of millions of people who died as victims of this despotism; and I am recalling here the interest of the youth of Germany of today, who should be protected from the demagogic effects of SS-meetings and from the flagrant and cynical misuse of democracy by criminals who have pledged by oath a blind obedience to the "Führer" and the destruction of human freedom.

Public meetings of the members of SS-Units can be prevented by the action of the Bundesminister des Inneren, Professor Dr. Werner Maihofer, Rheindorfer Strasse 198, Bonn 7; and these meetings could be stopped by decisions of the mayors and councillors of the above-quoted German towns.

I shall be grateful to you for any action which will let these gentlemen know that the free world does not approve (either by silent assent or otherwise) these public meetings of SS-criminals.

Yours sincerely,

Rudolf Vrba

Rudolf Vrba.

RV/elj

Enclosures 5 - documentation

P.S.: This letter is also to be issued to the press.

ROBIN: When was Carter in power?

ALAN: I'm not sure.

[She looks it up]

ROBIN: From [19]'77 to '81.

ALAN: And you came to Vancouver in '75.

ROBIN: Right.

ALAN: It sounds like you should have been more concerned about the police than the Nazis ...

[Laughter]

ROBIN: I was paranoid before I met Rudi. My father said I was paranoid.

ALAN: Growing up as a teenager?

ROBIN: No, as an adult. I moved to Boston. I got a job as a spy in a department store. I think I told you about this ...

ALAN: You did.

ROBIN: ... and I was really nervous about it. I think I lasted four days. I called home, and my father said to my mother, "It's 007 on the phone."

ALAN: As a store detective, did you ever catch anybody [shoplifting]?

ROBIN: No. I felt paranoid that they were going to catch me [being undercover]. In the end, I don't even think I got paid. It was probably my fourth job by then.

ALAN: But you seem self-assured.

ROBIN: Well, you can be self-assured and paranoid.

[Laughter]

Return To Auschwitz

ROBIN: Did I ever tell you about the time we went to Poland and Rudi was very nervous?

ALAN: No.

ROBIN: This was for the *Man Alive* program in 1991. After the Communists fell. They had wanted to do a film in the 1980s, but some Poles wrote to Rudi and told him, "Don't come to Poland now." They warned him that it wasn't a good idea to come.

ALAN: One questions whether it's ever a good idea to go to Poland.

ROBIN: This was right after the Communists fell. He never thought he'd ever go back to Prague. I remember we flew there with OK Airlines. It was kind of weird. They had portholes instead of windows. And if nobody was sitting in the seats, the seats went down automatically. There was a little bit of condensation in the plane when it took off. But it landed fine. As we were approaching the city, Rudi looked down and said Prague was even more beautiful than he had ever remembered it.

The military came to meet the plane and take us up to the terminal. Then we hired a driver, and the driver took us from Prague to Poland. Before we got to the border, Rudi put a band-aid onto his [concentration camp] number to cover it up. He was *so* nervous going through that border. That's why we had hired a driver, to help get us through to Poland from Czechoslovakia.

The taxi was old. It was some sort of Russian Cadillac. The trunk was in the front. The guy [driver] managed to skip the whole queue. At the border, they made us give them all the Czech crowns we had. They gave us a chit for it. We had a few hundred dollars in Czech crowns. Then they opened the hood.

I didn't know any Czech. I didn't know any Polish. I didn't know any Slovak. I didn't have a clue what was going on. Rudi knows all those languages. Sitting there, coming from the left window, these people are barking at us. Rudi gives them something. And then we have people on the right window barking at us. The Slovaks are at one window and the Poles are at the other, asking for documents, asking why we're travelling, asking us where we're going.

Rudi was so nervous. He had taken something like $4,000 in U.S. cash because you couldn't necessarily get money there. When the CBC crew came, Rudi asked [the producer] Robert Taylor to carry the money because he was afraid of going back through the border with all that cash. He knew that a Canadian would get away with it, but as a Czech or a Slovak, he could get into trouble more easily.

Even though Rudi had a Canadian passport, he was *really* uptight. I could see it. Rudi was never that uptight in Germany. He liked Germany. He had a good time there. And he hadn't been really uptight in Czechoslovakia. He had been a bit nervous about the [tattoo] number, but nobody even cared, nobody ever looked.

ALAN: I wonder if that was the first and only time he ever covered up his tattoo?

ROBIN: I don't know. Maybe.

ALAN: I know when he went to a swimming pool, he didn't cover it up.

ROBIN: No, never. If people asked what is that number, he'd tell people, "Oh, that's just one of my old girlfriends' numbers." He'd make a joke out of it. He was proud of that number. There was a special way they'd tattooed his. It was like a "nice" tattoo job. It wasn't ugly. He told me a story about [getting] it. It was somebody he knew.

ALAN: I've written about it on Rudi's website. The tattoo was made by a Slovakian locksmith named Ludwig Eisenberg.

ROBIN: There was something else funny from Poland. We were at the hotel in Katowice [capital of Silesian Voivodeship in southern Poland], and Rudi hired a taxi driver to go to Krakow. We were waiting for the Canadian crew. And the Polish taxi driver said, "But don't you want to go to Auschwitz?" And Rudi said to him, "What's Auschwitz?" [Laughter] And the guy thought he was totally imbecilic. The taxi driver gave him a big lecture about what Auschwitz was. Rudi got a kick out of that.

ALAN: Little anecdotes like that tell you so much about his character. How many people who survived Auschwitz would turn that into a humorous anecdote?

ROBIN: Well, he shared it with me. He thought it was funny.

ALAN: So, you are now traveling around Poland with a Canadian film crew.

ROBIN: Yes. The Canadian Broadcasting [CBC] was doing a *Man Alive* documentary tracing Rudi's escape. I remember we were in this little place called something Piciritza, which means "to the right." It's this little village on a farm road. The producer was Robert Taylor, a Canadian Englishman. He was very smart. We were high up.

Rudi says, "So, down below ... there was a train down below here."

And the interviewer, a guy named Downey, says to him, "Rudi, there's no train there."

And Rudi says, "There was definitely a train down below here."

Downey says, "Well, maybe they moved the tracks."

Rudi rolls his eyes and says, "They never move tracks."

Then all of a sudden you can hear a train going by. It was still right there. You just couldn't see it.

ALAN: And then you're also filming inside Auschwitz, and the gate was locked.

ROBIN: That was the same trip, yes. For that, we had a Polish film crew. They had this old Volkswagen bus. We were all traveling in that bus into Auschwitz. We were in Birkenau. In those days, at that time, Birkenau was not featured much [for visitors]. The Poles didn't think anything of it. They didn't treat it with any kind of respect. The local Poles had taken a lot of the stuff from the buildings there to rebuild houses and stuff. So, all you saw were chimneys all over the place. It was a skeleton of how Birkenau was.

I remember it was all kind of muddy. We were filming on top of the gas chamber. All of a sudden, there were about a million birds. I've never seen anything like it. When you have that many birds swarming above you, it makes an eerie swish. Rudi is talking about murdering all these people, on top of the exploded gas chamber, and you see this swarm of birds, making this eerie noise. It was surreal. It gave such a poignant feeling about where we were.

The film crew had a translator, but Rudi was a better translator than the guy they hired. Robin Taylor, the producer, was an Englishman and he had to deal with this film crew that was Polish. The *energy* was so different [because it was a Polish crew]. If Robin Taylor got angry, he just went quiet, but if the film crew got angry, they got noisy. [Laughter] The Poles communicated in a strange way. Of course, he [Taylor] wanted them to film those birds, but he couldn't communicate it.

I asked Rudi afterwards if he'd noticed the swarm of birds. It was so surreal. Rudi didn't even notice it because he was so focused on giving his testimony. He said, "You've gotta be kidding. If there were birds like that in Auschwitz, we would have eaten them!" He didn't see any metaphor involved. All he thought about was the birds as food.

They asked Rudi, "How do you feel about being in Auschwitz again?"

With his Cheshire cat smile, he said, "Much better than the first time."

Wetzler & the Escape

ALAN: I want to revisit that moment when Wetzler says, "I can't do this for another three days."

ROBIN: Right. Well, Rudi probably had more physical stamina. Or mental stamina. I mean, Rudi really considered himself a soldier. And don't forget, Rudi was part of the underground in camp, but Wetzler wasn't. Rudi was on the lower rungs of the Communist underground, and Wetzler was separate from all of that. Rudi wasn't that popular because he considered himself a soldier and he was treated like a soldier. Remember, Rudi took that beating for the *kapo*. It's in the book. He gained a big reputation from that.

ALAN: But I am curious about the moment when Wetzler says he can't take it anymore. Psychologically, at that point, it makes sense that Rudi would become the leader.

ROBIN: I think he was. I think he was. Because Wetzler did a couple of things that Rudi was really frustrated by. When they were out of the camp, he started to nag Rudi and complain that if it weren't for Rudi, he would be in his bed tonight. He complained so much that Rudi said he had to hit him to snap him out of it. Then Wetzler said he had money, which was a no-no. Wetzler wanted to go into a town. That was also a no-no. Then they ended up having to run up that hill, remember? They were running, and they were being shot at because of Wetzler. Rudi had to pretend that he was dead because he could not run fast enough.

ALAN: I didn't know that Wetzler brought money with him. Rudi was told [strictly] by the Russian, Volkov, "Do not take money." This is an interesting detail – that Wetzler took money anyway, against Volkov's instructions.

ROBIN: But Volkov wasn't Wetzler's friend. He was Rudi's friend.

ALAN: Yes, but Rudi was intending to follow the instructions of Volkov. It was because they followed those instructions they escaped so well. Then Rudi finds out Wetzler is carrying money!

ROBIN: I'm not 100 percent sure. But I think he [Wetzler] was [carrying money]. Rudi says he [Wetzler] said he wanted to go into the town because he was so popular with the women. "Then we ended up having to run up the mountain." [quoting Rudi] And then Rudi pretended he was dead when they were shooting because he couldn't run fast enough.

ALAN: But in Rudi's account of that incident, he doesn't mention that Wetzler did all that [took money; wanted to go into a town].

ROBIN: He didn't [mention it] because of a lot of the things ... These people [that he wrote about] were all alive. He did not want to create problems for them. It wasn't that he lied. He just left it out. He held some of those stories back. Like the reason they got into that predicament.

ALAN: Knowing Wetzler had money and wanted to use it explains the escape a little bit more in depth.

ROBIN: It's amazing, when I think about it, how many things he [Rudi] told me. Until you ask me these questions, I didn't realize he just told me so many things!

ALAN: Well, that's why we're talking! [Laughter]

ROBIN: But it's odd that I never thought about it.

ALAN: Well, if you don't tell me, nobody's going to ever know! There's this horrendously false Slovakian movie that fancifully says that Wetzler was the guy who led the way. That the Rudi character is a dum-dum! But he was the one who made their map.

ROBIN: Rudi had the logic, but he had a bad sense of direction. They got lost.

ALAN: But you're traveling mostly only at night.

ROBIN: You know, on the *Vrba-Wetzler Report*, the map that was drawn with the camp? That was definitely Rudi's map. I told you why it's like that, right?

ALAN: No.

ROBIN: How he had his signature on it, right?

ALAN: No. There's no signature.

ROBIN: Not a written one. Something else. When Rudi was in school, he had a teacher who was teaching them how to draw a map. And she always drew [her maps] with the south on the top of the map. Instead of the north. On his maps that Rudi drew in the *Vrba-Wetzler Report*, they have the south on the top. Nobody mentions that.

ALAN: Everyone in Žilina would have assumed the older person was in charge [Vrba was a 19-year-old].

ROBIN: I don't know. They were both pretty scrawny. He might not have looked that young. Rudi probably looked pretty old by that time. I saw pictures of him after the war. He was pretty gaunt.

ALAN: Do you know much about Wetzler after that?

ROBIN: Well, Rudi told me Wetzler came to the partisans, to join Rudi's unit. But the partisans were retreating and had a lot of wounded soldiers. So, they put Wetzler in charge of the wounded soldiers. There was some kind of underground pit. And the SS found them. And I think the job of the person in charge of looking after them is that you're supposed to die with them. But he talked himself out of it. All those wounded men got killed. But I think Wetzler went as a prisoner of war with the Germans.

ALAN: That's a big story. I hadn't heard that story.

ROBIN: That's all I know.

ALAN: And what was he doing marrying Eta [a notoriously harsh Block Leader]?

ROBIN: She was a prisoner. She was under duress. She didn't choose to go to Auschwitz. Rudi always said that. She was a Jewish prisoner. She didn't do what he would have hoped she would have done, but she still was a prisoner. She was not a free person. She was under duress. But Rudi wasn't in contact with her. He didn't send her money. He sent it to Wetzler.

ALAN: We know Wetzler was exceedingly bright, but he didn't do very well after the war. There was a lot of politics, but maybe he had some guilt about those [partisan] prisoners?

ROBIN: I don't know about that. I just know Rudi said he cracked when they left Auschwitz. Rudi said he cracked. So, he discounted [made allowances for] a lot of what he [Wetzler] was doing [later] because his stamina had been damaged irreparably.

ALAN: Due to the escape itself.

ROBIN: I can't give you a psychological analysis. Auschwitz can break most people. We all have a breaking point. His resolve was broken.

Unravelling Wetzler

ROBIN: I got the book that you recommended, the one about Mordowicz. [*The Auschwitz Protocols: Ceslav Mordowicz and the Race to Save Hungary's Jews* by Fred R. Bleakley]

ALAN: It was published in 2022. You'll find a fascinating story in there about how Rudi saved Wetzler's life.

ROBIN: I don't know what you're talking about.

ALAN: You will if you read it.

ROBIN: You're not talking about the escape from Auschwitz.

ALAN: No, this is different – but in the same year. It turns out that when they were all in hiding, in Bratislava, Mordowicz and Wetzler decided to visit Wetzler's brother in Nitra. They had fake IDs. Things were going smoothly until they were apprehended by Slovakian police, who took their false papers. They were being escorted to the police station when Mordowicz took out a revolver from the pocket of his trench coat and fired it into the air. The guards panicked and fled. Mordowicz was able to hide in the bell tower of a monastery, then he walked 15 miles to the next railway stop in Leopoldov. He got back to Bratislava where he pleaded with Rudi to go and find Wetzler, to bring him back somehow, to save him. Obviously, the police in Nitra were looking for them both. It was extremely dangerous. But Rudi went anyway. First, he found Wetzler's brother and his wife. That's how he learned Wetzler was hiding in a mountain cabin. Rudi had brought new identity papers for Wetzler. That's how Wetzler got out of Nitra and got back to Bratislava. Thanks to Rudi.

ROBIN: Are you sure that's not about Rosin and Mordowicz?

ALAN: No, their escape from Auschwitz is something entirely different. This is a story that Mordowicz told to his biographer.

ROBIN: Okay. Possibly this book is going to tell me something I don't know. I don't know a lot of things.

ALAN: It's one more chapter in the puzzling Vrba-and-Wetzler story. Their lives were separate and entwined at the same time. And they have storylines that don't always jive.

ROBIN: When Rudi left Czechoslovakia and wrote his book, the Communists were not very happy because they wanted things from a

Communist point of view. They got Wetzler to rewrite what he had written right after the war, so it had a Communist slant to it. Wetzler had written something right after the war, but they wanted to republish something after Rudi's book came out.

ALAN: Did you ever read Wetzler's book?

ROBIN: I didn't.

ALAN: It is bizarrely like a novel, but the narrative goes all over the place.

ROBIN: I understand it's a novel based on historical events and then he made up some things [according to Rudi]. For instance, he [Wetzler] said they took out the Zyklon B evidence [with them]. Rudi said that was ridiculous. Everyone knew what Zyklon B was. You didn't need to take it out.

ALAN: Much in the novel is very misleading, disturbingly so. People could read that book and assume it's based on fact. Wetzler borrows some details, I think, from Mordowicz' escape. Now there is a movie from Slovakia about the escape that has mostly been based on Wetzler's fictionalized account.

ROBIN: Well, that's also because they wanted the rights to Rudi's book, and I said somebody already had an option on it. I couldn't sell them [the rights] to them.

ALAN: This explains why the movie is so skewed in favor of Wetzler.

ROBIN: They were mad at me. They wanted Rudi's rights, too. They were connected with the walk [annual Vrba-Wetzler Trek]. That's who contacted me. So, I told them that I couldn't grant the rights to Rudi's book. They asked me a number of times. I said, no, I can't, because I have an option, a contract, with a film company already.

ALAN: Based in Los Angeles?

ROBIN: Right.

ALAN: Meanwhile that [Slovak] movie gives a completely false depiction of Rudi.

ROBIN: I haven't seen it.

ALAN: Don't. Cinematically, it makes a good attempt to depict Auschwitz. It's sophisticated in its visuals. But the storyline is bonkers.

ROBIN: They won an award, I think. From the European Union.

ALAN: So, you could have been involved but you chose not to.

ROBIN: I have a company called Rudolf Vrba Archives. My brother is my lawyer. He talked to the Slovaks. I don't remember the details. I just remember that we'd already optioned the rights and that was the issue. They were kind of angry with me, kind of abrupt. But I didn't really care [about their manners].

I had met one of them, the head of the Slovak walk [Trek]. The guy was Polish, a geologist. He had a stomach like this [she shows protuberance] but he was *very* fit. He was like a gazelle [on the Trek]. And they could drink slivovitz [plum brandy]! And then they could climb up the mountain. It was unbelievable. The Slovaks were quite impressive in that way!

He took [guided] the group. But it wasn't a very interesting tour. He didn't really follow the story. Then he started to read [from] Wetzler's book and Rudi's book. He started to put the readings together with where we were on the march. And on the third march day, he timed it so we could go by a certain area where Wetzler and Rudi were when a train went by [during the escape in 1944]. He timed it. It wasn't the same train, and it was going in the wrong direction. But he figured it was the right place. And then he found an area that he thinks was the park where Rudi and Wetzler pretended they were gay [hiding in the bushes]. Remember that?

ALAN: Yes.

ROBIN: The Nazis were coming by with the children. And the children found them in the bushes. And they [the Nazis] thought they must be gay and left them alone. In the bushes. And the guide found that area. It used to be a much larger area. If you look it up on Google maps. But he said this is probably where they were ... but he said, "But I think that was probably a figment of Rudi's imagination. What do you think?" [Laughter] I just said I don't know. But I think whatever Rudi wrote was as true to his memory as possible. Rudi was a good storyteller, but he used history and facts.

ALAN: Rudi's instinct was the opposite of fiction. It was more scientific. It was Wetzler who fictionalized. Maybe your guide didn't know that. It sounds like he didn't ... Movies supposedly based on history invariably go askew.

ROBIN: You're right. Rudi wrote big articles about not distorting things because it confuses the history. The company in Los Angeles also wants to distort it. I've read the script. They want to say they [Vrba and Wetzler] took things out of Auschwitz to prove what was happening. They say it works cinematically. But they took NOTHING out. They just took some clothes and some food. And some cigarettes. But they didn't take any [evidence of] Zyklon B. They didn't need to take that. Everybody knew what Zyklon B was. It was not anything unusual ... I told that to them [the would-be film producers in California]. They said, "It works. It makes the narrative work."

ALAN: That's terrible.

ROBIN: Well, Rudi [had] said to me, "When you sell the film rights, they'll distort it. They'll make a Hollywood movie out if it." You know what Rudi called Spielberg's film [*Schindler's List*]? He called it *Swindler's List*. All the children of all those people died [were murdered]. He did not save those children. He was not a great hero. He was not a bad guy, but he was not a great hero. All the children [of his slave labor force] were murdered.

ALAN: So, this film going to be made [in Hollywood] is going to end up verifying the false narrative in the Slovak film that is based on the false narrative that is in Wetzler's book.

ROBIN: Yes. Probably.

ALAN: Because anybody writing a film script today is going to seek out Wetzler's version, as well.

ROBIN: Right. Rudi said that everybody tried to present their own perspectives. So, the Poles presented that they were the great saviors in Auschwitz. The Israelis presented that the Jews were the great saviors in the underground. The Czechs and Slovaks did the same thing. And he tried to clarify the real history when he wrote the book.

ALAN: The book I have right here now is a perfect example. It's Józef Garliński's *Fighting Auschwitz* about the Resistance in Auschwitz. He arrived in Auschwitz on May 13, 1943, and he was transferred to Neuengamme that same year. Garliński's view is entirely pro-Polish. The Jews are invisible.

ROBIN: Rudi was different because he didn't have a nationalist perspective.

Somebody introduced Rudi once by saying, "This is the man who fought everybody during the Second World War."

ALAN: Wetzler's wife has always fascinated me. I think you met her once.

ROBIN: I did meet her once. We didn't have anything to do with her because she was a blood *kapo* in Auschwitz, but Rudi did say to me that she didn't choose to be there. She was there under duress. He gave her that. But he did not want to associate with her.

When I met her, they were honoring Rudi and Wetzler for being with the partisans. They put their names on one of the stones at Hippopotamus Hill. She was there for the celebration. This was after Wetzler had died. They never put the stone on while he [Wetzler] was alive.

ALAN: Was there any schism between Wetzler and Rudi partly because Wetzler and his wife were more in-line with the Communists? And Rudi was not?

ROBIN: No. Gerta was a snob, according to Rudi. She didn't like Wetzler and company [i.e., his wife, Eta]. So, she [Gerta] was not interested in that reunion. And Rudi did not like Wetzler's wife [Eta]. He liked Wetzler. Wetzler was very charming. Rudi told me a story: One day Rudi was in Prague, on the tram, and he saw Wetzler, on the street. The tram was going by, and Rudi reached out and pulled the cap off his [Wetzler's] head. And then they met up afterwards ... so they liked each other.

Rudi's Parents

ROBIN: When you ask me these questions, it kind of surprises me what's in the memory banks.

ALAN: Even though it might not feel that way to you, I think all these pieces of information are important.

ROBIN: Did I tell you about the one-room school?

ALAN: You certainly did not.

ROBIN: Rudi's sister, who I think was about fifteen years older, was named Fanči. She was often in charge of looking after Rudi. When he was about three years old, Fanči was babysitting and she had a friend who was a teacher in a one-room school. This must have been in Topoľčany. Rudi's father was still alive. It was her responsibility to look after Rudi, but Fanči was going out with Cedric, and she needed a place to leave Rudi for a while. She dropped him with her friend who was the teacher in this one-room schoolroom. All the kids were much older, but the teacher used to use Rudi as an example. "Look, little Walter can do that … and all you kids who are older …" He was the star in the one-room school.

ALAN: The schoolhouse story makes me realize we haven't talked much about Rudi's mother.

ROBIN: I don't know that much about his mother.

ALAN: I just want to get a fix on her character. She seemed to be overbearing. And bright. And obviously she doted on Rudi, her only child. You've actually met her.

ROBIN: In 1983, I met her in Vienna. She was there for a few days. And when the Communists fell, I met her twice, in 1991 and 1992. [The non-violent, so-called Velvet Revolution in Czechoslovakia occurred in November of 1989.] And she died, I think, in 1994.

ALAN: Did she like you?

ROBIN: I wasn't really concerned one way or the other. I'm always polite to people. I was polite to her. But we didn't speak the same language. And she was very manipulative. When we were walking around Vienna, there's a park at the top of Vienna, overlooking the city, and she and I were talking … and Rudi was with his cousin Max, and Ruth, his cousin-in-law … She [Rudi's mother] started to cry. And I said, "I don't understand what you're saying." And then she turned off the tears. That was it. We had no real communication … Rudi would sit, and he would tell her a few things, and then translate back to me. I think he was happy about that.

ALAN: That there was a language barrier.

ROBIN: Yeah. I think I told you that he would say we were very lucky in our marriage because my family was 3,000 miles away and his was 5,000 miles away. That makes for a good marriage … I didn't have very much to do with her. I mean, I sent her gifts. I told you about the calculator that I sent her, and she sold it on the black market? I sent her little things. That was kind of my relationship with her.

I didn't have a deep relationship with her, but she was nice to me. She made these doilies or she bought them, I'm not sure which. And she sent these Slavic embroidered shirts to me and Rudi. He went through a phase where he liked these Slovak embroidered shirts. He looked like a Slovak peasant. He liked that.

ALAN: Did Rudi like his mother?

[Pause]

ROBIN: She drove him crazy. He did say that she broke up his first marriage. His mother and Gerta had a fight in the People's Court of Czechoslovakia over a blanket. That's what Rudi told me. I don't know what the blanket was. That was in the divorce proceedings.

ALAN: You're suggesting that Rudi's mother never approved of Gerta?

ROBIN: No, she set up that marriage! Gerta's parents had died. And she [Gerta] was very intelligent. I told you that story. There's a picture of Gerta graduating from university with her doctor's degree, and Rudi's mother is holding the diploma like its hers. She was very proud of Gerta. I guess when Gerta started to show more independence ... But Rudi's mother said she [Gerta] was an orphan, and it would be good for Rudi to take care of her. She actually encouraged that marriage. I don't think he would have married her if his mother hadn't encouraged it. So, his mother must have had quite a bit of influence on his life, right?

ALAN: One would assume. We know Rudi spent several years under the care of his grandfather [in Nitra] and he was Orthodox. But what about his mother?

ROBIN: Of course she was from a mostly Jewish community, too. She lit the candles every Friday night. But mostly, I think, she was a very social person. I imagine that if she was at a party, she would be the center of attention. Rudi was like that, too. When he entered a room, there was like a light around him.

ALAN: Did he ever talk about his father [Elias Rosenberg]?

ROBIN: Not much. But he did remember when his father built a *sukkah* so they could have the train stop at their house. [A *sukkah* was a temporary hut built to recognize 40 years of Jewish wandering in the desert to escape slavery in Egypt.] He also told me a story about his father on his deathbed. Rudi didn't want to go into the room. They forced him to go in and say goodbye. That was one of the major memories he shared with me.

ALAN: What else?

ROBIN: After his father had died, he was walking down the street and some Slovak boys were teasing him. They joked with him and said, "Hey, little Jew boy, you should go home. Your father just rose up from the dead!" He went home and he was disappointed.

ALAN: Did he regard the death of his father as a tragedy? Or was it just a fact?

ROBIN: I don't think it registered as an emotional event. It was just part of his history.

Saving Fanči & Stefan

ALAN: Could you tell me a little bit about Rudi's half sister. Fanči?

ROBIN: She was from the [father's] first marriage. I think Fanči was a nickname, short for Francine or something. Or Fanny. Anyway, she was an interesting person. She was married to a bank manager. In order to stop him from getting deported to Auschwitz, the head of the bank accused Fanči's husband of embezzling funds. That was totally not true. But the accusation was made to save the family. After Bedrick – Rudi's half brother-in-law – was accused of absconding with funds, that meant Bedrick had to go to prison to await trial. I think it was in Nitra ... or a spa town. I can't remember exactly. But this was the way that Fanči's husband was able to avoid the first deportations. They had a son, Stefan, who had been born around 1941, I think.

When Rudi escaped from Auschwitz, he met up with Fanči in 1944. He put together false papers for the family. By this time, Bedrick was back in the town after the initial deportations. Rudi described for me how Fanči took those papers and said [imitating a haughty, imperious voice], "*I* don't use false papers!" [Laughing]

It was Stefan who later told us the rest of this story ... I guess Fanči must have kept those false papers because, at the last minute, there was another round of deportations from that town. That's when she and Bedrick used the false papers. To make sure Stefan would be safe.

They somehow arranged to have a peasant woman from one of the villages take Stefan away with her, back to her town, saying this was her illegitimate child. Her boyfriend broke up with her for saying this. She bonded with Stefan and Stefan bonded with her. After the war, Fanči wanted him back. But Stefan wanted to stay with the [adopted] mother. He was about four years old. They had bonded. Rudi had to get involved and he sorted it out. He sorted it out with the [peasant woman's] fiancé. He did it like a war hero. He did it with his uniform and his medals. So, Stefan went back to Fanči, but he was not very happy about it.

ALAN: So, Rudi's half-sister survived the war, but none of his half-brothers did.

ROBIN: Right. His brothers had already been deported by the time he got deported. He waved to one brother in Auschwitz. [In fact, this event occurred in Majdanek.]

ALAN: It's in the book.

ROBIN: His grandfather had been deported, too.

ALAN: One would assume there would be some bond between Rudi and his half-sister, Fanči, as the lone survivors.

ROBIN: Well, he was very good with children. He bonded with Stefan in Slovakia. Once he didn't even let Fanči know, and he took Stefan for a plane ride to Prague from Bratislava. And he never told her. What if the plane crashed? So, Stefan had a really good time with Rudi. Rudi was very good with children up to the age of six. When Stefan defected, I think Rudi signed for him [for entrance to Canada].

ALAN: When was that?

ROBIN: Probably in '68. I'm not sure about that.

ALAN: How well did you get to know Rudi's nephew? [Stefan Horny, 1942–2016]

ROBIN: Not very well. Rudi would go to Montreal every year and they would have a reunion. But he never took me. I don't think he really wanted me involved. Then, when Rudi turned eighty, Stefan came to Vancouver. We had a lovely holiday. He was very entertaining.

Rudi had this old, gigantic Cadillac. He *loved* that car. He did not like people to drive that car. He'd park it a mile away so nobody would scratch it. It was like a boat. Stefan was in the Army, and he was designated as a military driver. So, Rudi let him drive the car because he was a military driver. [Laughter] It was very funny.

We went to Butchart Gardens. Rudi was not very healthy. He could still walk but it wasn't great. But even Rudi had a good time. He wasn't too happy about having that party, but in the end, he really enjoyed it. We went for high tea.

ALAN: It's funny to see the three of you going to Butchart Gardens in a gigantic Cadillac.

ROBIN: We didn't go there in the Cadillac. We went to the mountains in the Cadillac.

ALAN: What color was it?

ROBIN: White.

ALAN: I hope you have some pictures.

ROBIN: There are a couple. When Gerta's neighbors came to Vancouver, we arranged to meet them at the Teahouse restaurant in Stanley Park. They parked a rental car and said, "Look at that white Cadillac," with their English accents. "It's so big!" And then they met Rudi in the restaurant. He said, "Where did you park?" They said, "Oh, we parked next to this gigantic, white Cadillac!" Rudi said, "That's mine." [Laughter]

ALAN: And you were the one telling me only the history matters.

ROBIN: He was really charming.

ALAN: It's little things that can help people become interested in the big things.

ALAN: When you met Gerta for the Vrba-Wetzler Trek, was it easy to talk?

ROBIN: Yes. She had lived in London for decades. She was very educated.

ALAN: I meant were you able to discuss things such as Rudi's mother?

ROBIN: She liked her. She called her grandma. After Rudi died, I think Gerta changed a lot of her stories in her mind. She was working on his legacy. Before that, she hated him. She wanted to bury him! [Laughter] People tell themselves stories. And those stories can change.

ALAN: You mean, after she hated him for decades, Gerta turned around to become pro-Rudi?

ROBIN: Yes. After Rudi died, Gerta was working with Zuza to make the Trek, and she was doing a lot of testimonies about the Holocaust. A lot of the interviews were about Rudi. Her [two] books were mainly important because they were [partially] about him. Otherwise, they

First wife Gerta, in Prague and London.

were not that interesting. Although she did escape from Czechoslovakia, dragging those kids up and down the mountains, and it was pretty dangerous. Pretty bold. Zuza told me that when she [Gerta] was being interviewed, it was really tough for her, having to say all these nice things about Rudi. [Laughter]

ALAN: Well, she certainly doesn't say many nice things about him in her books.

ROBIN: He read the first book, and Zuza told him about the second book. Zuza said to her mother, "Why are you going into the bedroom for the second book?" That was really unnecessary. She [Gerta] hated him! She really hated him. You can see it, right?

ALAN: Absolutely. Therefore, I don't think her book is a reliable barometer.

ROBIN: Well, I'm sure he was very promiscuous. And that really destroys a lot of relationships. It depends how the person takes it. And she was a Type A personality. She was competing with him. He wasn't really an A personality. He was more like a C+. He was competitive. But he was more like a lover than a barracuda. And she was kind of like a barracuda.

ALAN: But they were also very young. And they were both survivors [of Nazi persecution].

ROBIN: You're right. They both had gone through huge trauma.

ALAN: And suddenly there are two children to look after.

ROBIN: Zuza said a lot of things to me about her parents, and she did say, "I don't know how my parents ever got together – they were too much alike." Rudi would have been very angry with me if he knew I had become friendly with Gerta after he died. But I did. And I really liked her. I didn't talk to her about anything in any depth. I didn't talk about all the things Rudi had accused her of and hated her for. She tried to get me into conversations, and I just played simple. I went around it. Because I didn't think it was necessary to go into that. What was the point for me? To accuse her of things he had accused her of? I didn't do it. I was just sweet with her.

ALAN: You were much younger. Was she at all condescending to you?

ROBIN: No, she was really nice to me.

ALAN: She could tell herself, "Well, he's just married this young, pretty thing – and I really knew him much better."

ROBIN: I went to her 90th birthday party [2017]. I sat next to her. She almost treated me like I was her daughter. I stayed in her house. I was invited. It was kind of crazy that I went but I went anyway. [Laughter] You know, I think I was also very much missing Rudi. It was like a connection. And Zuza had died. And I had connected with her, and she was gone. So, that was a connection with Rudi. And Stefan had died. The only connection I had left was Gerta. I think it was a good thing for my grief.

ALAN: That could be a good place to start a movie of your life. And everything would be done in a flashback. [Laughter] It's poignant, just the two of you.

ROBIN: I was already in New York by that time. I flew to London. But, also, they had a celebration in Slovakia for Rudi, so she got me invited to that. I met her there, too. Like Rudi, she spoke probably eight languages.

Daughters

Zuza and Helena gather with their father for a formal photo. "They had told the girls that Rudi was dead." – Robin Vrba

ALAN: What was Zuza's view of her sister's so-called suicide?

ROBIN: Oh, it swung. I mean, she was devastated, totally devastated. Because Helena was almost like her mother. Her mother wasn't really like her mother. Gerta treated the children sort of like they were grown-ups, so it was Helena who sort of mothered Zuza. Gerta wasn't very nurturing with the children. And I think Helena resented that a bit. She took care of Zuza a lot.

But Helena tricked Zuza once. When they went to England, Helena said, "I'm not going to learn English!" So, Zuza said, "Well, I'm not going to learn English either." Meanwhile, Helena secretly learned English. [Laughter] So, she did things like that.

ALAN: But what about Helena's supposed suicide?

ROBIN: It was a grief that didn't really end. Zuza was devastated. It damaged her whole life. Sometimes she thought it was murder.

ALAN: Was she interested in getting to the bottom of it? Like Rudi was?

ROBIN: Zuza sent her significant other there [to Papua, New Guinea, to investigate]. Actually, Gerta sent him. But he was useless. He couldn't really follow what was happening. To be fair, that's a very strange country, too.

Helena was working for the natives, giving malaria treatments in the villages. The witch doctors were probably not that happy having this woman there. And there were huge politics going on in the [medical science] institute. Helena had had an affair with her department head. It's very confusing. I had a vision that it was a murder, but who knows?

ALAN: How well did you get to know Zuza?

ROBIN: We were actually friends. After Rudi had passed away, they were putting that placard for Rudi and Wetzler on Hippopotamus Hill, so they invited Zuza and me to come. I mean, they didn't pay for us but ... I met Zuza in Bratislava at the airport. We rented a car, and I drove around Slovakia. We stayed in a number of different places.

ALAN: And Zuza came out to Vancouver and stayed with you? When Rudi was dying?

ROBIN: Yes, she did. I'll never forget that Rudi asked her to look after me, after he died.

ALAN: What is your sense of Zuza's character?

ROBIN: She was a lovely personality. Like, *really* charming. She was very articulate and she was very connecting. People were really magnetized by her. I thought she was very attractive. People said that Helena was attractive, but I thought Zuza was more attractive. And she was kind of a hippie. A free spirit.

ALAN: She had more than a little bit of Rudi in her ...

ROBIN: Oh, yeah. Did I tell you that story when he met the two girls in London? Gerta left the two girls when she went to work. She left them in the yard by themselves. Did I tell you that story? He went there. And Helena remembered him. But they [Gerta and her husband] had told the girls he was dead. So, Rudi went to the fence and he saw them. Zuza was frightened. Helena said, "Zuza, that's Papa." She went over and looked at him. She said, "You're even more beautiful than you were in Prague."

ALAN: Very nice.

ROBIN: Both of them, I think, were attached to him. Helena told me a story. He took them for a trip to California. They were on this mountain road. And he was a terrible driver. There was a big cliff on one side. He didn't want to drive on the dangerous side. So, he drove on the wrong side of the road, all the way down the cliff. [Laughter] I said to her, "Weren't you afraid?" Helena said, "I was petrified."

Then she said there was a policeman who stopped them, about halfway down. And he said to Rudi, "Where do you think you are? In bloody England?" So, Helena said something, and then he [the policeman] thought they must be English. Then the police car escorted them down the rest of the winding highway. When Helena told me the story, she was just laughing.

ALAN: It's lovely that he was able to have that time with the two of them, together.

ROBIN: Every chance he could, he tried to see them. When he was in England, he had to go to court to fight for access to the girls. So, he had them every fortnight. He was with them every other weekend. They really loved him. Zuza used to come [to Vancouver]. I was more comfortable with Zuza than with Helena. Zuza was very down to earth. I was comfortable with her right away. Rudi and I would play tennis with her, and she was kind of jealous of Rudi and me, and things like that.

I told you the story when I told her to go for a walk to Wreck Beach? [Wreck Beach is a hard-to-get-to, nudist beach at the foot of cliffs, adjoining the University of British Columbia campus.]

ALAN: No, you didn't.

ROBIN: She came to visit us for a couple of weeks. I was 26 and she was 22. Not that much difference. She asked me what to do. I said, "Well, you know it's kind of interesting." She asked me to drop her off there and I said sure. I dropped her off at the beginning of the beach, and I told her where to walk. Then I get a phone call at about four o'clock at work. It's Rudi saying, "Where's Zuza?" I said I dropped her off at Wreck Beach ...

There was such a conniption! How could you drop the child at Wreck Beach? He treated her just like she was a child. He was screaming at me. I actually couldn't finish work. I was crying. I came home, and he was angry with me that I was just so irresponsible with the child ... And when she got back, she said, "It was horrible. I got lost!" Then he got even angrier with me. Years later, I told Zuza the story and, she said, "Sorry, Robin." [Laughter] She had found her way back eventually.

ALAN: Was this because part of it was a nude beach?

ROBIN: Well, I thought it would be interesting.

ALAN: What about later on?

ROBIN: After Helena died, Zuza came with her children, and they stayed with us in our apartment for about a month. I used to take her little girl to work with me.

ALAN: Did Zuza come to understand her mother had tried to give them a jaundiced view of Rudi?

ROBIN: Oh, I think she knew it all along. In fact, I don't think Zuza really liked Gerta [her mother]. She loved Rudi. Zuza was very pro-Rudi. She was very much a fan of his. [Hence, it was Zuza who had the original idea to have the Vrba-Wetzler Trek.] And she really hated Sidney Hilton [her stepfather]. She told me how cheap he was with the apples and things like that.

ALAN: Helena didn't feel that way so much?

ROBIN: No, she didn't.

ALAN: Would his daughters ever have wanted to come to Vancouver?

ROBIN: To live? Permanently? No, they had their lives. And they were English. And they were going through their things. Helena was an MD with a PhD in diabetes. She had a really good career ahead of her. Zuza had her degree in geology, and she was *so* personable! Such a good personality. In the end, she knew Rudi loved her.

Rosin & Mordowicz

ROBIN: Rosin loved Rudi. He really liked him. But Rosin was a thief. He had been a professional thief before the war. [Laughter] And he was a *lovely* person. Really lovely. Helena Karsai met Rosin, too. In Cologne. She liked him.

ALAN: She gave me some pictures of them together.

ROBIN: For a long time, Rudi thought Rosin was dead. We were in Canada, and it must have been in the 80s. Rudi got a message. Maybe it was a telegram. It said that Rosin was in Toronto. And Rudi realized it wasn't Rosin who had died. It was the brother.

Rosin was very funny. One time we were walking, and there was a bike path and a pedestrian path. Some bikes were on the pedestrian path. I was confused. "Where do we go?" I said. Rosin just said, "It's both. Mixed." The way it came out was funny.

ALAN: They split into pairs when they were hiding out in Bratislava, and Rudi chose to be with Rosin – not Wetzler.

ROBIN: That's right. There's a funny story about that. When Rosin escaped from Auschwitz, he took a roll of dimes.

ALAN: He must have stolen them! [Laughter]

ROBIN: It was a roll of gold dimes. So, later, when Rudi and Rosin were roommates, in Bratislava, Rosin was out of the apartment, right? This was just before Rudi went to the partisans. Rudi wanted to give his mother something. So, he stole two dimes from that package. Rudi took those two dimes, and he gave them to his mother ...

ALAN: Maybe he told himself if you steal from a thief, it's not really stealing.

ROBIN: [Laughter] When they reunited after the war, Rosin said, "How come you only took the two dimes? There was a whole roll." And Rudi said, "How did you know I took them?" And Rosin said, "Who would only take two? Most people would have taken the whole roll! [Laughter] Only you would just take two."

Rudi's mother had kept them in her safety deposit box. When she died, I got them ... So, when Rosin was in Toronto, he asked for his money back. And we wired him the money. I still have those two dimes.

ALAN: Do you think [Ceslav] Mordowicz was jealous of Rudi because Rudi got all the attention?

ROBIN: With Mordowicz, I'm not sure where the anger came from. Partly, it must have been because Rudi felt that Mordowicz took money from [Slovakian-born mining magnate Stephen Boleslav] Roman. He was not happy about that. Mordowicz went from Canada to Israel, and I think Rudi thought he had taken money from Roman. But I'm not sure. And Mordowicz was not Slovak, right?

ALAN: People might think Rudi must be braver because Rudi went back to fight with the partisans, but it was really Mordowicz who had a much more harrowing path. He got recaptured and had to chew off his tattoo. He went back to Auschwitz a second time!

ROBIN: I understand that. Look what he went through …

ALAN: History makes it look like Rudi was the braver guy, but actually Mordowicz went through the far worse hell.

Vrba & Fredy Hirsch

ALAN: During the lead-up to the liquidation of the Czech Family Camp, Rudi was the go-between for the Underground and Fredy Hirsch …

ROBIN: Regarding Fredy Hirsch, Rudi doesn't mention him too often. I think he was disgusted by how he acted. I've been taking a course on the Hindu *Gita* [700-verse *Bhagavad Gita*] and part of it reminded me of the story of Fredy Hirsch. I actually wrote an article on it, but I never did anything with it.

ALAN: What is the gist?

ROBIN: The *Gita* is about the Avatar, who is a god, and that's Krishna, and he arrives during a war. The character called Arjuna is supposed to be a metaphor for human beings. Part of Arjuna's family has stolen the crown and the family is split. The part of the family that stole the crown is considered evil. Arjuna is a top warrior, and it is his job to reclaim the crown. And he is given a choice. He can either have Krishna's Army on his side or he can have Krishna as his chariot driver. He doesn't know that Krishna is an avatar. He just liked him. He chooses Krishna, and the opposing side is really pleased. By default, they get all of Krishna's Army to fight with them. Arjuna comes into battle with his chariot, and he sees his family on the other side, his teacher who he loves, and his uncle. Everyone is fighting. He knows he is going to win, but he will have to kill all these people he has loved. It's a moral dilemma. He can't decide, so he collapses in the chariot. He couldn't make a decision.

ALAN: Like Fredy Hirsch.

ROBIN: It resonated that way for me. I had shared that with the class I was taking, but they didn't really understand. Rudi was acting like an avatar, but he really wasn't an avatar. He couldn't motivate Fredy Hirsch. The god was able to motivate Arjuna, but Rudi wasn't the same as the god. It was just a comparison. I don't know if you want to see it.

ALAN: Sure. I'm curious about it. Rudi mentions Fredy Hirsch in the context of trying to mount an insurrection, but there was so much more to Fredy's character. For instance, Fredy Hirsch got along well with Mengele. Apparently, they even looked a bit similar.

ROBIN: I don't know anything about that. I know that mentally, Rudi was a soldier. Even when we were married, he was actually a warrior. And a warrior that collapses in a chariot [ie. Fredy Hirsch] is not acceptable. It's just not acceptable. Rudi saw that happen a lot of times – when people collapsed. He also saw that when he was with the partisans ...

Vrba & Mengele

[While looking at photographs via Zoom]

ROBIN: Do you see this one?

ALAN: I've never seen it before.

ROBIN: They were doing that program, *Auschwitz and the Allies*. I think Bestic wrote this article for *Radio Times*.

ALAN: But it's ...

ROBIN: Gerta saw it, and she called them. She called *Radio Times* and said, "That's not my ex-husband."

ALAN: I was gonna say ... but ...

ROBIN: By mistake, they had used a photo of Mengele [Josef Mengele]. Is that even possible? Could they really have made a mistake like that? It was 1981. Or '82.

ALAN: As someone who ran a newspaper for 30 years, the answer is: Yes. Mistakes like that can easily happen.

ROBIN: They were very nervous that Rudi was going to sue them.

Rudolf Vrba spent hundreds of hours watching Dr. Josef Mengele on the so-called *Alte Judenrampe* at Auschwitz-Birkenau, making his selections, deciding who went to the left and was murdered and who went to the right and lived. *"I myself was almost always present at the unloading of the transports and at the 'selection' performed at each occasion by the SS-doctors. I do not know exactly how many times I witnessed the almost identical scenario, but it was certainly more than 100 times and certainly less than 300 times." – R.V.*

ALAN: What happened?

ROBIN: They wrote to him, asking for forgiveness. He wrote them back.

ALAN: What did he say?

ROBIN: "You don't have to worry about me suing you," Rudi said. "But you might have to worry about *Mengele* suing you."

APPENDIX 1

Timeline

1924 – Walter Rosenberg is born in Topoľčany, central Czechoslovakia on September 11.

1926 – His father, Elias Rosenberg, a timber exporter, moves the family to the remote village of Yaklovce Pika (also known as Jaklovce) in eastern Czechoslovakia, where he owns a steam sawmill and some adjacent forests.

1928 – His father dies of a liver ailment after his sawmill business falters. Later, Vrba recalled visiting his father's deathbed as a boy. His mother is unable to continue the family business.

1930–33 – Vrba's mother becomes a traveling saleswoman for female undergarments; Walter is placed in the care of maternal grandparents in Nitra. His grandfather Bernhard Grünfeld introduces him to Orthodox Judaism. Grünfeld's only son Alec had immigrated to the U.S., so Walter becomes a substitute son. The grandfather hopes Walter will become a rabbi.

1933 – Dachau is established as Hitler's first concentration camp, initially for political dissidents.

1934–37 – After Walter's grandmother suffers a bad fall, Walter is sent to a Jewish orphanage in Bratislava run by "Jewish Secular Authorities" [Vrba's description], as his mother increasingly has misgivings about her own father's influence. After two years, at the instigation of his mother, Walter passes the entrance exams for the Gymnasium (high school) in Bratislava.

1938 – Hitler demands Czechoslovakia surrender Sudetenland (or *Sudetengebiet*) to Germany. British Prime Minister Neville Chamberlain and French Prime Minister Édouard Daladier meet Hitler in Munich and announce "Peace in Our Time" in September. In November, *Kristallnacht* (Night of Broken Glass) unleashes lootings of Jewish businesses throughout Germany and Austria, the burning of synagogues and the murders of 91 Jews. Goebbels admits there were some isolated incidents of looting for Christmas trinkets and suggests all Jews should be prevented from using public parks. Heydrich suggests every Jew should wear a badge. Hitler suggests to Göring, leader of the Nazi Party, that all Jews could be forcibly resettled in Madagascar. In December, it is decreed that all Jewish businesses must be "Aryanized."

1939 – Czechoslovakia is partitioned; a quisling government makes Jews subject to the Nuremberg Laws; Walter is banished from classes and will live with his mother in Trnava (50 miles from Bratislava) for three years. Among the banished Jewish students who meet at "The Pond" in the nearby fields to educate themselves is a precocious younger student named Gerta Sidonová, his future wife, who was born in Trnava, Czechoslovakia, in 1926.

1939–1942 – Forced to work as a laborer in Trnava, Walter wears a yellow Star of David but disobeys Slovak People's Party orders and teaches himself (and Gerta) chemistry, as well as foreign languages. Meanwhile, his mother has remarried to a Jewish clerk, Ignaz Reichsfeld.

1940 – With its first crematorium from the firm of Topf & Söhne, the original Auschwitz camp implements a new mass murder system less upsetting for the German soldiers stationed there, achieving a "performance rate" of more than 100 corpses a day.

1942 – Deportation of Jewish families begins on April 11; there are five main transit camps in Slovakia (Patrónka, Nováky, Poprad, Sered', Žilina) through which approximately two-thirds of the Jewish Slovakian population (approximately 80,000) will be deported via 57 transports (March 25, 1942 to October 20, 1942). Some 57,628 Jews are removed in seven months.

1942 (March) – Appalled at the prospect of being "deported like a calf in a wagon," Walter, at 17, rips the yellow Star of David from his shoulder and sets off in a taxi from his hometown of Trnava toward the border, hoping to reach Budapest in order to join British or Yugoslavian forces. He is eventually captured, badly beaten (twice) and taken to a barbed wire compound in Nováky where he is the youngest of several hundred men marooned inside a "resettlement camp." He vows to escape and he succeeds.

1942 (April) – Vrba's escape companion from Nováky fails to keep his word; Vrba is recaptured by a solo policeman with a bicycle. He is beaten by police and returned to Nováky, where he is beaten again.

1942 (June 14) – Vrba is deported to Majdanek, Poland, where he glimpses his brother, Sammy.

1942 (June 30) – Vrba volunteers to be transferred for "farmwork" at an unknown place called Auschwitz where he is tattooed as prisoner #44070.

1942–44 – Vrba works at a variety of jobs at Auschwitz I, II and III: as a Buna laborer (briefly), then as a *Judenrampe* laborer in the *Aufräumungkommando*. He is transferred on January 15, 1943 to Birkenau to work as a *Kanadakommando*. He gains the favorable job of registrar or *Blockschreiber* in the quarantine section for men in the summer of 1943 — he retains the job for 21 months and seven days. He estimates the death toll during that time at 1,760,000.

1944 (April 7) – Vrba commences his escape with Alfréd Wetzler.

1944 (April 10) – They commence their getaway trek back to Slovakia.

1944 (April 21) – The duo reaches Žilina, Czechoslovakia, where they are given refuge in the basement of a former old folks' home.

1944 (April 25) – The pair generate an (uncredited) report on the Auschwitz camps, providing a history of events prior to April of 1942. He soon assumes the *nom-de-guerre* Rudolf Vrba with a new birthdate on his identity papers, April 7, 1924, to recognize the date his escape began.

1944 (June) – The yet-to-be-named *Vrba-Wetzler Report* reaches the Allied governments in June 1944, but Jewish lawyer Rudolf Kasztner prefers to conduct private and self-serving negotiations with Eichmann rather than ensure all Hungarian Jews are made aware of their fate if they board the trains, as bidden by the Nazis.

1944 (summer) – Vrba reunites with teenage friend Gerta (or Gerti) Sidonová but they do not become lovers. She types a version of the *Vrba-Wetzler Report* for his secret meeting with the Papal Nuncio. The gist of this report will reach the Vatican and help save 200,000 Jews. None of her close relatives will survive the war. "Perhaps that summer," she later recalled, "Walter and I became as close as we would ever get, though the distance and barrier between us never disappeared. The friendship and trust we had shared before these fateful two years, which I so hoped would return, was never recaptured. Somewhere in Auschwitz, Walter had lost his capacity to trust anyone."

1944 (September) – Vrba joins the Czechoslovak Army's Partisan Units in a unit commanded by Sgt. Miloš Uher (Hero of the Slovak National Uprising); he swears allegiance to the Czechoslovakian government in exile in London, and he fights mainly alongside communists despite their widespread antisemitism.

1944 (November) – Having learned from Vrba about the fate of Jews who boarded the trains, Gerta makes the painful decision to abandon her mother as she leaps from a second story window to escape from the Gestapo headquarters in Bratislava.

1945 – Vrba continues with the partisans until war's end and subsequently receives the Czechoslovak Medal for Bravery, the Order of Slovak National Insurrection (Second Class) and Order of Meritorious Fighter. He legalizes his *nom-de-guerre* and gains entry to the Czech Technical University in Prague.

1947 – Partly at the behest of his mother, Helena, Vrba marries Gerta Sidonová, since orphaned, who accepts the surname Vrbová. The pair had studied together with two of her friends in order to receive high enough marks on university entrance exams to pursue careers.

1945–49 – Vrba is employed at the Department of Organic Chemistry, Czech Technical University, Prague. He graduates in Chemistry, Ing. Chem (Engineer of Chemistry) and receives a post-graduate fellowship in his final year.

1949–51 – Vrba is employed at the Dept. of Biochemistry & Fermentation, Czech Technical University, Prague.

1951–52 – Vrba receives his doctorate in Technical Science under supervisor A. Kleinzeller for a thesis entitled "On the metabolism of butyric acid." He is employed at the Dept. of Physiology, Czechoslovak Academy of Science, Prague, where he continues his biochemical research.

1952 – His first daughter, Helena Vrbová, is born, named after his mother (May 26).

1952–53 – He is employed at Penicillin Factory, Prague - Roztoky.

1953–58 – He conducts research at Charles University Medical School in Prague under Professor J. Teysinger. During this period, he is also employed at the Institute of Industrial Hygiene & Occupational Diseases, Ministry of Health, Prague. In 1956, he publishes "Metabolic changes in brain during physical exercise."

1954 – Second daughter Zuzana Vrbová is born in Prague (May 3).

1956 – Vrba receives a post-graduate degree from the Czechoslovak Academy of Science; he will produce more than 50 research papers on the chemistry of the brain with additional research work relevant to diabetes and cancer; Gerta is co-organizer of an international conference in Prague to discuss the influence of nerves on muscle at which she is attracted to English physiologist Sidney Hilton. He has come to Prague with his pregnant wife.

1957 – Vrba gains his first confirmation that his reportage with Wetzler saved lives when he reads *The Final Solution: The Attempt to Exterminate the Jews of Europe, 1939–1945* (Beechhurst Press, 1953); its British author Gerald Reitlinger suggests (only) 100,000 Hungarian Jews were spared and under-estimates the overall number of Jews killed during the Holocaust at (only) 4.2 to 4.5 million.

1958 – Having paid for her "emotionally damaging" divorce and found a flat for herself and the children (in 1956), then having visited Budapest (in 1957) where she felt people were still attached to "fascist ideas," Gerta illegally and dangerously crosses the Czechoslovak-Polish border, subjecting her two young daughters to a wilderness trek (unbeknownst to their father). Her goal is to re-unite with Hilton who will divorce his wife and marry her, but the trio of escapees will first end up being marooned in Sweden for a year.

1958–60 – Having been invited to attend an international conference in Israel, Vrba defects in 1958 and works as a biochemist in Israel. He is employed at Veterinary Research Institute, Ministry of Agriculture, Beth Dagan, Israel, during which time he has an affair with Baroness Bethsabée Louise Emilie Beatrix de Rothschild (who had assumed the first name Batsheva after moving to Israel in 1956) and she will remain a longtime friend.

1960 – Vrba receives money from Batsheva (who also becomes the main patron for the Martha Graham dance company) to marry a beautiful Swiss woman he has wooed in Israel, but he gets cold feet once he reaches Switzerland and meets her family.

1960–62 – With a Rockefeller Grant for research in neurochemistry, Vrba immigrates to Great Britain to work for the British Medical Research Council's Neuropsychiatric Research Unit, Carshalton, Surrey, U.K. for two years. This move will enable him to see his daughters again.

1961 – After Adolf Eichmann has been captured by Mossad in Buenos Aires and brought to Jerusalem, public interest in the trial of Nazi Adolf Eichmann results in five newspaper articles in a London daily paper by Rudolf Vrba, teamed with journalist Alan Bestic. Vrba also provides a written testimony for the Eichmann trial, disappointed not to be asked to appear in person.

1962 – Vrba works as a member of the Research Staff of British Medical Research Council in London from 1962 to 1967 and chiefly resides in a rented flat in Surrey. He becomes romantically involved with his former research assistant, Gillian Bryant, after she has helped him (in 1963) with (uncredited) research for an important article that he publishes in *Nature* (April 1964), *Utilization of Glucose Carbon In Vivo in the Mouse,* which is important for his career. Bryant also greatly assists in his rapprochement with daughters Helena and Zuza.

1963 – Vrba and journalist Alan Bestic co-write *I Cannot Forgive,* later retitled *I Escaped from Auschwitz.* Bryant, as one of the first readers of the manuscript, will reveal (in 2024) that the chapters were not written in the order they appear in the book. The book will appear in German (1964), French (1988), Dutch (1996) and Czech (1998).

1964 – Vrba appears as a witness at the Frankfurt Auschwitz trials. Bryant has become like a second mother to his daughters seeing them on a fortnightly basis, organizing joint outings, etc., and meanwhile Vrba also has a short-lived love affair with the Canadian artist Mary Filer. For the rest of his life Vrba will decorate his living quarters with a series of her sketches of him at work in his laboratory. She leaves and he resumes seeing Bryant.

1965 – As Vrba is preparing to emigrate, Bryant informs Vrba she is pregnant with his child. He is a reluctant, expectant father. Legalized arrangements are made for child support after she goes against the wishes of her friends and family, insisting she will have the child and continue to pursue her PhD. The fetus dies in utero after six-and-a-half months of pregnancy in 1965. It would have been a son.

1966 – Vrba becomes a naturalized British subject. According to future wife Robin Vrba, at some point he has an affair (more than a fling) with a beautiful academic from Scotland who wants to marry him.

1967 – In August, Vrba is appointed as an Associate of the Medical Research Council of Canada, via the University of British Columbia. Departing for Canada, Vrba intentionally leaves behind his Partisan medal with Bryant (who takes over his flat) because he does not wish immigration officials to ask any questions about his associations with Communists.

1967–72 – He chiefly teaches pharmacology. Subjects include anti-cancer agents, insulin and oral hypoglycemics, sex hormones and oral contraception, thyroid diseases, as well as anti-inflammatory, anti-allergic and immunosuppressive drugs.

1971–73 – In Vancouver, Vrba maintains a tempestuous sexual relationship with feminist playwright and single mother Betty Lambert, a Simon Fraser University lecturer who challenges him intellectually and sometimes attacks his male ego.

1972 – Vrba gains Canadian citizenship.

1973 – Vrba attends the Ninth International Congress of Biochemistry in Stockholm, Sweden and co-publishes a significant research paper with L.N. Epps and A. Winter. He also accepts a two-year position as a Visiting Lecturer on Pharmacology in the Department of Medicine, Harvard Medical School, as a Research Fellow in Medicine at the Gastrointestinal Research Unit, Massachusetts General Hospital, Boston.

1974 (April) – Vrba meets his future wife Robin Lipson at a party in Boston.

1975 (June) – Vrba receives the "substantial news" from his University of British Columbia (UBC) Faculty Dean David Bates that he will soon be accorded tenure within the pharmacology department.

1975 (September 13) – Vrba marries Robin Lipson in her parents' home in Boston, primarily at the behest of her father. She had been willing to go to Vancouver without being married. Vrba could remain at Harvard, but he rejects an offer to continue as a medical researcher in Boston, to be funded solely by grants; coincidentally, his half-sister Fanci takes up permanent residency in Montreal. There is a brief honeymoon in San Diego.

1975 (November 1) – As anticipated, Vrba receives "Appointment without Term" (aka tenure) for teaching Pharmacology at the Faculty of Medicine. Vrba has taken temporary lodgings near the university; now, for the first time since his infancy, he will have some financial security. The couple will reside at Penthouse 6, 5775 Toronto Road, on the UBC campus while he teachs as an Associate Professor of Pharmacology.

1978 – Filmmaker Claude Lanzmann literally begs on his knees (according to Robin Vrba) to get Vrba's cooperation for a Central Park interview in New York that is used extensively for the Holocaust documentary *Shoah* (1985). Vrba never signs a consent waiver for the interview; instead, he asks Lanzmann to promise to make a sizable donation to Hermann Langbein's International Auschwitz Committee (for which Vrba was listed as on the executive). Lanzmann never fulfills this promise. More than 30 years later, Lanzmann will make a fool of himself in a New York restaurant by drunkenly trying to fondle Vrba's widow during their business meeting with the Coen brothers to discuss a possible movie about Vrba.

1979 – Vrba commences a five-year stint as a member of the Editorial Board of the International Society for Neurochemistry, to be followed by a four-year stint as a member of the Admission Selection Committee for the Faculty of Medicine at UBC.

1981 – Future friend and supporter Martin Gilbert publishes *Auschwitz and the Allies.*

1982 – Having returned to Papua, New Guinea for a second term as a malaria researcher and public health coordinator, Dr. Helena Vrba deliberately takes an overdose of malaria prevention medicine after having driven her married lover to the airport. Seemingly distraught because he is returning to Australia to be with his family, she commits suicide in their love shack on the beach. The body is shipped back to London. Rudolf Vrba is deeply affected and suspects foul play. Years later Zuza will show Gillian Bryant-Greenwood her sister's suicide note. Vrba is guilt-ridden because he had harshly forewarned her not to go back to New Guinea, whereupon she had cut off communications with him.

1985 – In January, Vrba takes over as the chief prosecution witness for the Toronto trial of Holocaust denialist Ernst Zundel after historian Raul Hilberg was rattled in the witness stand. Zundel is convicted. Interviewed in his laboratory at UBC, in August, by Maurice Samuelson of the Jewish Telegraph Agency, Vrba expresses criticism of the Canadian Jewish establishment for its nervous reluctance to bring the pro-Nazi apologist Zundel to trial. The case had to be led by the independent Holocaust Remembrance Association, headed by Sabina Citron, an Auschwitz survivor. "From experience," Vrba says, "we know that by pretending the Nazis do not exist we will not make them disappear. Instead, they will just be able to behave more uninhibitedly."

1987 – In December, Vrba is visited by "Franz Marmalade," the Viennese *kapo* who had bought him for a lemon and enabled him to work at the SS food store. "I owed my life to Franz," he wrote.

1988 – Alfréd Wetzler dies in Slovakia.

1989 – Along with the courageous diplomat George Mandel Mantello, Vrba goes to Detroit to receive a Righteousness Award. The keynote speaker is Michigan Governor James Blanchard.

1991 – Vrba attends an investiture ceremony at Hippopotamus Hill, Slovakia, with Robin Vrba, for a new plaque honoring his services as a partisan, along with the services of Alfréd Wetzler.

1992 – The American Holocaust denialist David Irving assists Ernst Zundel in a retrial and the American Holocaust expert Christopher Browning takes over as the main prosecution witness. Again, Zundel is convicted. Four years later, the Supreme Court of Canada votes 4–3 in favor of Zundel's acquittal.

1993 – Vrba receives "Laufberger Medal for Physiology" from the Czech Academy of Science and Medical Society in Prague.

1994 – Vrba provides a presentation for a conference at the United States Holocaust Memorial Museum in Washington, D.C. to mark the 50th anniversary of the Hungarian Holocaust and challenges the audience to ascertain who is the better historian — "those of us who saw the Nazis in action in Auschwitz" or "those who did not have direct experience of the Nazis?"

1995 – Vrba attends the 50th anniversary of the liberation of Pilsen, [Plzeň] in Czechia by the U.S. Army in May of 1945.

1997 – Gerta informs Vrba in a "Dear Rudo" letter dated February 22, 1998, that she has had a slight heart attack, and she references monetary needs and their daughter Zuza's struggles.

1998 – Correspondence (from solicitor Jo Goldby of the law firm Theodore Goddard) notifies Vrba that he and Gerta will each receive 6,707 pounds from their daughter Helena's estate.

1998 – Vrba receives an honorary doctorate, Doctor of Philosophy, Honoris Causa, at the University of Haifa [shown above] "in recognition of his heroism and daring in exposing the horrors of Auschwitz during the war, which led to the saving of Jewish lives, and in profound appreciation of his educational contribution and devotion to spreading knowledge about the Holocaust." This unprecedented recognition within Israel is instigated by Ruth Linn. A translation of his book is finally made available in Hebrew for Israeli readers.

2001 – The Rudolf Vrba Award for films about human rights is established in Prague for the One World International Human Rights Documentary

Film Festival under the auspices of Mary Robinson, United Nations High Commissioner of Human Rights and Czech Republic President Václav Havel. The festival continues to exist, but the prize named in honor of Vrba does not.

2004 – Ruth Davis of the Czech and Slovak Jewish Communities Archive states the *Vrba-Wetzler Report* ought to be credited with saving 200,000 lives, a figure endorsed by historian Sir Martin Gilbert shortly before he died. This has since become the standard estimate.

2006 – Rudolf Vrba dies of bladder cancer at home with Robin and daughter Zuza in attendance (March 27). Auschwitz demons resurface during his suffering and hallucinations. Vrba is attended by his friend, Dr. Arthur Dodek, a Vancouver cardiologist and GIM (General Internal Medicine) doctor who accompanied him to medical appointments. Zuza Jackson (née Vrbová) had stayed with her father and Robin for three months prior to the death.

2008 – The first annual Rudolf Vrba Memorial Lecture is held at the Frederic Wood Theatre at the University of British Columbia on November 30, hosted by Prof. Chris Friedrichs, with reminiscences from Prof. John Conway and nephew Dr. Stefan Horny. The inaugural Keynote Lecture is presented by Ruth Linn of Haifa University: "Genocide and the Psychology of Memory: The Case of Rudolf Vrba."

2013 – Before Zuza Jackson (née Vrbová), dies in Cambridge (September 17), she proposes an annual Vrba-Wetzler Trek to honor her father.

2014 – The annual Vrba-Wetzler Trek is inaugurated. Vrba's two wives will participate the following year.

2017 – Robin Vrba attends Gerta's 90th birthday party in London.

2020 – Robin Vrba and Nikola Zimring co-edit a new version of *I Escaped from Auschwitz* with new maps. Fearing criticism due to one error regarding an undocumented visit to Auschwitz by Himmler, the pair decide to leave out Rudolf Vrba and Alan Bestic's brilliant opening chapter "When the Music Stopped."

2021 – A Slovak film directed by Peter Bebjak makes a laudable attempt to achieve the impossible – representing the grim reality of Auschwitz-Birkenau within an entertaining movie – but this fictionalized version of the escape and report leans heavily in favor of a character meant to represent Alfréd Wetzler and misrepresents the character one assumes is meant to represent Rudolf Vrba. The lopsidedness of the Slovak movie only makes sense if one knows Vrba's wife was unwilling to grant film rights because a Los Angeles-based film project based, on Vrba's story, was in development. The Bebjak movie consequently depicts the younger escapee as an ineffectual character.

2022 – Jonathan Freedland's faux-thriller *The Escape Artist*, packaged as airport fiction, is closely modeled on Vrba's autobiographical account. In cruder terms, anyone who cares to read both books can be excused for using the slang term rip-off. Robin Vrba's brother, a lawyer, identifies 88 instances of alleged plagiarism. Despite competing film projects, she opts to not attempt a lawsuit against the well-connected journalist.

2023 – After generating a million-word website about Rudolf Vrba, Alan Twigg contacts Robin Vrba and commences a series of interviews that last for the next year-and-a-half. With her consent, Rudolf Vrba's private papers are examined and copied at the Franklin Delano Roosevelt Presidential Library in New York State in 2023 and 2024.

2024 – Vrba's long-time nemesis in Israel, historian Yehuda Bauer, dies on October 18, at age 98.

2025 – Research for this biography uncovers proof that *Reichsführer* Heinrich Himmler did indeed visit Auschwitz in mid-July of 1942. This squelches any claims from Holocaust denialists that Vrba & Bestic's opening chapter [first published in *I Cannot Forgive*, 1963] could be disregarded as fiction. During ten years of negotiation to have his book finally published in Czechoslovakia, Vrba was forced to jettison that riveting chapter in order to have his memoir made available in his native land. Later, when a Czech academic and Robin Vrba oversaw its re-publication in English in 2020, they cautiously deferred to the Czech version because they, too, were unable to find proof that Himmler had visited Auschwitz on July 17, 1942.

In fact, Vrba had his facts right …

In the first chapter of the original version of *I Cannot Forgive* (1963), Vrba described his face-to-face encounter with Heinrich Himmler by writing "… he passed closed to me, close enough for me to touch him, and for a moment our eyes met." Having been in Auschwitz for 17 days,

Vrba was still very fit and therefore he had been placed in the front row for Himmler's inspection ... There is now inconvertible evidence that Himmler – after he made his first visit to Auschwitz with construction chief Karl Bischoff and the SS architect Fritz Ertl in 1941 – returned in mid-July, 1942 to inspect development of "I.G. Auschwitz." Proof has been found in the construction journal that was kept by Buna's chief construction engineer Maximilian Faust. He noted in his weekly report: "July 18. Visit from the Reichsführer SS with a big entourage, including Obergruppenführer Schmauser und Obersturmbannführer Höss, to whom the Reichsführer SS personally conveyed his promotion to Obersturmbannführer. The Reichsführer was greeted by the undersigned at the Feierabendhaus. Then we drove to the powerhouse and, from the vantage point of the high-rise bunker, gave our high-ranking visitor an overview of the entire plant, explaining the complex as a whole by using a site plan prepared for this purpose ..." This excerpt [above] is from Wochenbericht [weekly report] No. 60/61 for the period July 13–26, 1942, sgd. Faust, NI-14551. Archive of the Fritz Bauer Institute, Subsequent Nuremberg Trials, Case VI, Prosecution Exhibit 1991, reel 033, pp. 353–355, here p. 354. (Transl. KL)

Corroboration for the evidence in Faust's notebook was then found in "Genesis of the Camp," the first section of an essay by Danuta Czech called *Konzentrationslager Auschwitz – A Historical Outline* within *Auschwitz Nazi Extermination Camp,* a very detailed but seldom-cited publication by Interpress Publishers in Warsaw in 1978, supported by the Council for the Protection of Monuments of Struggle and Martyrdom. Danuta Czech (1922–2004) was a highly respected Polish Holocaust historian as well as the deputy director of the Auschwitz-Birkenau State Museum in Oświęcim. Her essential essay on the origins of the Auschwitz concentration camp states on page 22 that Reichsführer SS Himmler came to Oswiecim for the first time on March 1, 1941 accompanied by SS-Brigadeführer Fritz Bracht, SS-Obergruppenführer Ernst Schmauser, SS-Oberführer Glicks and representatives of IG Farben. Then, on pages 27–28, Danuta Czech the states, "On 17–18 July 1942, Himmler visited Oswiecim for a second time accompanied by [SS-Brigadeführer Fritz] Bracht, [SS-Obergruppenführer Ernst] Schmauser and the chief of

Front row: SS-Reichsführer Heinrich Himmer (left) listens to Max Faust (fedora) along-side Auschwitz commander Rudolf Höss during Himmler's two-day visit to Auschwitz, July 17–18, 1942.

Amtsgruppe C of WVHA, SS-Gruppenführer Heinz Kammler, who was in charge of construction for the concentration camps, the army, the SS and Police, as well as the armaments industry." The two-day visit is re-confirmed by Franciszek Piper, chair of the Historical Department at the Auschwitz-Birkenau State Museum, on page 115, who confirms the presence of Bracht and Schmauser but omits Kammler. There are at least three photos of Faust guiding Himmler.

APPENDIX II

The Genesis of Auschwitz

AUSCHWITZ BEGAN AS an old-fashioned prison. It was never initially conceived as an industrialized murder site. Yet it became mankind's most infamous murder factory consisting of three distinct camps with separate administrations and functions. Rudolf Vrba was a rare survivor of all three places:

Konzentrationlager Auschwitz 1 – *Stammlager*
Konzentrationlager Auschwitz 2 – *Birkenau*
Konzentrationlager Auschwitz 3 – *Aussenlager*

Today, Auschwitz is a global tourist destination where you can visit vestiges of Auschwitz I and Auschwitz II (Birkenau). Lesser-known, but largest by far in terms of its geographical size, was Auschwitz III, an industrial complex known as the Buna-Werke or Monowitz (a German variation for the village of *Monowice*). Now barely recognizable, its once-massive presence has been obviated by urban sprawl.

As Nazism spread like a cancer beyond Germany and Austria, mass arrests of the local population in southwestern Poland were deemed necessary to maintain control. By 1939, prisons in Upper Silesia and the Dabrowa Basin were full. The Nazis knew more arrests would be necessary to stem the rise of an intensifying resistance movement.

To alleviate the over-crowding of prisons, the Nazis formed a commission headed by SS-Oberführer Arpad Wigand to address the problem.

In January 1940, SS-Oberführer Richard Glücks, the newly appointed director of the Concentration Camps Inspectorate, subsequently sent a small delegation, led by SS-Sturmbannführer Walter Eisfeld, to inspect an abandoned Polish military barracks.

Eisfeld found a derelict wooden shell near the fork of the Vistula and Sola Rivers, at the village of Oświęcim, about twenty miles southeast of Katowice. According to the most notorious Auschwitz commandant, Rudolf Franz Ferdinand Höss, during statements he made during his Warsaw war crime trial, the disused barracks at Oświęcim were deemed uninhabitable by Glücks.

Reichsführer Heinrich Himmler consequently ordered inspections to be made beyond the immediate Oswęicim vicinity. Himmler had only promoted Glücks to the post of Concentration Camps Inspector on November 15, 1939 after Glücks' boss, Theodor Eicke, had become field commander of the SS Division Totenkopf.

The situation changed on January 25 when Himmler accepted a contrary, favorable report on the Oświęcim barracks by SS-Gruppenführer von dem Bach-Zelewski, whereupon Glücks opted to contradict his earlier report. Glücks conceded those former barracks at Oświęcim could be adapted as a "quarantine camp" whereby Polish prisoners could be detained temporarily until they could be sent to concentration camps inside Germany. Glücks had an "almost unbelievable fear" of Himmler, according to Höss, and was therefore motivated to give Himmler the answer he most wanted to hear.

Another commission, this time headed by SS-Hauptsturmführer Höss, visited Oświęcim in mid-April and submitted a favorable report that speculated that a camp at Oświęcim could detain 10,000 prisoners. Consequently, Himmler gave an order on April 27 for Höss and five SS men to go to the site and commence preliminary construction. He was designated as the Commandant of *Konzentrationslager Auschwitz* on May 4, 1940.

~

ESCORTED BY THE notorious sadist Rapportführer Gerhard Palitzsch, the first thirty prisoners arrived at Oświęcim, renamed Auschwitz, on May 20, 1940. These prisoners were not Jews. They were convicted German criminals from the Sachsenhausen prison camp in Oranienburg, 22 miles north of Berlin. Accorded green triangles on their tunics and serial numbers from 1 to 30 – but no tattoos – these criminals would soon be designated as camp disciplinarians whose chief occupation would be to oppress and terrify the other prisoners in order to maintain order in the camp.

Prisoner #1 at Auschwitz was Bruno Brodniewicz, soon to be nicknamed "The Black Death." He was camp elder in the Gypsy section of Auschwitz and then he worked in four satellite camps and ended up in Bergen-Belsen where he was reputedly lynched by inmates as soon as the camp was liberated in April 1945. "Brodniewicz was a beast," said fellow Green kapo Willi Brachmann [according to Hermann Langbein], "He was king of the camp. What he ordered had to be done."

On June 14, 1940, a transport of 728 Polish political prisoners arrived from Tarnów, in southeastern Poland, and received the next set of prisoner numbers from 31 to 758. Among them would be the first person to escape from Auschwitz, prisoner #220, a Pole named Tadeusz Wiejowski. Born in Kołaczyce in 1914, Wiejowski was a professional shoemaker. Disguised as a village laborer, he escaped on July 6, 1940 when he accompanied members of the Polish resistance movement who were hired as local "civilian workers" for the nascent site. He remained in hiding in his hometown for more than a year before he was apprehended in the autumn of 1941. According to the Auschwitz Museum, he was not identified as an escapee from Auschwitz during interrogation but was shot soon afterwards.

In the aftermath of Wiejowski's first escape, camp officials soon enforced an edict of collective responsibility – sometimes killing one-tenth of those associated in any superficial way with the escapee. Beatings and torture became commonplace for those had any dealings or friendships with an escapee or a would-be escapee. As a result, the Polish underground, inside and outside the camp, soon adopted a policy of not assisting in escape attempts until 1943 – by which time camp authorities had stopped punishing families of escapees as well as their comrades in the camp. Only after someone did manage to successfully escape, would the Polish underground assist.

The Auschwitz administration also saw fit to evict most of the Polish population in the surrounding area, without compensation, and allotted their homes, in some cases, to the families of SS guards. The eviction of Poles within a "Zone of Interest" (Interessengebiet) for approximately 40 square kilometers around the camp served to limit the probability of success for any escape attempts simply because most of the local inhabitants were now Nazi loyalists.

By mid-1940, the Auschwitz staff was bolstered by the arrival of 100 SS men, plus officers and SS-Obersturmführer Josef Kramer from Mauthausen. Later dubbed the Beast of Belsen, Kramer would ascend the ladder of tyranny to become Commandant of Auschwitz-Birkenau (May-to-November, 1944) and Bergen Belsen (December 1944-April 1945) before he was hanged in December of 1945.

Initially, neither Auschwitz nor its spin-off Auschwitz-Birkenau were conceived for the mass murder of Jews.

The first major infusion of captives in the Auschwitz-Birkenau compound consisted of 10,000 Soviet prisoners in the autumn of 1941. After they were installed in rudimentary conditions, only a few hundred of those Soviet soldiers would be alive after five months. During this period, experiments to murder Soviet captives with Zyklon B commenced, overseen by the ambitious Auschwitz commander Höss.

Józef Paczynski, a Polish political prisoner at Auschwitz, witnessed some of Höss' initial murder experiments to kill Soviet POWs with the use of Zyklon B near Höss' office headquarters at Auschwitz I: "I went into the attic. I stood on a crate. I lifted a roof tile and I could see everything that was going on right there in front of me. They were very polite with those people, very polite. 'Undress, pack your things here, this here, that there …' Then an SS man climbed onto the flat roof of the building. He put on a gas mask, opened a hatch, and dropped the crystals in."

Similar experiments were conducted with more secrecy at a cottage outside the camp known as the Little Red House, or Bunker 1, where windows and doors were replaced by bricks. A second nearby structure called the Little White House was built for more gassing experiments. it was this converted house, called Bunker 2, that would be used to impress Himmler with the gassing procedure during his two-day visit in July 1942. Hence, the genesis for the mass murder of Jews on a daily basis at Auschwitz-Birkenau occurred with non-Jewish victims. "It was most important that the whole

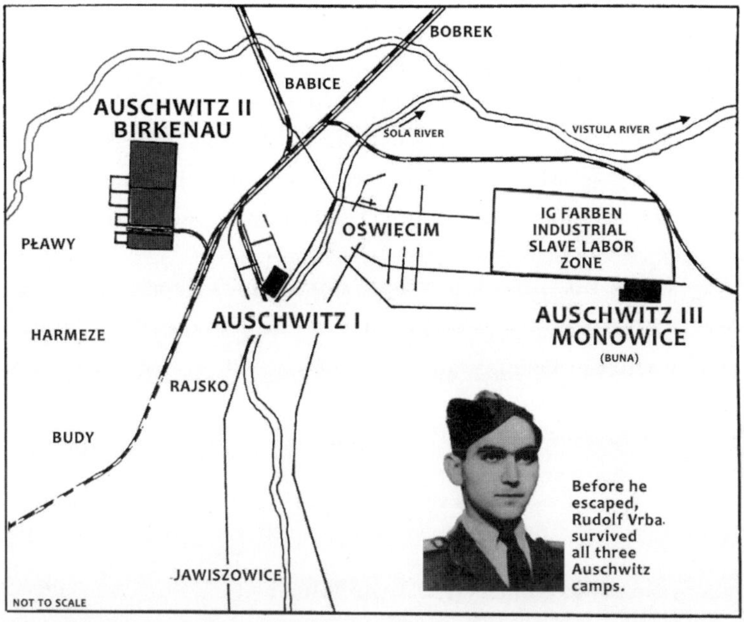

There were three separate camps at Auschwitz — for slave labor, for genocide and for industry.

business of arriving and undressing should take place in an atmosphere of the greatest possible calm."

Meanwhile, Nazi leaders beyond Poland had significant roles to play in the development of the Auschwitz complex.

Heinrich Himmler, one of Hitler's earliest followers, had pursued a degree in agricultural at the Technical University of Munich. He wished to develop land beyond the prison camp as a farming zone (*Gutsbezirk*) for experiments in farming, livestock raising and fish breeding. The so-called Architect of Terror made his first of three visits to Auschwitz on March 1, 1941, resulting in formalized plans to expand the overall complex by June of 1941. Reinhard Heydrich, as the chief of the Reich Main Security Office, named Auschwitz and officially intended for it to house prisoners who were "not serious offenders." Auschwitz II (Birkenau) would be for "more serious offenders, but still capable of being educated and reformed." As early as 1940, Heydrich envisioned an offshoot for Auschwitz I before he was assassinated in Prague on June 5, 1942.

Reichsmarschall Hermann Göring worked in concert with IG Farben and other major German companies from 1940 onwards to develop synthetic fuel oil and synthetic rubber for the war effort. As early as January 1941, a member of the IG Farben board, the German chemist Otto Ambros, had commenced the planning process that determined Dwory, near Oswiecim, as the site for a massive chemical works built by slave labor. This was the scheme that gave rise to Auschwitz III.

The local Polish populations of Babice, Broszkowice, Brzezika, Budy, Harmeze and Rajsko were therefore evicted or killed for the "Buna-Werke" construction as of April of 1941. Auschwitz III, or Monowitz, would occupy about half of its projected area in 1942 and the site would reach its maximum size by the summer of 1943.

~

THE REMAINING 945 Soviet POWs in Auschwitz I were transferred to the crude beginnings of the "Brzezinka camp," later known as Auschwitz-Birkenau, on March 1, 1942. Meanwhile, preparations were made at the main camp for ten blocks to be set aside the for Women's Section (*Frauenabteilung*) to handle the simultaneous arrival of two contingents: 999 tough, female German prisoners from the Ravensbruck prison and 999 frightened, young Jewish women and girls from Slovakia (eastern Czechoslovakia) who arrived via the internment camp at Poprad.

Both groups were accorded serial numbers from 1 to 1998. It was almost a month later, on April 27, when 127 Polish women, all deemed political prisoners, were added to the female Auschwitz population, with numbers from 6784 to 6910. It was not long after that Rudolf Vrba arrived in Auschwitz I on June 30. He came face-to-face with Heinrich Himmler during the latter's second visit to Auschwitz, July 17–18, 1942 when Himmler witnessed the new gassing procedures for mass murder as well as the construction progress at Buna, aka Auschwitz III.

The Final Solution was not set in motion during the first two years of Auschwitz' existence. It was only officially launched when until Hitler convened a meeting in a fashionable Berlin suburb, at 56/58 Am Grossen Wannsee, on January 20, 1942. While Hitler and Reinhard Heydrich were

APPROXIMATE ESTIMATES OF HOLOCOUST VICTIMS

	Gilbert 1982	Reitlinger 1953	Hilberg 1981
CHELMNO	360,000)		
BELZEC	600,000)		
SOBIBOR	250,000)	Close to 2 million	
TREBLINKA	840,000)		
AUSCHWITZ [Vrba & Wetzler] 1944	2,500,000	900,000	1,000,000
Einsatz-Gruppen [Krausnick & Wilhelmi] 1981	2,250,000	1,250,000	1,250,000
	6-7 millions	4-5 millions	more than 5 millions

Rudolf Vrba kept this simple graph to remind himself how people behind desks in universities could know more about Auschwitz than he did. Rudolf Höss, the longest serving Auschwitz commander, estimated the overall death toll at Auschwitz was three million, in a 1946 affidavit. This figure aligned with Rudolf Vrba's somewhat lower estimate but they were merely eyewitnesses to genocide. How could they know?

Always wary of being accused of exaggeration, historians have tended to whittle down death toll estimates. Vrba was unimpressed by Raul Hilberg (1926–2007) whereas Sir Martin Gilbert (1936–2015) eventually became his close friend. *The Final Solution* (1953) by Gerald Reitlinger (1900–1978) was significant because it first alerted Vrba to how many Hungarian Jewish lives were saved by his co-authorship of the *Vrba-Wetzler Report* (within the Auschwitz Protocols).

Vrba's relationships with various historians such as Randolph Braham (1922–2018) and David S, Wyman (1929–2018) will be considered in Volume II.

the chief strategists for industrialized annihilation of Europe's Jews, a relative underling named Adolf Eichmann recorded the minutes.

Administratively, the decision to officially split Auschwitz into three camps was made by SS-WVHA chief Oswald Pohl on November 11, 1943.

Rudolf Vrba escaped to finally effectively blow the whistle on the Holocaust – making it undeniable – in April of 1944. These words at the end of the first Rudolf Vrba biography are being written in March of 2025. The world of cruelty is on the rise. The world of virtue is collapsing. The bravery of Rudolf Vrba is a shining example of how we must proceed – with valor and determination and truth.

– A.T.

An estimated 15,000 labour, death and concentration camps were established by Nazi Germany from 1939 to 1945 based on the information compiled in *Le Livre des Camps* (1979) by Ludo Ven Eck, *Perpetrators Victims Bystanders: The Jewish Catastrophe 1933-1945* (1992) by Raul Hilberg and *Atlas of the Holocaust* (1993) by Sir Martin Gilbert.

1 Arbeitsdorf
2 Bergen-Belsen
3 Buchenwald
4 Dachau
5 Flossenburg
6 Gross-Rosen
7 Hertogenbosch
8 Hinzert
9 Kaiserwald
10 Kauen
11 Krakow-Plaszow
12 Majdanek
13 Mauthausen
14 Mittelbau-Dora
15 Natzweiler-Struthof
16 Neuengamme
17 Niederhagen
18 Ravensbruck
19 Sachsenhausen
20 Stutthof
21 Vaivara
22 Warsaw
23 Klooga
24 Rumbula Rorest
25 Ponary
26 Westerbork
27 Treblinka
28 Chelmno
29 Sobibor
30 Starachowice
31 Drancy
32 Belzec
33 Auschwitcz-Birkenau
34 Janowska
35 Theresienstadt
36 Babi Yar

A seven-volume encyclopedia, prepared by the Jack, Joseph and Morton Mandel Center for Advanced Holocaust Studies at the United States Holocaust Memorial Museum, has identified and examined more than 40,000 camps and ghettos operated by the Nazis and their allies from Norway to North Africa, from France to Russia.

Bibliography

Here is a partial bibliography of books and other sources that have been consulted in the preparation of this book.

Books

Adderson, Carol, *A History of Forgetting*. Key Porter, 1999.

Adler, H.G., *Theresienstadt 1941–1945: The Face of a Coerced Community*. Cambridge University Press, 2022.

Alma, Ann, *Brave Deeds: How One Family Saved Many From the Holocaust*. Groundwood, 2008.

Arendt, Hannah, *Eichmann in Jerusalem: A Report on the Banality of Evil*. Penguin, 2006.

Avey, Denis with Rob Broomby, *The Man Who Broke into Auschwitz*. Hodder & Stoughton, 2011.

Bascomb, Neal, *The Nazi Hunters: How a Team of Spies and Survivors Captured the World's Most Notorious Nazi*. Scholastic, 2013.

Bauminger, Dr. Arieh L., *Roll of Honour*. Yad Vashem—Martyrs and Heroes' Remembrance Authority, 1970.

Bird, Kai, *The Chairman: John J. McCloy & the Making of the American Establishment*. Simon & Schuster, 1992.

Black, Edwin, *The Transfer Agreement: The Dramatic Story of the Pact Between the Third Reich and Jewish Palestine*. Carroll & Graf, 1983.

Bleakley, Fred R., *The Auschwitz Protocols: Ceslav Mordowicz and the Race to Save Hungary's Jews*. Post Hill Press, 2022.

Bluman, Barbara, *I Have My Mother's Eyes: A Holocaust Memoir Across Generations*. Ronsdale, 2008.

Boder, David P., *I Did Not Interview the Dead*. University of Illinois Press, 1949.

Boraks-Nemetz, Lillian, *The Old Brown Suitcase: A Teenager's Story of War and Peace*. Ben-Simon Publications, 1995; Ronsdale, 2008.

Borkin, Joseph, *The Crime and Punishment of I.G. Farben: The startling account of the unholy alliance of Adolf Hitler and Germany's great chemical combine*. The Free Press, 1978.

Braham, Randolph L., *The Politics of Genocide: The Holocaust in Hungary*. Wayne State University Press, 2000.

Bresheeth, Haim, Hood, Stuart, Janz, Litza, *Introducing the Holocaust*. Icon Books, 2000.

Browning, Christopher R., *Ordinary Men: Reserve Police Battalion 101 and the Final Solution in Poland*. Penguin 2001.

Buck, Tobias, *Final Verdict: The Holocaust on Trial in the 21st Century*. Hachette, 2024.

Buckman, Alex, *Afraid of the Dark: The Memoir of Alex Buckman*. Writing Lives project, 2016–2017.

Cambell, Olga, *A Whisper Across Time*. Jubaji Press, 2018.

Caplan, Sonia, *Passport to Reprieve*. The Azrieli Foundation, 2011.

Cherish, Barbara U., *The Auschwitz Kommandant: A Daughter's Search for the Father She Never Knew*. The History Press, 2009.

Cernyak-Spatz, Susan, *Protective Custody Prisoner 34042*. N&S Publishers, 2005.

Cornwall, Claudia, *Letter from Vienna: A Daughter Uncovers Her Family's Jewish Past*. Douglas & McIntyre, 1995.

Davidovits, Paul, *Holocaust Memories: Annihilation and Survival in Slovakia*. Amsterdam Publishers, 2021.

Donat, Alexander, *The Holocaust Kingdom*. Holt, Rinehart and Winston, 1963.

Drabek, Jan, *Thirteen*. Caitlin, 1991.

Drabek, Jan, *Vladimir Krajina: World War II Hero and Ecology Pioneer*. Ronsdale, 2012.

Drabek, Jaroslav, *The Memoirs of Jaroslav Drabek 1901–1996* (*Unpublished memoir of Auschwitz prisoner #94692*) translated by Jan Drabek, edited by Alexandra Drabek. Self-published, 2011.

Drysdale, Magaret Melanie, *Three Times Betrayed: The Sudeten Germans of Tomslake*. Malaspina College, Master's thesis. 2002.

Fairweather, Jack, *The Volunteer: The True Story of the Resistance Hero who Infiltrated Auschwitz*. William Morrow, 2019.

Frie, Roger, *Not in My Family: German Memory and Responsibility After the Holocaust*. Oxford University Press, 2017.

Frie, Roger, *History Flows Through Us: Germany, the Holocaust and the Importance of Empathy*. Routledge, 2018.

Frinton, Ernst, *Memories, An Autobiography*. Self-published, 1994.

Gallant, Mary J., *Coming of Age in the Holocaust: The Last Survivors Remember*. University Press of America, 2002.

Garlinski, Josef, *Fighting Auschwitz: The Resistance Movement in the Concentration Camp*. Fontana/Collins, 1975.

Gilbert, Martin, *The Holocaust: A History of the Jews of Europe During the Second World War*. Henry Holt & Company, 1985.

Gilbert, Martin, *The Jews in the Twentieth Century, An Illustrated History*, Key Porter, 2001.

Gilbert, Martin, *The Righteous*. Key Porter, 2003.

Gold, Joe, *Two Pieces of Cloth, One Family's Story of the Holocaust*. Page Two, 2021.

Goldberg, Adara, *Holocaust Survivors in Canada: Exclusion, Inclusion, Transformation, 1947–1955*. University of Manitoba Press, 2015.

Goldhagen, Daniel Jonah, *Hitler's Willing Executioners: Ordinary Germans and the Holocaust*. Abacus, 1997.

Goldman, Rene, *Childhood on the Move: Memoirs of a Child-survivor of the Holocaust*. Island Blue, 2014.

Granirer, Pnina, *Light Within the Shadows: A Painter's Memoir*. Granville Island, 2017.

Greeks in Auschwitz. Greek Foreign Ministry, 2009.

Hájková, Anna, *The Last Ghetto: An Everyday History of Theresienstadt*. Oxford University Press, 2020.

Harvey, Stella, *Nicolai's Daughters*. Signature, 2012.

Hay, Peter, *Ordinary Heroes: Chana Szenes and the Dream of Zion*. Putnam, 1986.

Ordinary Heroes, The Life and Death of Chana Szenes, Israel's National Heroine. Paragon House, 1989.

Hemmendinger, Judith, Krell, Robert, *The Children of Buchenwald: Child Survivors of the Holocaust and their post-war lives*. Gefen, 2000.

Hilberg, Raul, *The Destruction of the European Jews*. Holmes & Meier, 1985.

Hobbs-Birnie, Lisa, *In Mania's Memory*. Read Leaf, 2010.

The Holocaust Chronicle: A History in Words and Pictures. Publications International Ltd., 2000.

Hoffman, Eva, *Lost in Translation: Life in a New Language*. Penguin, 1989.

Jelínek, Yeshayahu Andrej, *Star of David under Tatra Mountains* (English language translation). National Museum of Jewish Culture, 2020.

Kamenec, Ivan, *On the Trail of Tragedy: The Holocaust in Slovakia*. H & H Publishers, 2007.

Kaellis, Rhoda, *Keeping the Memory: Fifteen Eyewitness Accounts of Victoria Holocaust Survivors*. Vancouver Holocaust Centre Society, 1991.

Kahn, Leon, *No Time to Mourn: The True Story of a Jewish Partisan Fighter*. Ronsdale, 2004.

Kalla, Daniel, *The Far Side of the Sky*. HarperCollins, 2011.

Karwowska, Bozena (ed), *The More I Know, The Less I Understand: Young Researchers' Essays on Witnessing Auschwitz*. Auschwitz Birkenau State Museum Publishing House, 2017.

Kraus, Ota and Kulka, Erich, *The Death Factory*. Pergamon Press, 1966.

Krell, Robert, *Memoiries: Sounds from Silence*. Self-published, 2016.

Krell, Robert, *Sounds from Silence: Reflections of a Child Holocaust Survivor, Psychiatrist and Teacher*. Amsterdam Publishers, 2021.

Langbein, Hermann, *People in Auschwitz*. Fitzhenry & Whiteside, 2004.

Lanzmann, Claude, *Shoah: An Oral History of the Holocaust: The Complete Text of the Film*. Pantheon Books, 1985.

Larson, Erik, *In the Garden of Beasts: Love, Terror and an American Family in Hitler's Berlin*. Broadway Paperbacks, 2011.

Lederman, Marsha, *Kiss the Red Stairs, The Holocaust, Once Removed*. Penguin Random House, 2022.

Lengyel, Olga, *Five Chimneys: A Woman Survivor's True Story of Auschwitz*. Ziff-Davis Publishing, 1947.

Lester, David, *The Listener: Memory, Lies, Art, Power*. Arbeiter Ring, 2011.

Levi, Primo, *Survival in Auschwitz: The Nazi Assault on Humanity*. Simon & Schuster, 1986.

Levy, Alan, *The Wiesenthal File*. William B. Eerdmans Publishing, 1993.

Linn, Ruth, *Escaping Auschwitz, A Culture of Forgetting*. Cornell University Press, 2004.

Lloyd, Alexandra, *Defying Hitler: The White Rose Pamphlets*. The Bodleian Library, 2022.

Matas, David with Susan Charendoff, *Justice Delayed: Nazi War Criminals in Canada*. Summerhill Press, 1987.

Mazzeo, Tilar J., *Irena's Children*. Simon & Schuster, 2016.

McKay, Paul, *The Roman Empire: The Unauthorized Life and Times of Stephen Roman*. Key Porter, 1990.

McKenzie, James E., *War Criminals in Canada*. Detselig Enterprises, 1995.

Mermelstein, Robert, *My Life: A Journey from Mukacevo to Vancouver, Prevailing Over Adversity and Challenges*. Self-published, 2018.

Mielnicki, Michel, *Bialystok to Birkenau: The Holocaust Journey of Michel Mielnicki*. Ronsdale, 2000.

Milman, Isa, *Afterlight: In Search of Poetry, History and Home*. Heritage House, 2021.

Moszkiewiez, Helene, *Inside the Gestapo: A Jewish Woman's Secret War*. Macmillan, 1985.

Müller, Filip, *Eyewitness Auschwitz: Three Years in the Gas Chambers*. Stein and Day, 1979.

Nicholls, William, *Christian Anti-Semitism: A History of Hate*. Jason Aronson, 1992.

Nyiszli, Miklos, *I Was Doctor Mengele's Assistant: The Memoirs of an Auschwitz Physician*. Auschwitz-Birkenau State Museum, 2010.

Patai, Raphael, *The Jews of Hungary: History, Culture, Psychology*. Wayne State University Press, 1996.

Porter, Anna, *Kasztner's Train: The True Story of Rezso Kasztner, Unknown Hero of the Holocaust*. Douglas & McIntyre, 2007.

Pringle, Heather, *The Master Plan: Himmler's Scholars and the Holocaust*. Viking, 2006.

Rabinovici, Doron, *Eichmann's Jews: The Jewish Administration of Holocaust Vienna*. Wiley-Blackwell, 2011.

Rogow, Sally, *They Must Not Be Forgotten: Heroic Catholic Priests and Nuns Who Saved People from the Holocaust*. Holy Fire Publishing, 2005.

Roland, Paul, *The Nuremberg Trials: The Nazis and their Crimes against Humanity*. Arcturus, 2010.

Rozett, R., Spector, S., *Encyclopedia of the Holocaust*. Jerusalem, 2006.

Ryback, Timothy W., *Hitler's Private Library: Books that Shaped His Life*. The Bodley Head, 2009.

Salcudean, Martha, *In Search of Light - The Azrieli Series of Holocaust Survivor Memoirs, 59*. The Azrieli Foundation / Second Story, 2019.

Schallie, Charlotte, *Under Swiss Protection: Jewish Eyewitness Accounts from Wartime Budapest*. Columbia University Press, 2017.

Schochet, Simon, *Feldafing*. November House, 1983.

Shandler, Rhodea, *A Long Labour: A Dutch Mother's Holocaust Memoir*. Ronsdale, 2004.

Slyomovics, Susan, *How to Accept German Reparations*. University of Pennsylvania Press, 2014.

Sonnenschein, Bronia, *Victory of Nazism, The Journey of a Holocaust Survivor*. Memory Press, 1998.

Stafford, David, *Endgame, 1945: The Missing Final Chapter of World War II*. Black Bay Books, 2007.

Stoddard, Lothrop, *Into the Darkness: An Uncensored Report from Inside the Third Reich at War*. Indo-European Publishing.com, 2011.

Świebocki, Henryk (ed.), *London has been informed: Reports by Auschwitz Escapees*. Auschwitz-Birkenau State Museum, 1997.

Tanenbaum, Roy D., *Prisoner 88: The Man in Stripes*. University of Calgary Press, 1998.

Thau, Isaac, *Killing Me Off: The Many Lives of Rubin Thau*. Self-published, 2021.

Vadkerty, Madeline, "Aspects of the Holocaust During the Slovak Autonomy Period (October 6, 1938, to March 14, 1939." *Occasional Papers on Religion in Eastern Europe*: Volume 42, Issue 1, Article 2. George Fox University, February 2022.

Venezia, Shlomo, *Inside the Gas Chambers: Eight Months in the Sonderkommando of Auschwitz*. Polity Press, 2009.

Vrba, Rudolf, *I Escaped from Auschwitz: The Shocking Story of the World War II Hero Who Escaped the Nazis and Helped Save Over 200,000 Jews*. Skyhorse Publishing, 2020.

Waisman, Robert, *The Boy from Buchenwald: The True Story of a Holocaust Survivor*. Bloomsbury, 2021.

Ward, James Mace, *Priest, Politician, Collaborator: Jozef Tiso and the Making of Fascist Slovakia*. Cornell University Press, 2013.

Wetzler, Alfréd, *Escape from Hell: The True Story of the Auschwitz Protocol*. Berghahn Books, 2007.

Wiesel, Elie, *A Mad Desire to Dance*. Knopf, 2009.

Wyman, David, *The Abandonment of the Jews: America and the Holocaust, 1941–1945*. The New Press, 1984.

Zimring, Nikola, *The Men Who Knew Too Much: Reflections on the Historiography of Rudolf Vrba and Alfred Wetzler's Escape from Auschwitz-Birkenau and their Attempt to Warn the World*. Master's Degree thesis, The Lester and Sally Entin Faculty of Humanities, Department of Jewish History, Tel Aviv University, 2024.

Interviews

Oral interviews available online have been useful, most notably Claude Lanzmann's interviews with Vrba, including segments that do not appear in the documentary *Shoah* [transcripts now available at rudolfvrba.com], as well as the oral history interview with Joseph Neumann, August 21, 1988, United States Holocaust Memorial Museum Collection, Gift of the Illinois Holocaust Museum and Education Center. There is also an extensive video interview with Ceslav Mordowicz, in Polish, with a rough English transcript made available via U.S. Holocaust Museum, and an oral history interview with Arnošt Rosin, only available in German, in which he recalls Vrba and Wetzler.

Websites and Articles

These are a few of the hundreds of websites and articles that have been consulted.

Cohen, M.J.: "Churchill and the Jews: The Holocaust." *Modern Judaism* 6:27–49, 1986.

Friedrich, Otto: "The Kingdom of Auschwitz," *The Atlantic Monthly*, September 1981.

Hlavinka, Ján. "I never negotiated with the Jew." On the Aryanizations of Slovak writer L'udovít Mistrík-Ondrejov. Historický časopis, 2020, 68, 6, pp. 1029–1048, Bratislava.

Hlavinka, Ján (ed.). *Uncovering the Shoah: Resistance of Jews and Efforts to Inform the World of Genocide* / Proceedings from the Conference held in Žilina, Slovakia, August 25–26, 2015.

Kunt, Gergely, "An Open Secret? The Dissemination and Reception of News about Auschwitz in Hungary in 1944," in S.I.M.O.N.- Shoah Intervention. Methods. Documentation 6 (2019) 1, 35–51. Vienna Wiesenthal Institute for Holocaust Studies.

"Mäilander, Elissa: A specialist: the daily work of Erich Muhsfeldt, chief of the crematorium at Majdanek concentration and extermination camp, 1942–44." https://doi.org/10.7228/manchester/9780719096020.003.0003 November, 2014.

Medoff, Rafael, "The Roosevelt Administration, David Ben-Gurion and the Failure to Bomb Auschwitz: A Mystery Solved." http://new.wymaninstitute.org/wp-content/uploads/2017/03/TheFailureToBombAuschwitz.pdf

Nižňanský, Eduard, "The history of the Escape of Arnošt Rosin and Ceslav Mordowicz from the Auschwitz-Birkenau concentration camp to Slovakia in 1944." Institute of History of the Slovak Academy of Sciences; Prague: International Christian Embassy Jerusalem, 2016.

Vadkerty, Madeline, "Aspects of the Holocaust During the Slovak Autonomy Period (October 6, 1938, to March 14, 1939)," *Occasional Papers on Religion in Eastern Europe*: Vol. 42: Iss. 1, Article 2. DOI:e, 2022. https://digitalcommons.georgefox.edu/ree/vol42/iss1/2

Films Related to Vrba

1966 – *Die Advokaten des Feindes* (a four-hour film, directed by Werner Rings, Swiss Television, Zurich)
1973 – *The Holocaust* (in the World War II series, one-hour documentary film, directed by Jeremy Isaacs, British Broadcasting Corporation, London)
1982 – *Auschwitz and the Allies* (two-hour film in collaboration with the historian Sir Martin Gilbert, directed by Rex Bloomstein, British Broadcasting Corporation, London)
1984 – *Survival* (one-hour film, directed by N. Downie, British Broadcasting Corporation, London)
1985 – *Shoah* (nine-and-a-half-hour documentary film, directed by Claude Lanzmann, Paris)
1990 – *Witness to Auschwitz* (30-minute documentary film, directed by Robin Taylor for the series "Man Alive," Canadian Broadcasting Corporation, Toronto (Program #Y8L 9006)
2007 – *Auschwitz, The Great Escape* (British documentary, directed by Alex Nikolic-Dunlop, Firefly Productions)

Internet falsifications about the lives if Vrba and Wetzler keep spreading. A 15-minute *Unpacked* documentary accords credit to Vrba and Wetzler for planning their own escape and once more we are told they carried Zyklon B cannisters to prove victims were being gassed. A new Slovakian documentary focused on Wetzler also exaggerates the escapees' role in formulating the escape, once again not affording any mention of how the pair double-crossed the men who planned the escape.

Some Articles by Vrba

1966 – Footnote to the Auschwitz Report (*Jewish Currents* (New York) v.20, No.3, pp.22–28.

1968 – The Camps, An Inside View. *History of the Second World War* Vol.5, pp.2148–2156. Editor Sir Basil Liddel Hart. Purnell and Sons, London, U.K.

1988 – The Role of Holocaust in German Economy and Military Strategy during 1941–1945. *Remembering for the Future. International Scholars Conference, Oxford.* Vol.2, pp.2263–2273. Pergamon Press, Oxford. U.K.

1992 – Personal Memories of Actions of SS-Doctors of Medicine in Auschwitz II (Birkenau). *Medical Science Without Compassion, Past and Present.* pp.15–38. Edited by Charles Roland, Henry Friedlander, Benno Muller-Hill. Hamburger Stiftung fur Sozialgeschichte des 20 Jahrhuderts. Arbeitspapiere – Atti – Proceedings No 11

1993 – SS-artsen in Auschwitz. *Nexus,* No.6, pp.20–37. Kok Agora voor de Stichting Nexus. Tilburg, Holland.

1996 – Die missachtete Warnung Betrachtungen uber den Auschwitz-Bericht 1944. *Vierteljahrshefte fur Zeitgeschichte,* v.44, Heft 1, pp.1–24

1997 – The Preparations for the Holocaust in Hungary: An Eyewitness Account. *The Holocaust in Hungary. Fifty Years Later.* Editors Randolph L. Braham and Attila Pok. pp.227–283. Columbia University Press.

1997 – Bericht uber eine Flucht aus Auschwitz: Die missachtete Warnung. *Die Erfahrung des Exils. Exemplarische Reflexione.* pp.105–124. Editors Wolfgang Benz and Marion Neiss. Netropol Verlag, Berlin

1998 – The Preparations for the Holocaust in Hungary: An Eyewitness Account. *The Nazis' Last Victims: The Holocaust in Hungary.* Wayne State University Press, Michigan, edited by Randolph L. Braham with Scott Miller

Awards

Czechoslovak Medal for Bravery
Order of Slovak National Insurrection (Class 2)
Medal of Honour of Czechoslovak Partizan
Laufberger Medal for Physiology, bestowed by Czech Academy of Science and Medical Society J.E. Purkinje, Prague (1993)
Doctor of Philosophy, Honoris Causa, University of Haifa (1998)
Order of the White Double (Class 1), Slovakia (2007)

Books by Vrba

In a partnership with Alan Bestic, Rudolf Vrba co-wrote a memoir about his escape from Auschwitz and the making of the *Vrba-Wetzler Report* entitled *I Cannot Forgive* (London: Sidgwick and Jackson, 1963, and New York, 1964). It was subsequently republished in Great Britain (as *Factory of Death*, 1964), Germany (as *Ich kann nicht vergeben*, Munich, 1964), France (*Je me suis evade d' Auschwitz*, Paris, 1988), Holland (*44070 – Ik ontsnapt uit Auschwitz*, Kempen, 1996), Czech Republic (*Utekl jsem z Osvetimi / I Escaped from Auschwitz*) Prague, 1997) and eventually Israel (Haifa, 1998). A little-known version of *I Cannot Forgive* was also reissued in 1989 under a new title, *44070: The Conspiracy of the Twentieth Century* (Star and Cross Publishing). The French/Czech title was adopted in English for a Barricade Books edition in the United States in 2002 and, again, in Great Britain for a Robson Books edition in 2006. The latest version from Racehorse/Simon & Schuster is co-edited by Robin Vrba and Nikola Zimring, a New York University history grad student who became a PhD candidate in Prague in 2024. (Zimring and Robin Vrba participated in the annual Vrba-Wetzler Trek in the second year of its existence, and their version continues to credit the London journalist Alan Bestic as Vrba's co-author. According to Robin Vrba, the newest edition incorporates some editorial changes in compliance with Rudolf Vrba's requests that were made in 1998 when he was consulted for a Czech language edition, and an editorial decision was made to jettison the book's opening chapter. The full title in English was changed to *I Escaped from Auschwitz: The Shocking True Story of the World War II Hero Who Escaped the Nazis and Helped Save over 200,000 Jews.*

Slovakia issued this commemorative coin to mark the 80th anniversary of the *Vrba-Wetzler Report*. By 2025, Canada and Vrba's hometown had still not provided any public recognition of Vrba, a Canadian citizen for 34 years (1972–2006).

Memorials

To mark the 80th anniversary of the *Vrba-Wetzler Report*, the Bank of Slovakia issued a 10-Euro coin [90 percent silver, 10 percent copper] that honors "Wetzler and Vrba." As manufactured by the Kremnica Mint in 2024, it celebrates their escape from Auschwitz and making the 140-kilometer journey to Žilina to generate "one of the most important Slovak entries in the pages of world history." The obverse side contains their prisoner numbers, a representation of a rail line, raised dots to represent guard posts and a teddy bear representing all personal effects stolen from victims.

The names of Rudolf Vrba and Alfréd Wetzler are inscribed at Slovakia's most impressive monument honoring its Partisan soldiers at Roh Hill (Hippopotamus Hill) outside of Lubin, in the Trenčín Region of western Slovakia.

Between the villages of Skalité and Zwardoń, near the border between Slovakia and Poland, at 685 meters above sea level, artist Fero Guldan erected an iron-concrete, memorial signpost on August 19, 2014 as a border-crossing landmark for participants in the annual Vrba-Wetzler Trek from Auschwitz to Žilina. It provided a shelf upon which trekkers could place stones to recognize the victims of the Holocaust.

Robin Vrba (left) and Gerta Vrbová (center) participated in the 2015 Vrba-Wetzler Trek.

Fedor Gál co-created the Vrba-Wetzler Trek as envisioned by Rudolf Vrba's daughter, Zuza.

Since 2014, in memory of Vrba and Wetzler's bravado, the Vrba-Wetzler Memorial March has been held every year, except for cessations due to the Covid pandemic. The Trek's primary organizer Fedor Gál was motivated to organize an annual trek after getting to know Rudi Vrba's first wife, Gerta Vrbová, who came to him in Prague and said, "My [second daughter] Zuzana has died [in 2013]. She once had a dream that an international community would walk the trail that her father took as he fled from Auschwitz to Žilina."

The trek ends at the building of the former Jewish old folks' home in Žilina that was declared an historic site in 2021. The Vrba and Wetzler Memorial Rooms at Hollého 9 in Žilina were officially opened in 2021 as a historical site by the Jewish Religious Community in cooperation with the city of Žilina and the Malá Fatra Regional Tourism Organization. As well, in 2020, the borough of Ružinov, in Bratislava, renamed a park after Alfréd Wetzler in front of its Pan-European University because he had worked in the Ružinov library while writing his novel under the pseudonym of Jozef Lánik. A small square in Žilina was named after the pair in 2023.

To finally honor Rudolf Vrba in his home province of British Columbia, the Schara Tzedeck cemetery board will erect a memorial stone and plaque near its Holocaust memorial in New Westminster. This will be the first outdoor commemoration for and about Vrba in Canada. Schara Tzedeck Cemetery is a private cemetery dating back to the 1920s.

A Note on Pronunciation

For pronunciation, Rudolf Vrba's surname in Slovakian requires a rapid fluttering of the tongue. In English, "Verba" tends to suffice.

Vrba's Academic C.V.

Available at rudolfvrba.com

Index

Note: **Bold** type indicates an image

ACKNOWLEDGMENTS

With the exception of photos taken by the SS and Vrba's Partisan medal from the author, images were sourced mainly from the personal archives of Rudolf Vrba with the consent and permission of Robin Vrba, or were provided by Gillian Bryant-Greenwood. The author is particularly grateful for the vital cooperation and facilities of the Franklin Delano Roosevelt Presidential Library, Hyde Park, NY.

This book would not exist without the enduring assistance and friendship of Sharon Jackson (graphics, researcher, Auschwitz map, website), Michelle Madden and Nicole LeCody (FDR Library researchers), Michael Worek (editor), Lionel Koffler (publisher), David Lester (Beyond Auschwitz map), Helen Karsai (translations), Shane McCune (proofreader), Robert Krell and Yosef Wosk (advisors). The book is dedicated to Yosef because he was the only person who believed, without any doubt, that the job had to be done and I was the one to do it. Thanks also to John and Gustavo for creating Casa de Piedra and to loved ones who were obliged to accept the Holocaust into my life on an ongoing basis. Thanks must also be extended to Robin Vrba who accepted my journalistic resolve to tell the truth, whatever it turned out to be, and never sought to hinder or control the contents in any way.

INTERVIEWS WERE CONDUCTED WITH

George Bluman, Gillian Bryant-Greenwood, Arthur Dodek, Jan Drabek, Geoffrey Druker, Chris Friedrichs, Marketa Goetz-Stankiewicz, Helen Karsai, Robert Krell, Dr. Ruth Linn, Joseph Ragaz, Dan Sonnenschein, Peter Stenberg and Robin Vrba.

OTHERS CONTACTED

Richard Bestic, Christopher Browning, Noam Butterfield, Rabbi Abraham D. Cooper, Lady Esther Gilbert, René Goldman, Anna Hájková, Robert Jan van Pelt, Dagmar Wertheim, Nikola Zimring.